BRITISH
Motorcycles
OF THE 1940s AND 1950s

BRITISH Motorcycles
OF THE 1940s AND 1950s

**Roy
Bacon**

First Published in 1989 by Osprey Publishing,

British Library Catologuing in Publication Data.

Bacon, Roy
    British Motorcycles of the 1940s and 1950s : a
    comprehensive guide to 79 post war marques from
    Aberdale to Zenith.
    1. British motorcycles, to 1983
    1. Title
    629.2'275'0941

This edition published 1993 by The Promotional
Reprint Company Limited exclusively for Bookmart
Limited, Leicester, UK and Treasure Press in Australia.

ISBN 1 85648 125 5

Printed in Malaysia.

Half-title page **Typical prosaic model and background of a road test
of those times. The 1956 Panther 10/4 was powered by a 9E Villiers
engine.**

Title page **Prime Minister Harold Macmillan accompanies President
'Ike' Eisenhower along Fleet Street during his 1959 visit, flanked by
the inevitable Triumph outriders.**

Contents

Foreword	6	Douglas	87	Pullin	150
Austerity to boom	7	Dunelt	94	Radco	151
Aberdale	13	Dunkley	94	Rainbow	152
ABJ	14	EMC	95	Raleigh	152
AJS & Matchless	16	Excelsior	97	Raynal	153
AJW	25	FLM	102	RCA	154
Ambassador	28	Francis-Barnett	103	Reynolds	155
Ariel	32	Greeves	107	Royal Enfield	155
BAC	42	GYS	111	Scott	163
Bantamoto	43	Harper	112	Sun	165
Bikotor	44	Hercules	113	Sunbeam	168
Bond	45	HJH	115	Swallow	173
Bown	47	Indian	116	Tailwind	174
Bradshaw	48	James	118	Tandon	174
Britax	50	Lohmann	122	Teagle	177
BSA	52	Mercury	123	Triumph	177
Cairn	65	Mini Motor	124	Turner	186
Commander	65	New Hudson	125	Velocette	187
Corgi	67	Norman	126	Velosolex	194
Cotton	69	Norton	130	Villiers	195
Cyc-Auto	71	OEC	137	Vincent–HRD	200
Cyclaid	72	Oscar	139	Wabo	208
Cyclemaster	73	Panther	140	Watsonian	209
Cymota	76	Phillips	144	Wooler	210
Dayton	77	Phoenix	145	Zenith	214
DKR	79	Power Pak	147	Model charts	215
DMW	80	Powerwheel	148	Acknowledgements	240
Dot	85	Progress	150		

Foreword

There are few people to whom we owe such a debt as we do to Roy Bacon, whom I count a friend since the days, alas, long ago, when we raced together in the early years of 50 cc racing in Britain. That he would rise to be a world authority on classic motorcycles and one of the most prolific – if not *the* most prolific – I had no way of knowing, and as an engineer in the aircraft industry, I doubt if Roy did either!

Roy was one of the first to write about what are now known as 'classics'. His many one-make histories in the Osprey Collector's Library series are an enormously valuable source of information and the books in his 'Restoration' series are invaluable, covering absolutely every aspect of the subject, even colour changes year by year.

This book neatly complements Roy's *British Motorcycles of the 1930s* and *British Motorcycles of the 1960s*. Nearly 80 makes are covered. Some of them are ephemeral and a few scarcely got beyond the proto-type stage. It is almost entirely thanks to Roy that their brief histories will be preserved.

Roy knows the 1950s, as the subtitle 'Austerity to boom' indicates, and he shows a rare understanding of economic forces that shaped – and eventually destroyed – the British industry. As ever, he has written an entertaining book, as well as an instructive one. Enjoy it.

Brian Woolley
TECHNICAL EDITOR
The Classic Motor Cycle

Left **Near the end of the decade, and a difficult choice between the Goldie the heart desires and the Leader the head and purse dictate**

Right **Post-war racing at Scarborough in late 1946, with Allan Jefferies on his Triumph ahead of Denis Parkinson and Roy Evans on Nortons**

Austerity to boom

Peace came to Europe in May 1945, and by June there was a modest ration of two or three gallons of petrol per month for motorcyclists. Modest indeed, but after years without any private motoring, it was better than nothing, and in those days a restrained throttle hand could easily wring over 100 miles from a gallon of fuel.

Before then, in March, there had been news of the new Triumph range, hints as to the form of the big Vincent-HRD, and a patent for BSA relating to an ohv twin and its valve gear. Later came articles in the magazines on how to get the most from your fuel ration, and on how to persuade reluctant machinery back into life after the long period off the road.

The results of some backroom work appeared with a preview of the Wooler and its flat-four beam engine, but of rather more practical interest was the announcement, in June, that AJS were about to return to civilian production. A week later the equivalent Matchless models were unveiled and, as the months rolled by, more and more firms introduced their wares.

Some machines were really new, such as the Vincent and Douglas twins, while others simply picked up the reins again after the six long years of war. The latter were either exactly the same as those from the 1939, or the aborted 1940, range, or were the same with the exception of a fresh coat of paint and the addition of the new telescopic front fork design. Rear suspension remained virtually unknown. For most of the industry, it was a case of restarting with black paint in the spray-guns instead of khaki.

Machine prices were high thanks, in part, to the imposition of purchase tax at $33\frac{1}{3}$ per cent. This was to prove the bane of the car and motorcycle industry, until it was replaced by VAT, as its rate was varied by the government to either stimulate or retard the economy as it thought fit. Early post-war writers thought that this tax was temporary, for it had been introduced in April 1940 as a wartime measure. On some goods it had risen to as much as 100 per cent in the darker days of war, and although, in time, it was reduced, it was never to drop to zero.

The early post-war years were a period of continued hardship in Britain; the people had been

drained by their six-year struggle for existence, but faced a battle for economic survival. Rationing of many items continued for some years, and everything was in short supply.

All manufacturers, regardless of product, were exhorted to produce more and more, the phrase 'export or die' being frequently quoted by politicians. The task was not made easy by the acute shortages of many materials and a plethora of wartime controls, which the bureaucrats were reluctant to relinquish.

For all these reasons, it was a time to concentrate on producing the goods, and most firms did this with as few changes as possible. In general, the new designs came from the smaller firms, many of which had been shifted from motorcycles to other work during the war. A considerable number of them never produced complete machines again, for they found that they had viable businesses which could switch to peacetime parts production with little trouble and minimal investment.

The major firms, which had been kept in production, were better placed to continue much as before but, under these conditions, kept innovation to a minimum. Most of their production went for export, and this was to continue for some years. Even in the early 1950s, certain new models were restricted to export markets when first introduced, and later only released at home in a trickle. In 1945 supply was even more restricted, and before being able to buy a new machine, the purchaser had to obtain a 'licence to acquire', which was only issued where an essential need could be shown.

This situation altered only gradually during the 1940s. Worldwide there were many changes as the old British Empire broke up, new nations were formed, and East-West attitudes hardened. Times were austere for most, and rationing and controls remained in Britain as a new socialist government sought to give fair shares to all, nationalize major industries, and to introduce substantial social reforms.

Motorcycling played its traditional role in that period as a means of getting to work, plus giving an occasional outing at the weekend. Despite the bombing, many workers, both office and manual, still lived close to where they worked, often only a few streets away. New towns, high-rise blocks, and longer journeys to work were still a decade away, so for many the daily round included a bus, tram, train or bicycle ride. Few aspired to cars,

and anyway these were restricted in their supply which, for a period, was hedged with covenants on resale.

The motorcycle became a means of easing longer journeys for many. Some had little option if their route did not coincide with public services, while others found it less costly and gradually came to prefer the freedom of their own road. Despite the rationing, which continued until 1950, and the shortages, it always seemed better to ride past the bus queue than stand in it, even in the rain.

Many machines were pre-war types, often repaired with guile and whatever came to hand, for there were few spares available. Exceptions soon became the ex-WD models, for many of these were auctioned off to the trade for resale. Most were given a quick, all-over respray in black, although a few of the avant-garde used maroon, but more likely because it was to hand than for aesthetic reasons.

It was a time for making do, and the reliance of the services on a few models, nearly all fitted with an Amal carburettor and Lucas electrics, was a great help. The same parts could be used on many pre-war models, and were just as effective for those riders lucky enough to obtain a new machine.

The magazines were full of hints and tips on how to repair, renovate, modify and make good, while, in the main, the machines would run with minimal service. Tyres were a major problem, as they were hard to find and none too good when obtained. Most riders learnt to ride on bald ones and to deal with the inevitable punctures.

In time, the situation improved, but the pre-war machine remained a common sight well into the 1950s, as did the ex-WD one. Before then, there were additions to the manufacturers' ranges, most major firms fielding a vertical twin before the end of the 1940s. These differed in many details, but all followed the same outline and all used many parts from the singles of the same marque.

So, whether with one or two cylinders, many models continued in much the same form as they had in the 1930s. The engine remained separate from the gearbox and had a vertically-split crankcase. The barrel was invariably iron, but a few of the more adventurous did turn to light-alloy cylinder heads. Valve gear was generally simple, but over the years the side-valve models were dropped, until only the services, and the AA and

Preparing Bob Ray's Ariel twin with puncture sealant for the 1951 ISDT, in which it was a member of the Trophy winning team

George Buck and Bob Ray about to set off on an ACU observed test through seven countries in seven days, late in 1953, to launch the new Huntmaster

RAC road patrols were using this type.

The electrics featured a magneto and dynamo, with a change to the alternator during the 1950s, but this was by no means universal. Lubrication was normally dry sump, with the oil tank under the saddle and twin pumps in the engine. The carburettor of larger machines was invariably an Amal, and most singles carried their exhaust system on the right.

The chassis was much the same as it was in 1939, with the addition of telescopic forks. Frames were still brazed, using forged lugs and pinned tubes, while rear suspension was slow to catch on. Where offered, it was often in plunger form, with little or no damping, other than that provided by the inherent friction of the system.

Larger machines had a four-speed gearbox, and virtually all used a positive-stop change mechanism. The gear pedal gave an up-for-down movement, in most cases, and it was on the right of the machine, together with the kickstarter. The primary and secondary drives were both on the

Far away in Japan, this Meguro twin followed the copy route, with its BSA lines, and remained in the Kawasaki list into the 1970s

left, as was the rear brake pedal; the first had a pressed-steel or cast-alloy case. Rear chain enclosure was rare.

Wheels had steel rims with wire spokes, and the 19 in. size was by far the most common, except for competition use, where a 21 in. front rim was fitted. A few models did use 20 in. wheels, but none 18 in. Tyres tended to be studded front and rear, except for sports models, which would have a ribbed front. Sections were invariably 3.25 in. front and the same, or 3.50 in., rear on the larger models, and 2.75 or 3.00 in. on the smaller ones. Brakes were offset, single-leading-shoe, drum types in most cases.

Supporting the traditional 350 and 500 cc singles, together with the newer 500 cc twins, were a line of similar, lighter 250 cc singles and many small two-strokes. The former were built on the same lines as the larger models, and some used common parts, but usually they were lighter and cheaper. The latter models were nearly all powered by Villiers engine and gearbox units, which were so numerous that they have a section of the book to themselves. The cycle parts were often minimal, but these models fulfilled their role of basic transport and, while the detail parts often gave trouble and caused annoyance, the machines normally completed their journeys.

By the beginning of the 1950s matters began to improve, with better petrol, fewer restrictions and more machines on the market. Many of the scars of war began to disappear as new buildings rose on bomb sites in the cities, and air-raid shelters in parks and suburbs were filled in or demolished.

Styles began to brighten, and the motorcycle followed suit with such models as the Golden Flash and Thunderbird, which broke away from the traditional black finish. Other colours were less successful, such as the blue used by Tandon but, in time, Barnetts became a pleasant green, James maroon and, of course, the Speed Twin was always in its Amaranth red.

Part of the reason for this was to suit the export market, and it was the American sector that sparked off the gradual increase in vertical-twin capacity. With vast stretches of straight roads, plus a performance and sports market on both coasts, the Americans needed more power, and the easy way to get it was with more 'cubes'. The big Vincent shone in this respect, as did the bigger twins from the major firms.

This process continued through the decade, together with a gradual refining process which, too often, was too slow. Detail changes only became the norm for each year's models, showing

Typical 1959 scene at the dealers on a Saturday morning with decisions and deals to be made

the complacency that lay behind the façade of prosperity.

There were new designs, but too few came from the home industry, while those that did were usually under-funded and never really got off the ground. Often, as with the Wooler, the designer tried to do too much at once, combining a new engine, transmission and cycle parts, so was unable to develop any one area completely.

The conservative nature of the buyer was no help, but too many had seen friends burn their fingers on the radical for them to risk their own money. Too often, final development was left to the riders of the initial production machines, and the word soon went round to let someone else buy the new design. Thus, too many would put off purchase for a year or two until the model was

sorted out, and the resultant low level of sales would hold the price too high.

While there may have been little that was innovative and which reached volume production, there were exceptions, such as the LE Velocette and Ariel Leader. Neither was fully sorted when launched, but both were closer than most and near enough to be successful. Thus, they ran on from slightly shaky starts to a reasonable lifespan.

The one really good feature the traditional singles and twins had going for them was that the steady improvements made them reliable. At the same time, the parts that wore out tended to remain the same, so spares were easy to stock and obtain, while problem areas became well known. At club and dealer level, the solutions to problems were passed around, and any modified detail parts could usually be bought or machined by a friend in industry.

The ACU National Rally finished at Weymouth in 1958, where this mass of machines is parked

Meanwhile, the world moved on, and other events affected motorcycling. The Korean war, early in the 1950s, caused a worldwide shortage of nickel, so chrome plating was restricted by government decree. Petrol-tank styles changed to suit, and some never went back to the older arrangement of chrome, painted panels and lining, for the new designs were often cheaper.

Later came the Suez crisis and, once more, there was petrol rationing, although it did not last for long and time spent building up stocks in advance proved to be wasted. Prior to the appearance of the coupons, there were queues at the pumps, which were repeated in the 1973 oil crisis, but the affair came and went with little long-term effect, except that petrol never cost under five shillings a gallon again.

At various times during the 1950s, there were booms in clip-on attachments, scooters, mopeds, and bubblecars, but few British firms had any significant investment in these. In the main, the industry kept to its solid, worthy models, which it produced in ever-increasing numbers up to 1959,

after which the numbers began to fall away. Total sales were to rise again in the 1970s, but these were nearly all imports, and sales figures fell again in the following decade.

That final year of the 1950s was a great one for motorcycling, as the sun shone, the economy was buoyant and even motorcycle dealers smiled. Motorcycles and scooters were in demand to beat the traffic jams and parking problems, while the appearance of the Mini and the Japanese had not yet made any impact. The former was to kill off the bubblecar and sidecar market, virtually at a stroke, while the latter were looking for expansion outside their home market to accommodate their enormous production rate.

Soon learners would be restricted to 250 cc machines, and later other measures would further limit the appeal of motorcycling, but that fine summer of 1959 was a good way to end the decade. John Surtees won every 350 and 500 classic, albeit on the Italian MV Agusta, the M1 opened, and the industry thought that good times had come to stay.

It was downhill from then on, but the legacy remained and was resurrected 30 years later with the classic revival.

Aberdale

The Aberdale company of Edmonton, London, announced its autocycle to readers of *Motor Cycling* in March 1947, but failed to make the pages of its rival, *The Motor Cycle,* which that week produced three issues as one. This was due to the fuel crisis of the times, which closed some magazines and shut many factories, while others only worked a three- or four-day week. Lack of coal was the problem, but as the Aberdale was made at the Bown factory in Wales, this might have given them an edge in supplies.

The machine itself was a typical autocycle, being powered by a Villiers Junior de Luxe engine. This 98 cc, single-speed unit was hung from a simple tubular frame with dropped top tube and no rear suspension. At the front were basic blade girders. Both wheels had small drum brakes and heavy-duty bicycle rims and tyres.

The petrol tank held about $1\frac{1}{2}$ gallons of fuel (16:1 mixture) and fitted into the space formed by the top, down and seat tubes. Below the tank detachable side panels concealed the engine while, aft of these, there were guards for both the cycling and power chains. A toolbox was provided, together with a steel carrier over the rear mudguard. The pedalling gear revolved in the bottom bracket to the rear of the engine.

Equipment included lights, a bulb horn, and a speedometer driven from the front wheel. The controls were simple, with a throttle lever on the right, clutch on the left and inverted levers on each side for the brakes. There was also a catch to hold the clutch out and a decompressor.

All told, it was a smart example of the type and able to run up to around 30 mph, while fuel consumption could be almost 150 mpg, which gave a good range for working journeys. It continued in production as the Aberdale until 1949, but at the end of that year was revised in form and then sold as the Bown, under which name it is described further on page 47.

The 1947 Aberdale autocycle with Villiers Junior de Luxe engine and very typical of the type

ABJ

This make was announced in July 1949, the correct company name being that of its chairman, A.B. Jackson. They were located in Pope Street, Birmingham. Pre-war, they had produced the Raynal autocycle, which was a production version of the 1937 Jones prototype, and they also made bicycles, so they were not strangers to two wheels. As with many other marques, their range was based around Villiers engines and was launched with two 98 cc models.

The machines were very similar in appearance, the first being the Autocycle, powered by a 2F engine, and the second, the Motorcycle, with the 1F. Both had more of a motorcycle than autocycle look, having a simple, rigid loop frame and telescopic front forks. The Autocycle frame had its

ABJ Autocycle of 1950 with 2F engine and pedals, but very similar to the two-speed Motorcycle from the same firm

pedal shaft fitted aft of the engine, and both had a low top tube and a single saddle on a pillar tube, which gave it height adjustment.

The forks had compression and rebound springs in each leg, with an arrangement of cones and split bushes to act as dampers. They were packed with grease and had seals to retain the lubricant. The upper tubes supported a deeply-valanced mudguard. The rear mudguard was a simple blade, but was hinged for easy wheel removal, while its stays acted as a luggage grid. A toolbox was attached to the left side on the Motorcycle, and a rear stand was provided for both.

The wheels had wire spokes and 2.25 × 26 in. tyres, while the hubs contained minute drum brakes, the rear one, at 4 in. diameter, being the larger. Fuel was carried in a $1\frac{1}{2}$ gallon tank mounted on four rubber blocks. The electrics of both models were powered by the flywheel magneto, but the Motorcycle had a rectifier and battery, so it was also equipped with an electric horn.

The controls were all on the bars for the Autocycle, both brakes being operated by inverted levers, but the Motorcycle had a foot pedal on the left for the rear brake. Both machines had a twistgrip and decompressor. They were finished in black with gold lining, although other colours were said to be available as options. These did not materialize and were not mentioned again,

The ABJ Minor cyclemotor introduced in 1952 with friction drive to the bicycle front tyre

but the two models continued to be offered up to 1952.

In July of that year they were joined by a cyclemotor, listed as the Auto Minor, and this drove the front wheel by means of a carborundum roller bearing on the tyre. The unit could either be supplied with a special front fork for fitting to any bicycle, or as a complete machine based on a single- or three-speed bicycle.

The two-stroke Auto Minor engine unit was pivoted to the fork so that the drive could be disengaged; its cylinder was on the left of the wheel and was inclined close to the horizontal. Its capacity was 49.9 cc. The iron barrel had an

alloy head, a downdraught Amal carburettor on top, and a drum-shaped silencer below. An over-hung crankshaft with needle-roller big-end was fitted, and the mainshaft extended through the drive roller to the Miller flywheel magneto on the right. This provided both lights and ignition. The petroil mixture was carried in a $\frac{1}{2}$ gallon tank clipped to the fork above the engine.

The cycle that ABJ supplied with this engine had hub brakes, heavy-gauge spokes and oversize tyres, which made it more suitable for its intended use.

At first, the two existing machines and the cyclemotor were listed for 1953, but before the year arrived the range had been reduced to the Auto Minor alone. This continued in production for that year, but then was dropped and the company reverted to making bicycles only.

AJS & Matchless

As the 1930s moved to their close, the differences between AJS and Matchless models came closer to being limited to badge engineering. The process was delayed by the war, but accelerated after it, so for the purposes of this book the two are considered as one, as indeed they had become when joined together as Associated Motor Cycles, or AMC, in 1937.

It was well known that the machines were built on the same production line, largely with the same parts but, for all that, each marque had its adherents. The firm fostered this attitude with competition riders on both makes and separate advertising in the press, but at club level we all knew that only the badges and, up to 1951, the magneto position distinguished one from the other.

During the war the firm built little other than the 348 cc G3L Matchless model, and post-war continued with this, although the AJS models were announced first. There were two of them:

the 348 cc model 16M and 497 cc model 18, which were almost identical, except for the cylinder bore and, curiously, the run of the exhaust pipe. On the smaller machine it was above the right foot-rest, but on the larger it ran below.

The engines were typically British in design, with built-up crankshaft, vertically-split crankcase, and timing gear on the right. Both head and barrel were in iron, but the rocker box was in light alloy and had a side cover for tappet adjustment.

Tall pushrod tunnels ran from crankcase to head, and on the AJS the magneto was mounted on a platform ahead of the engine, where it was driven by chain from the exhaust camshaft. This, at least, allowed some access to the dynamo, which was fitted into the engine plates behind the engine and above the gearbox. It was chain driven from the left-hand end of the crankshaft, so its removal meant disturbing the primary chaincase, the seal of which was notorious for leaking. It enclosed the clutch and chain drive to the sep-arate Burman four-speed gearbox with its foot-change.

The engine and gearbox went into a rigid cradle frame, and front suspension was by the Tele-draulic forks developed, and used by the G3L, during the war. These had hydraulic damping and a long, smooth action, which gave the owner a comfortable ride. Both wheels had offset hubs with single-leading-shoe brakes and 19 in. rims.

The cycle parts were much as those which had been used by the military, with the oil tank on the right and battery on the left beneath the

First post-war G3L Matchless of 1946, which was based heavily on the wartime model

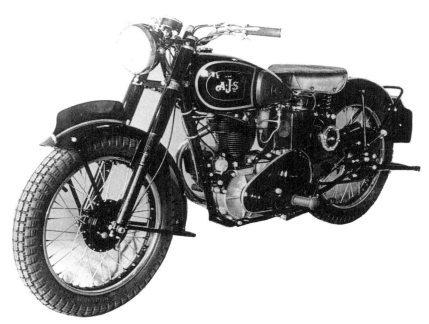

Similar 1947 AJS ohv single with conventional construction and fine finish

saddle. The toolbox was on the right above the upper chainstay, and the machine had Lucas lights and switches. Less usual was the provision of a prop-stand, in addition to the usual rear stand, although not all liked the way it sprang up when the machine's weight came off it.

The finish, which was to a very high standard indeed, was all black with gold lining and very little plating. For a while AMC had owned the Sunbeam firm and, before selling it to BSA, had learned how the famous Sunbeam finish was achieved. They continued to use the techniques for many years after the war, quickly gaining a reputation for producing one of the finest jobs in the industry.

A week after the AJS announcement, the equivalent two Matchless models appeared as the 348 cc G3L and 497 cc G80. They were known as Clubman models, as if to distinguish them from tourers. However, there were only the two of them, so the additional name had little real meaning, other than to remind owners that these were not the army versions.

As expected, the two machines were the same as the AJS models, except for the badges and the magneto position. On the Matchless this was behind the engine, where it took its drive from the inlet camshaft, and thus made the dynamo hopelessly inaccessible. The horn was ahead of the engine, but it was aft on the AJS, as it used the space vacated by the dynamo. The tank lining was silver with a red pin-stripe running through it.

Of interest to devotees of the two marques were two patents noted at the end of 1945. One concerned a system which ensured that the rear wheel would hold its alignment when moved to adjust the chain tension; the other applied to a pivot for a rear suspension fork. The firm had done some work on the latter aspect during the war, and the patent concerned how the fork pivot pin was first fixed to the machine and later lubricated with oil when in use.

In March 1946 the standard machines were joined by competition versions, which were built in small numbers. There were 50 of each marque, this number being split into 30 of the 348 cc size and 20 of the larger model. To identify them, a letter 'C' was added to the model number, for example the 498 cc AJS became the 18C. The actual changes, however, were minimal and based on the works models.

The front wheel gained a 21 in. rim, and the rear one a 4 in.–section tyre, while both had extra-heavy-gauge spokes. Competition tyres and alloy mudguards were fitted, and the silencer was canted upwards to deal with water splashes. The gearing was lowered, the lighting became optional, and the clutch and throttle cables were duplicated. Otherwise, it was all stock, with the unwanted frame lugs being removed to reduce the weight a little.

With production being the key issue, there were few changes to any model range in the 1940s, and AMC's was no exception. There were alterations and improvements to the engine for 1947, but only minor details changed on the cycle side. The most obvious of these on the 348 cc models was the exhaust pipe, which was run under the footrest. It was the same in the following year, although the brake size did increase a little. Another step towards rationalization took place during that year when the crankcase and crankshaft from the 497 cc engine were adopted by the smaller unit to make them common.

There was one new model for 1948, but this was for racing rather than the road. It was the 348 cc 7R with chain-driven overhead camshaft, and was intended for sale to private owners, as well as for use by the works team. The firm was already campaigning the Porcupine twin in the 500 cc class, and the addition of the smaller single allowed them to run in a second class.

The 7R followed the pattern set by the pre-war ohc models as far as the engine was concerned, although it was totally new. It followed the British layout, but its camshaft was driven from a half-speed timing gear by a chain with a Weller blade tensioner. The engine was all alloy with magnesium crankcase halves, and other parts were finished in a gold paint to protect them from corrosion.

The valve gear was fully enclosed, despite the hairpin valve springs, and the magneto was behind the barrel, where it was gear driven. There were twin-gear oil pumps in the timing chest for the dry-sump lubrication system, and the whole motor was very well made and oil-tight.

The gearbox was a close-ratio, racing Burman driven by an exposed chain and dry clutch. Together with the engine, it went into an all-welded duplex frame with pivoted-fork rear suspension controlled by AMC-designed-and-made spring-and-damper units. Teledraulics were used at the front, and at both ends the wheels had massive twin-leading-shoe drum brakes in conical hubs. These were in magnesium alloy and, curiously, spoked into high-tensile steel rims, although light-alloy ones were an option. Sizes were 21 in. front and 20 in. rear.

The fixtures and fittings were to suit road racing, so there was a large wrap-around oil tank with filler on the left. It looked nice, but suffered the snag that stones could be thrown over the tank by the rear tyre and often went down the bellmouth. A sponge block formed a cure.

The light-alloy fuel tank held nearly five gallons, and both tanks were rubber-mounted. There was a dualseat for the rider and passenger, which was

Left **A 1951 348 cc Matchless competition springer in action at a Normandy scramble**

Right **Fine, traditional Matchless springer in the form of a 1953 G80S with jampots at the rear and the comfortable dualseat**

an improvement over a saddle and pad, but it lacked any hump at the rear. The megaphone fitted at the end of the exhaust pipe was enormous and became a sore point for riders who tried to slipstream the AJS. The 7R was first called the Junior, but within weeks became the Boy Racer, which stuck to it, as did the type code.

The range expanded a good deal for 1949, with both spring frames and twin-cylinder engines making their debut on the road models. Unlike many of their contemporaries, AMC did not bother with the plunger frame at all, but went straight to the pivoted rear fork. Both rigid and sprung models used the same front frame half, the alternative rear sections being bolted in place. The rear end was controlled by the AMC spring-and-damper units, which became known as 'candlesticks'. They were never to be renowned for their stable damping or long life but, as they had clevis fork ends, it was not easy for the average owner to change to a proprietary unit.

The remainder of the rear end was altered to suit the rear suspension, the toolbox being in the rear subframe corner. A separate saddle and pillion pad remained, and the rear mudguard and its supports were amended to suit. There was a centre stand instead of the rear-mounted one,

and the models were identified by the addition of a letter 'S' to the existing codes. They came in both marques and engine sizes to produce the AJS 16MS and 18S, while the Matchless models were the G3LS and G80S.

The rigid models ran on in standard and competition forms, as did the racing 7R, and all the ohv engines had a new iron cylinder head with hairpin valve springs. At the same time the appearance was improved by moving the valve lifter to the rocker box. There were also other detail changes.

The remaining new models for 1949 were the 498 cc twins, which were coded 20 for AJS and G9 for Matchless. The engine used in both was a parallel twin made in the British mould, except for a third, central main bearing. The camshafts were fore and aft with a gear drive to both of them and the dynamo and magneto, which were mounted fore and aft respectively.

The iron barrels and alloy heads were separate, the rocker pedestals being cast integrally with the latter. The rockers were enclosed by alloy covers. Internally, there was a one-piece crankshaft, while twin-gear pumps in the timing case looked after the dry-sump lubrication system. The timing covers bore the marque logo and differed a little

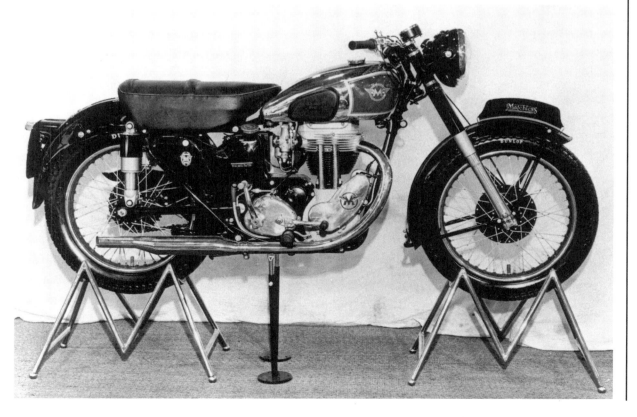

in shape, but otherwise the engines were identical.

The rest of the twin was based on the sprung single, so the gearbox, frame and forks were common, as was a large number of the detail fittings. There were minor differences between the two marques, and the most obvious were the seats and silencers. The Matchless had a dualseat and very neat megaphone-shaped silencers, but the AJS stuck to the saddle, pillion pad and tubular silencers, as on the other models. Both the sprung singles and the twins were produced for export only at first but, after a while, a few reached the home market. They were quickly snapped up and highly regarded as being some of the nicest motorcycles of their day.

There were few changes to the road models for 1950, but more to those on the competition side. For this field, the ohv engines went to an all-alloy top half, while the wheelbase was reduced, as was the tank size, to produce machines that looked much more like proper trials models, rather than converted roadsters. The 7R was given a number of detail engine improvements and a new Burman gearbox. The oil tank was slimmed down so it no longer grilled the rider's legs, and a shorter exhaust pipe with a smaller megaphone fitted.

There was a further expansion of the range for 1951, when competition springer singles appeared as the 16MCS and 18CS, or G3LCS and G80CS. Effectively, they comprised the all-alloy engine in the sprung frame, and were aimed more at scrambles use than trials. At the rear end were much fatter suspension units, which were immediately called 'jampots'. They were an improvement over the slimmer versions, as the internal pressure was lower, but they were still prone to variable damping as the temperature changed. The works riders had to use them, but everyone else changed to something better, and AMC still fitted them to all the sprung road models and the 7R. All the road singles were given an alloy head.

The whole road range ran on with little change until the end of 1955, for it was very much a case of annual detail improvements at AMC. There was a new Burman gearbox for 1952, when the Matchless single finally had its magneto moved ahead of the barrel like the AJS. The distinction between the marques was continued with the timing-case logo, while the shape of the case itself also differed. That year saw the underslung pilot lamp appear, but it was replaced by twin pilots, one on each side of the headlamp shell, for 1954.

Before then 1953 had brought detail alterations

only, plus a dualseat for sprung models, but 1954 saw a full-width front hub and auto-advance for the 497 cc road singles. The rigid competition singles were given an all-welded front frame that year, and the sprung ones a dualseat.

Nearly all models received Monobloc carburettors for 1955, together with another full-width front hub, the fins of which were in a barrel profile. There was a full-width rear hub to match it, a deeper headlamp shell to accommodate the speedometer, auto-advance for the 348 cc road singles, and many detail changes. The exception to the new Monobloc was the scrambles engine, which used the racing TT.

The 7R also progressed during this period, receiving a decrease in valve angle for 1953 and many detail improvements. The frame was new and narrower, while the forks were shorter, and 19 in. wheels were fitted. The front retained its twin-leading-shoe brake, but the rear became a single, which was all that was needed. Many of the cycle parts were also revised, either to suit the new frame or simply as improvements, and this process continued for the following two years.

For 1953 the 7R was joined by the Matchless G45, which was based on the 498 cc twin engine. The twins had previously run in the 1951 Clubman's event, and later that year a hybrid had come fourth in the Manx. This machine used a tuned twin engine in a 7R chassis, and the exercise was continued for 1952, when it won the Manx. This caused some controversy at the time, for works prototypes were not supposed to run in an amateur event, although it was not unheard of. AMC had made the mistake of winning, but all was forgiven when the firm announced that a batch of machines would be built for 1953.

The G45 was only ever built as a Matchless, just as the 7R was only an AJS, and its engine followed the G9 design closely. The camshafts and pistons were changed for racing parts, and alloy barrels were used. The covers were cast in a magnesium alloy, and triple valve springs fitted. On the outside were twin Amal GP carburettors, a racing magneto and a rev-counter. The cycle side was 7R with a minor alteration to suit the two exhaust pipes and megaphones, while the petrol tank carried the 'flying M' transfer.

There were detail alterations only for the next two years, and the machine soon took its place on the racing scene. It was never very successful, and no one seemed able to get the engine to run cleanly, but it filled a gap on the racing circuits.

Despite the packing, there is a Matchless G45 under there en route to Venezuela

It also enabled the AMC rider to run in the 350 and 500 cc classes using machines with common cycle parts, which was a great asset, as Manx owners already knew.

There were major changes to the range for 1956, when all the rigid models were dropped and the road models had a new frame. On the competition side, the trials machines were given a new frame with pivoted-fork rear suspension,

and the scrambles ones were given short-stroke, all-alloy engines.

The model codes continued unchanged, so the road singles were the 16MS and G3LS in 348 cc size, and 18S and G80S in 497 cc capacity. The new frame was still bolted together, much as before, but its appearance was improved with a long, slim oil tank on the right-hand side. This was matched by a combined toolbox and battery

A 1957 AJS model 16MC built for trials use only, hence the small saddle and raised silencer

The Matchless G9 twin in 1958 when it still had the lovely megaphone silencers, which set it off so well

carrier on the left, and there were further panels to tidy the machines up.

The twin had the same set of cycle parts and was joined by a larger version. This was of 593 cc, which gave it more power to meet the demands both at home and abroad, and was listed as the model 30 or G11. For export there had been a 550 cc G9B a year or two earlier, but this was produced as a temporary measure only.

The trials single was only built in 348 cc size and kept its 16MC or G3LC code, which was confusing, as it now had a pivoted-fork frame. This was of all-welded construction and had a shorter wheelbase to suit the model's use. The scrambles machines had new engines and were listed as the 348 cc 16MCS or G3LCS and the 497 cc 18CS or G80CS. Both had shorter strokes than before and integral pushrod tunnels, while the frame had extra bracing and stiffer suspension.

On the racing side, the 7R had revised engine dimensions, so its capacity came out at 349 cc. Together with the G45, it had various alterations to the cycle parts. Both tanks were altered, there were reverse—cone megaphones for the exhaust pipes, clip-on bars and other minor details. In fact, the machines were beginning to struggle a little to keep up, and the following year was to be the last for the G45. It was fitted with Girling rear units for that season, as was the 7R, which was to continue.

All road and competition models were fitted with the AMC gearbox from the middle of 1956, and this was based heavily on the pre-war Norton design, which had its roots in the Sturmey-Archer

Right **A special press test on a Matchless 248 cc G2 at Silverstone in 1958, when the model was set the task of covering 250 miles in the same number of minutes, but it took just five more**

box of the early 1930s. This came about because AMC had taken over Norton in 1953 and wished to use more of their own gear-cutting facility.

The gearbox also went into the Norton range, where it was to continue until 1977, and while the change mechanism was new, the gears were unchanged. It was a very good gearbox, but it worked better with its old Norton clutch than the AMC one it carried from then on.

The whole range went over to Girling rear units for 1957, but they remained unusual with clevis fork ends. Otherwise, the range ran on as it was, but there were plenty of changes for 1958. The most obvious of these appeared on the road singles, which went over to alternator electrics with the generator in a neat alloy chaincase. This was used on the twins as well, although they kept their magneto ignition. All road-equipped machines lost the twin pilot lights, which had never been too successful.

Two new 593 cc twins joined the range; both were more sporting, using the scrambles frame and an engine with raised compression ratio. One was the 30CS or G11CS which was, in effect, a street scrambler with siamezed pipes, small tank, fat tyres, alloy mudguards and quickly detachable lights. The second was the 30CSR or G11CSR, the first of the line quickly dubbed 'Coffee Shop Racer'. It used the CS engine, frame and exhaust

with the standard tank, but kept the shorter competition dualseat and special lights.

There was also a new road racing machine to replace the G45; the 496 cc G50. It was simply a bored-out 7R, and no one could understand why it had not been built back in 1948, for AJS had produced both 350 and 500 cc ohc singles in pre-

war days. The prototype G50 ran in the 1958 TT, and production versions arrived later in the year. The 7R had a number of changes, which also applied to the G50, and most concerned the engine details. In addition, the racing version of the AMC gearbox was used and there were other minor chassis changes.

Late AMC single in the form of the 1959 AJS, which used the same cycle parts for both models 16 and 18

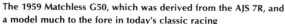

The 1959 Matchless G50, which was derived from the AJS 7R, and a model much to the fore in today's classic racing

During 1958 one more road single appeared to create the beginning of a lighter line. Although the new model, listed as the 248 cc 14 or G2, was always referred to as the lightweight single, this was simply to distinguish it from the other, heavyweight, models, and at 325 lb it hardly qualified.

The engine followed AMC practice in many respects, having a built-up crankshaft with roller big-end, iron barrel, alloy head, hairpin valve springs and access plate on the side of the rocker box. It differed in having the oil for the dry-sump lubrication system carried in a chamber within the vertically-split crankcase, and in having the gearbox strapped to the rear of the case. This gave the appearance of unit construction, but the box was housed in a drum-shaped casting which could be turned to adjust the primary chain. It contained four speeds with foot-change on the right, as usual, and its primary drive was enclosed by an alloy case, which also held the alternator.

The engine unit went in a built-up cradle frame with telescopic front and pivoted-fork rear suspension, the 17 in. wheels having full-width hubs with drum brakes. The mudguards, seat and side panels reflected a touring image or a machine for learners and riding to work.

The road singles had their type numbers changed, but little else for 1959. They became the 16, 18, G3 and G80, for the 'S' suffix was superfluous, as all had rear suspension. The trials models became the 16C and G3C, but with a new frame and small offset hubs to reduce weight, and the smaller scramblers became the 16CS and G3CS for what was to be their final year. The larger versions kept their existing codes and form.

The twins were changed, the 593 cc machines being replaced by 646 cc models, coded as the model 31 or G12. These, and the 498 cc machines, were listed in four versions; standard, de luxe, CS and CSR, with appropriate suffixes to the code. The first two were effectively the same machine with a variation only in finish and were little changed from the 1958 versions. The standard differed from the de luxe, and the others, in having an alternator and coil ignition, while the sports models followed the same format as before.

The 248 cc single ran on as it was for 1959 and was joined by a scrambles version, listed as the 14CS or G2CS. This had a tuned engine, heavier frame and forks, 19 in. wheels, and suitable fittings and fixtures, but it was not successful, as it was too heavy and too expensive.

On the racing front there were detail improvements for both the 7R and G50, which were no longer competitive in the classics. However, they continued to do their job well, giving the private owner reliability and no real troubles so that he could race consistently over the season.

That brought the decade to a close, with AMC ready to move to a duplex frame for 1960 and, later still, to an even closer amalgamation with the Norton name and component parts.

AJW

Although always on the fringe of the industry, AJW kept going for a long time. The name came from the initials of the founder, Arthur John Wheaton, whose background was publishing. In pre-war days he used various bought-in engines and other parts to create his machines. In the 1930s this could mean anything from a 172 cc Villiers to a big 994 cc JAP or Anzani, and the range size varied from one to a dozen. By 1940 it was down to three.

After the war the firm changed hands, and it was late in 1948 before any more AJW motorcycles appeared. When they did, there were two models. One, the Speed Fox, was a speedway machine fitted with the usual 498 cc JAP engine running on dope and driving the rear wheel via two chains, a countershaft and a clutch. It was built in very small numbers indeed, and the records suggest that only a round dozen were made, some being produced in a grass-track form.

The other model for 1949 was in road trim and listed as the Grey Fox. It was powered by a 494 cc

JAP vertical twin, which broke with that firm's tradition of building V-twins. The engine had been seen earlier in 1946 and was a very simple side-valve unit with one-piece alloy head and similar iron block. This last had well-splayed exhaust ports with the single inlet between them, so that the carburettor had to face forward and sat, well warmed, between the exhaust pipes.

The block was mounted on a vertically-split alloy crankcase, which extended downwards to include a sump for the oil. The crankshaft was originally in one piece, running in ball or roller races, and the connecting rods were forged in light alloy. In production, a built-up crankshaft was used. The camshaft ran across the front of the engine with tappets above and, at first, was driven by a chain, which also drove the front-mounted dynamo. This carried the ignition points at one end. Later, a separate duplex chain was used to drive the dynamo, and a vernier adjustment was added to the valve timing. Tappet adjustment remained by shims under the tappet-head caps. A simple cover enclosed the timing gear.

Lubrication was by the ancient dipper system. With this, the connecting-rod caps had hollow extensions which entered the oil near bottom dead centre so that it was forced up and into the plain big-ends. The timing gear was lubricated via pressure valves by the crankcase mist, and the oil simply drained back into the sump once it had done its work.

AJW fitted this very basic engine, together with a four-speed Burman gearbox, into a cradle, which

The 1949 AJW Grey Fox with its 494 cc JAP vertical twin, side-valve engine

could be readily removed from the machine for maintenance. The main frame had a single top tube, but was duplex elsewhere and fitted with plunger rear suspension. This was undamped, with load and rebound springs to control the light-alloy fork ends, which were bronze bushed and greased to slide on the steel pins. There were gaiters top and bottom to keep the lubricant in and the outside clean.

At the front were Dowty Oleomatic telescopic forks, which relied on air as the suspension medium, backed up by oil to provide hydraulic damping. They were an offshoot of the firm's work in the aviation field, and were both good and bad

news. The good was their progressive action and rise in spring rate as the fork moved. The bad was the dependence on fine-tolerance parts; once wear began to take effect, repairs were difficult.

For the rest, the Grey Fox had a saddle, with the battery below, as there was no oil tank to share the space, a toolbox ahead of it above the gearbox, clean handlebars with inverted levers, and a centre stand. The two exhaust pipes ran to the rear of the machine without change of diameter, but incorporated absorption silencers. The petrol tank had a gutter to keep rainwater away from the rider's legs, a welcome pre-war AJW feature, and was finished in red and blue. Detail fittings were of the period.

In production, the finish was azure blue for the tank, mudguards, rim centres and rear suspension gaiters. The other painted parts were in black,

AJW Fox Cub with 48 cc FBM engine unit, as imported and sold at the end of the decade

AJW prototype built in 1952 with JAP 500 cc ohv engine. This was laid down with the gearbox above and mounted in a spine frame

while the wheel-rim edges and other usual items were chrome plated. Virtually all the initial production went for export, but the numbers were limited by the availability of the JAP twin engines. Manufacture continued into 1950, when the engine supply dried up, so there were no more Grey Foxes.

The firm continued with the Speed Fox and also a speedway sidecar outfit, which had its third wheel hinged like a castor, but spring-loaded. This was arranged so that under power, and when cornering, it turned out to run parallel with the front wheel, which would point the same way on the tracks' right-hand bends.

Around 1952 the firm built two prototypes with horizontal, single-cylinder engines fitted into spine frames with pivoted-fork rear and telescopic front suspension. The larger used a 500 cc JAP ohv engine with an Albion gearbox mounted above it. This forced the rear fork pivot to be higher than normal, and it had a bell-crank lever to connect to the suspension springs in monoshock style. The rear of the machine was enclosed by a tail-unit, which carried a pillion pad behind the saddle.

The second machine used a 125 cc JAP two-stroke engine, which was built in unit with its three-speed gearbox. It was of conventional construction with built-up crankshaft, roller big-end, iron barrel and alloy head. Less usual was a cast-iron piston, but the gearbox was straight from the Villiers of the same capacity, Wipac supplied the ignition and generator unit, and Amal the carburettor.

As on the 500, the engine was positioned with the gearbox above it and in a spine frame with partial rear enclosure, but with just a short dual-seat. Brakes were drum with a 7 in. diameter at the front and 5 in. at the rear, both wheels being fitted with 2.75 × 19 in. tyres.

The 125 was listed as the Fox Cub for 1953, but the other models were to special order only. They included the Speed Fox speedway machine, the sidecar to go with it, and the Flying Fox. This last used a sports 500 cc JAP engine coupled to a four-speed Albion gearbox in a frame with pivoted-fork rear and telescopic front suspension.

Unfortunately for AJW, the supply of JAP engines, except for speedway, dried up, so their production of road models ceased. They left the market for a while, but returned in 1958 with another Fox Cub; this time a 48 cc light motorcycle.

In truth, it was an import with an FBM engine and three-speed gearbox hung from a pressed-steel spine frame with front and rear suspension. However, they continued to produce it into the next decade, when it was joined by others. The company remained in the motorcycle business until 1964.

Ambassador

This concern was founded by Kaye Don, an ex-Brooklands rider and driver, who sought to expand his business, after the war, to include motorcycles. His company produced well-finished lightweights with Villiers engines and, from around 1954, also imported Zundapp mopeds, motorcycles and scooters.

One of Don's early prototypes, built in 1946, was very different and used the 494 cc vertical-twin JAP engine with side valves and coil ignition. This was fitted into a substantial cradle frame with girder forks at the front, but no rear suspension. The cycle parts were typical of the period, with drum brakes and saddle, but no more was heard of this machine.

The first production model appeared in 1947 and used the Villiers 5E 197 cc engine unit with twin exhausts, side inlet with long inlet tract, and three-speed gearbox. This went into a simple, rigid loop frame with pressed-steel blade girders at the front. There was a saddle, a petrol tank finished in silver with black and red lining and John Bull kneegrips, and Dunlop tyres. A bulb horn gave notice of approach, and the lighting was direct.

This first machine was listed as the Series I, becoming the Series II for 1948. Logically, it was the Series III for 1949, but of particular importance was a change to a 6E engine with single exhaust pipe. It continued for 1950, but with battery lighting, and was joined by two more models fitted with the 6E engine.

The first of the new machines was the Series IV, but this was better known as the Popular and was, in effect, the Series III from the previous year with its direct lighting. The second was the Series V, which differed from the others in being fitted with MP telescopic front forks in place of the girders. It became known as the Embassy in 1951, when the Series II became the Courier. Together with the Popular, they ran on much as before.

They were joined by the Supreme, still with the same 6E engine unit, but this had plunger rear suspension in addition to the telescopic forks and battery lighting, so it was the top model of the range. To enhance this, the finish was in grey for all painted parts plus the battery and footrest rubbers, while the petroil tank was chrome plated with lined grey panels.

There were only three models for 1952, as the Courier was dropped, but the range was expanded again for 1953. Of the existing models, the Supreme was fitted with larger 6 in. brakes and smaller 18 in. wheels, plus a deeper, valanced front mudguard. New was the Self Starter version, which was a Supreme with a Lucas starter motor tucked in under the front of the tank. The motor drove the engine by belt, so a large cover appeared on the right to enclose it, while two large batteries were hung in pannier boxes on each side of the rear wheel. The power needed to recharge them, and cope with all the extra weight, must have nearly exhausted the poor little engine.

If the Self Starter was tiring to the engine, the second new model put an almost impossible strain on it, for this was the Sidecar machine. For this, the firm hung a single-seat sports sidecar on to their Embassy machine, which was fitted with special Webb girders, and sold it as a complete outfit only. The gearing was lowered to suit, and the battery lighting retained, while the sidecar came complete with hood and screen.

During 1953 the range experienced a change in engine type, from the 6E to the very similar 8E. For the Supreme this was a short-lived alteration, as it was amended again for 1954, when it was fitted with the 224 cc 1H engine with its four-speed gearbox. At the same time, it was given a new frame with pivoted-fork rear suspension and dualseat. The Embassy took over its role, receiving the plunger frame, and the Popular was fitted with telescopic forks.

All the models continued for 1955, the Embassy being given the option of a four-speed gearbox, and there was one new machine. This was the Envoy, which continued with the 197 cc 8E engine and three-speed gearbox, but in the pivoted-fork frame with dualseat.

Above right **Ambassador prototype of 1946, with the 494 cc JAP vertical twin side-valve engine in rather dated cycle parts**

Right **A batch of early Ambassador models in 1947, when they still used the pre-war-style 5E Villiers engine**

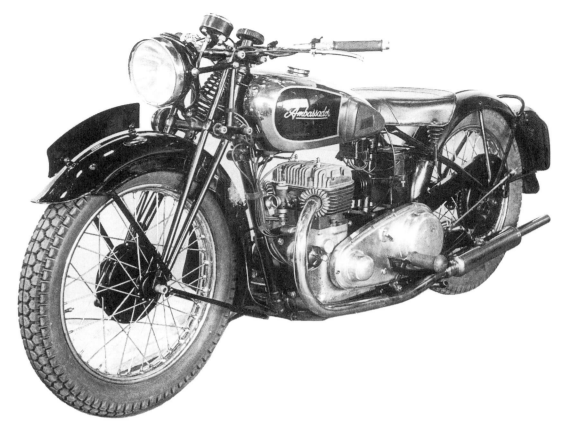

Right **The Ambassador Sidecar model, with its girder forks, was only sold as a complete outfit and gave the 8E engine a hard time**

Ambassador Supreme of 1953 with plunger frame and Villiers 8E engine

The range was reduced to three models for 1956, the Envoy and Supreme being joined by a new version of the Popular. This used the 147 cc Villiers 30C engine with three-speed gearbox, which were fitted into the pivoted-fork frame. It was finished in a rather more basic manner than the other models, so some parts did not blend together very well, but it offered basic transport.

Effectively, there was a fourth model for 1956, as the Envoy was also offered with the 9E engine and four-speed gearbox instead of the 8E. Of the range, it continued alone into 1957, when it was listed with only the 9E engine, but with a choice of three or four speeds. At the same time, the Popular switched to the 148 cc 31C engine, again with a choice as to the number of gears, and the Supreme to the 246 cc 2H engine. This had the word 'Single' added to its name.

The 1957 range was completed with the Supreme Twin model, which was fitted with the

249 cc Villiers 2T twin engine unit in place of the 2H. All the models had full-width, light-alloy hubs. These contained 6 in. drum brakes for all models, except the Popular, which had to manage with 5 in. versions.

The entire range ran on for 1958 with little change, the Popular and Envoy continuing to be offered with a choice of gearbox. The Supreme remained on offer as a Single or a Twin, but to this selection could be added the Statesman model. This used the 174 cc Villiers 2L engine, again with a choice of three or four speeds, so it slotted in between the other two singles.

This did not last for long as, for 1959, the 148 cc model was dropped and the 174 cc one took its name to become the Popular. The Envoy continued, but only for the first few months of the year, and the two Supreme models were also dropped. In their place came the Super S, which had the 249 cc 2T engine and a new, more enclosed, style. This was all the rage towards the end of the decade, and Ambassador followed the

trend with a rear enclosure that ran from the seat nose to the rear number plate, but which kept the wheel in view. To go with it, there was a well-valanced front mudguard and 17 in. wheels with 7 in., full-width hubs.

In April 1959 the Envoy was replaced by the Three Star Special, which was similar to the Super S, but fitted with the 9E engine offering a choice of three or four speeds. The rear panels had a trio of stars to decorate each side, while the front mudguard enclosed even more of the wheel. The style was enhanced by a pressing over the bars and controls to conceal the cables, and there was a grab handle to the rear of the dualseat. An option of a rear chaincase was listed. The finish was in Tartan red and black.

All three models ran on for 1960, when the Super S was fitted with the front mudguard from the Three Star. However, in 1962, Kaye Don retired and the make was taken over by DMW, who continued to produce the marque for a few years only.

The Super S Ambassador of 1959 with its Villiers 2T twin engine, some rear enclosure and full-width hub

Ariel

Ariel built one of their overhead-valve singles for the services during the war and, afterwards, simply continued with this in civilian guise. They added four more singles to expand the range and completed it with their unique Square Four model.

The wartime single became the 346 cc NG, which differed from the others in having the service frame with extra ground clearance, derived from the pre-war competition one. Except for this feature, and minor details such as mudguard valancing, the five singles were very similar. However, one, the 598 cc VB, had a side-valve engine.

Those with ohv were the NG already mentioned, plus the larger 499 cc VG, both of which were listed as de luxe models. The two capacities were then duplicated as the sporting Red Hunter models, coded NH and VH respectively. These had improved internals and a larger carburettor, so they were able to breathe more easily and produce more power. Their finish was also brighter, with red tank panels and wheel-rim centres, as in pre-war days.

The single-cylinder engine design dated from 1926, when Val Page had laid down its basic form. It replaced a truly elderly layout, and with the magneto being moved behind the cylinder in the following year, it assumed the shape it was to keep for over 30 years.

The engine was simple, sturdy and very tough indeed. It was laid out in traditional British form, with a built-up crankshaft, bearings to support it, and a vertically-split alloy crankcase. The timing gear was the simplest, with two spur pinions and followers to move the tappets or pushrods. The camshaft drove the mag-dyno and the oil pump for the dry-sump system, a cover being fitted to conceal both drive and pump.

Both head and barrel were cast in iron for side- and overhead-valve engines, with the former having a tappet chest with lid to enclose the valves. The ohv engine had stud fixings for the barrel and separate bolts to hold the head to it. The pushrod tubes ran up to the underside of the head from the crankcase, and each rocker had its own alloy box, which fitted on top of the head.

All the ohv models were said to be available with twin-port heads and either standard or upswept exhaust systems. It was also stated that a request for either, or both, features could delay delivery, so there can be few who asked for them at a time when new machines were in such demand. In all cases, the single-cylinder engine drove a four-speed Burman gearbox with foot-change. The primary drive was housed within a sleek, polished alloy chaincase, which had an outer space for the clutch. Consequently, this ran dry under its own domed cover.

The engine and gearbox went into a rigid frame with a duplex arrangement beneath them and single tubes for the main section. The front suspension remained as girders, although the firm was known to have a fully-developed telescopic fork. This was promised as soon as production would permit it.

The remainder of the cycle parts were pre-war in form and laid out in a traditional manner. Thus, the oil tank and battery were under the saddle, to right and left, while the toolbox was between the right-side chainstays. The mudguards varied, valanced, flared examples being provided for the de luxe VG and side-valve models, and more sporting ones for the smaller de luxe and Red Hunter machines.

In pre-war style, there was an instrument panel set in the top of the petrol tank, front and rear stands, and single-leading-shoe brakes in wheels with offset hubs and 19 or 20 in. rims. The headlamp was hung on the top of the fork girder and carried the light switch and ammeter, while the front number plate was in a style common to the Ariel marque.

The final machine in the range was the 995 cc Square Four, which was virtually unchanged from its 1939 form. It retained its then unique engine layout, but in other respects was much as the singles, having a rigid frame, girder forks and Burman four-speed gearbox. The one obvious change from pre-war days was the fitting of tubular silencers in place of the Brooklands cans, although this style was to be seen on the VB, possibly to use up stocks.

The four-cylinder engine had first appeared in its 1-litre, ohv form for 1937, but its origins could

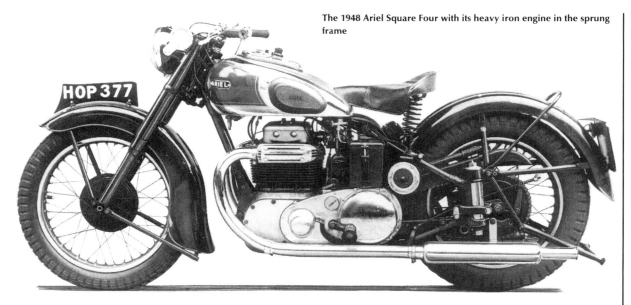

be traced back to 1931, when it was of 500 cc, but had an overhead camshaft. The larger engine was built much in the traditional British style with vertical crankcase joint, but inside it there were two crankshafts.

Each crankshaft was a one-piece forging, to which a central flywheel was bolted, and these were offset so that they could overlap, allowing the distance between the shaft centres to be kept to a minimum. The two crankshafts were coupled by large spur gears mounted on their left-hand ends within an alloy case, from the outside of which a chain took the drive to the gearbox. Connecting rods with split big-ends were used, and the four pistons moved in a very heavy, cast-iron block.

A one-piece, cast-iron head carried the valves in two vertical rows, and on top was an alloy rocker box. This was in the form of an open tray with a lid, the rockers being mounted in two lines. Incorporated into the box was the induction passage. This ran forward from a Solex carburettor to the centre of the box, from where it was directed down into the head and four inlet tracts. The exhaust ports ran out to the sides of the head casting, and to each was bolted a finned manifold, the pipe curling down from its forward end.

In the lower half of the engine, the camshaft was positioned high up in the crankcase, between the cylinders. It operated a line of tappets and pushrods, and was driven by chain from the crankshaft. This chain also drove the rear-mounted electrics and had a Weller tensioner to keep it under control. The twin-plunger oil pump

was driven from the camshaft nut. A special twin-spark magneto, which ran at engine speed, not only had the dynamo mounted on its back, but also drove a distributor via skew gears.

When this range was announced, in July 1945, there was mention of another multi, the telescopic front forks, and the unusual plunger-type rear suspension, which had been devised by Frank Anstey in 1939. The new model was a twin, which was to take some time to reach production, but the other items were soon in use.

In the middle of 1946 details of a patent relating to saddles were released. In the new design, the usual springs were dispensed with. They were replaced by a single, central, telescopic spring unit, which could include a hydraulic damper if required. The support this gave could be varied by changing either the spring or the top fixing position.

No more was heard of this, but two weeks later came news of the telescopic front forks. These were essentially simple with external springs between the seal holder and the bottom crown, while inside there was oil for the hydraulic damping. Initially, the new forks were used on the Square Four and the two Red Hunter models, and with them there was a new front hub with a knock-out spindle. The front brake was also revised with a wedge adjuster at the shoe fulcrum, as had been used at the rear wheel since pre-war times.

When the 1947 programme was announced, all the models had telescopic forks and the modified front wheel, and all, in theory, became available with the special Ariel rear suspension. In practice, production was limited, so most examples went to the Four and the sports singles, export requirements taking priority.

The rear suspension was the same as in 1939, with plungers incorporated into the frame. Each had a very short, pivoted arm, which carried the wheel spindle at one end, was attached to the plunger slider in the middle, and was pivoted on a link at the front. This link was nearly vertical and ran down to a pivot on the frame's lower chainstay.

The effect of the linkage was that the wheel spindle moved in an arc about the gearbox sprocket, which kept the chain tension constant. It did this, however, at the expense of restricted wheel movement and the addition of several pivot points, all of which had to be kept well greased. If this was not done, they soon wore and put an even greater strain on the wheel spindle, as it alone kept the two sides working as one and the wheel itself upright. There was no damping, other than that provided by the friction of the pivots and sliders, so not all riders were totally convinced that the system was worth having at all.

At the time, many solo riders preferred a rigid frame, rather than undamped plunger suspension, for a good saddle gave just as comfortable a ride. Where a sidecar was attached, this applied to an even greater extent, and most outfits of the day had rigid frames and often girder forks as well. It was to be some time before the traditional sidecar driver was to consider any change in suspension systems as desirable, even though the option may have been taken from him.

One of the magazines ran a test with a Red Hunter and sidecar, using girders and telescopics. The result was a preference for the latter, although the fixed, solo trail did make the steering heavier. However, the traditional owner would have none of it and muttered about rigidity and feel.

The range had remained the same with six models, but the existence of the twin was now well known, a photograph appearing in the press late in 1946. It finally made its debut for 1948 and appeared as two models, the KG being the de luxe one and the KH the Red Hunter version. Both had a 499 cc vertical twin engine with overhead valves.

They were nearly identical, with many common parts, and the engines differed only in compression ratio, carburettor size and degree of polish to the cylinder head. Construction was conventional with vertically-split crankcase containing the one-piece, forged crankshaft with central bolted flywheel.

The mains were plain timing and roller drive, while the big-ends were plain shells in light-alloy rods. The camshafts ran high in the crankcase, to front and rear, and had a chain drive from the crankshaft. Each cam had a tappet above it, running in a guide. These, and the pushrods, were placed at the four corners of the cast-iron cylinder block.

Above the block was a cast-iron, one-piece head with integral rocker boxes, each pair of which had a single alloy cover held by one bolt. An Amal carburettor was bolted to the rear of the head, and twin pipes and silencers to the front. The inlet camshaft drove a long, vertical shaft, which ran down to the duplex-gear oil pump of the dry-sump lubrication system. Its drive sprocket had a gear fitted behind it, which drove a rear-mounted magneto. A similar arrangement on the exhaust camshaft drove the dynamo, which was clamped to the front of the crankcase.

For the rest, the twins were as the singles, having a four-speed gearbox driven by a dry clutch and a chain within a polished alloy case. The frame was amended a trifle to clear the dynamo, and the models were offered as rigid or with the rear-link suspension as an option. At the front there were telescopic forks and a 20 in. wheel for the Red Hunter, while the de luxe kept to the 19 in. size. The finish of both matched that of the singles.

These all continued with no significant change, as did the Square Four, and it was the latter that had the only real alterations for 1949. These were made in an attempt to reduce the very considerable weight, and this was done by switching to an all-alloy engine. While doing this, the manufacturers replaced the magneto by coil ignition with a special dynamo and skew-gear-driven points housing and distributor.

The result was considered by many to be the most handsome Squariel of all, with its chrome tank with red panels and matching wheel rims. The rear link suspension continued to be listed as an option, but few machines were built without it, and they continued to be supplied with a very comfortable saddle and pillion pad.

The suspension gave a very civilized ride, for the machine was fast for its era and accelerated well. The handling was adequate for most owners, although it would weave on rough roads if

Competition 1952 Ariel VCH model with an all-alloy engine in a rigid frame and with an odd exhaust-pipe run

pressed, but few who bought the model did this, preferring to use the acceleration to get back to their cruising speed.

For 1950 there was one new model in the form of the competition Hunter VCH, which could be supplied in trials or scrambles specification. Both presented the owner with a racing magneto and alloy mudguards, but no lights. The engine was all-alloy with the pushrod tunnels cast into the barrel. The internal specification, gearing and tyres were to suit the intended use, and the rigid frame was special with a shorter wheelbase. No rear suspension was offered, but there were telescopics at the front and standard hubs.

The rest of the range had detail alterations only, but the Square Four and the twins had their speedometers moved to the fork bridge where they were easier to read. All road models had a new top crown for 1951, which did this job, but the NG and VG models were no longer listed. The tank-top instrument panels were no more, although the Four and the twins still had an oil gauge set in the tank, and there were many detail changes.

The de luxe twin was no longer listed in 1952, but there was a new single in the form of the all-alloy VHA, which used the cycle parts from the other singles and either the rigid frame or the link

Ariel 499 cc vertical twin in 1950, when it was still built to KG or KH specification

Nice line of Ariel models at the 1950 New York motorcycle show, with the new, all-alloy Square Four at the front

suspension. There was also a new Burman gearbox for all models and an alloy head for the side-valve VB engine.

There were two more models for 1953, plus detail changes and a dualseat option for the ohv singles. One of the new machines was the KHA, which was an alloy-engine version of the twin with the dualseat option and a Wedgwood blue finish. The last was also used that year by the Four and Hunter singles and twins. The second model was another version of the Square Four, which became the Mark II, while the original continued as the Mark I.

The new model had a new cylinder head with four separate exhaust pipes, which became the main distinguishing feature. Inside, there was a gear-type oil pump and other improvements, but on the cycle side the two machines used common parts.

During the year, the firm tried Earles leading-link front forks on various models, with a view to putting them into production. They reached the catalogue, but then a combination of technical problems and the tragic death of Les Graham, who died in the TT when riding an MV with Earles forks, caused them to drop the idea. At the same time, their general manager also died. His successor, Ken Whistance, decided to keep to telescopics and to pursue other ideas.

The end of the 1953 season saw the Mark I Square Four, alloy KHA twin, alloy VHA single and competition VCH dropped from the range. This left the NH, VH and VB singles, the KH twin and

the Mark II 4G, to which another four models were added.

The smallest of these was a 198 cc ohv single, which revived a pre-war Ariel name, the Colt, and was listed as the LH. It owed a good deal to the BSA company, which had owned Ariel since 1944, and their Bantam and C11G designs. The result was a very simple engine, with alternator electrics and coil ignition, which drove a separate four-speed gearbox. The pressed-steel primary chaincase was a typical BSA design, having a row of small fixing screws, and the cycle parts showed their Small Heath lines as well.

There was telescopic front and plunger rear suspension, oil tank and battery beneath the dual-seat, and offset hubs with drum brakes, the rear brake being from a Bantam. It added up to a neat workaday machine, but was effectively a C11G reduced to fit in the 200 cc class.

At the other end of the scale was the 647 cc ohv twin FH, also known as the Huntmaster, which simply used the BSA Golden Flash engine with the minimum of changes to disguise the fact. No mention of the matter appeared in the press of the time. To help the model along, it had a new frame with pivoted-fork rear suspension.

This was also used by the smaller twin and ohv singles, and had duplex downtubes and single top and seat tubes to form a full cradle. Unlike others in the industry, the rear fork arms were built up from pressings welded together, which was an indication of the direction in which the Val Page design team was heading.

The Ariel all-alloy VHA was only built for 1953 and is seen here in the sprung frame

To suit the new frame there were new cycle parts and a dualseat fitted as standard. The finish became deep claret, as the blue had not been to the taste of many, but the Four and the VB went to black and the Colt to Brunswick green. The two black models also retained the link suspension, while it remained an option for the side-valve machine. The Four was given an SU carburettor in place of its earlier Solex instrument. As well as the new frame, the VH also gained an alloy cylinder head and an iron barrel with integral pushrod tunnels. The KH twin switched to an alloy head which, as on the all-alloy engine, had the rocker chambers formed differently. Each had its own cap.

The other two new models were both for competition, the HT having a rigid frame with saddle for trials, and the HS a pivoted-fork frame and dualseat for scrambles. Both had the all-alloy 499 cc engine, but with different internals, and cycle parts to suit their purpose.

After this major redesign, it was no surprise that little was altered for 1955 when the Monobloc carburettor was the most noticeable change. It went on to all the road singles and twins, plus the HT, but not the HS or 4G. The VB finally made it into the pivoted-fork frame, but the rigid one remained available for the diehards, who saw both the frame and side-valve engine as the only way to go.

The four-pipe Ariel Square Four, of 1953, hitched to a sporting sidecar to make a fast road outfit

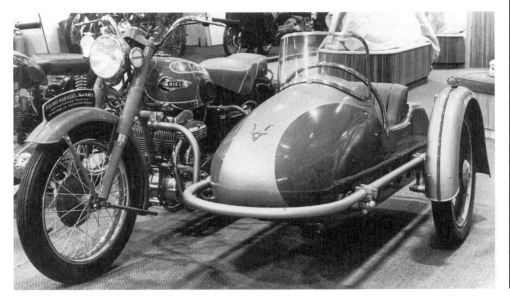

There was a headlamp cowl for all road models in 1956, and full-width, light-alloy hubs front and rear for all singles and twins, except the Colt in either case, but only for the front of the Square Four. That model did receive the benefit of a much larger oil tank, which extended down behind the gearbox, so the toolbox had to be moved. It was mounted on the left, which can hardly have been helpful to sidecar owners, but at least they could pack their gear in the chair.

Of the singles, the NH finally received an alloy head and iron barrel to match the VH, and the VB was no longer listed with the rigid frame. The HS had its oil tank moved to the left to make way for a massive air filter, and also went over to a Monobloc. The HT was altered more drastically to a new frame with pivoted-fork rear suspension, but designed to retain the short trials wheelbase. In this form it became the HT5.

For 1957 it was joined by the smaller HT3 with an all-alloy, 346 cc engine, but otherwise this model was as the 499 cc one. The road models, except the Colt, were given a deeper valanced front mudguard, and there was a one-bolt tank for all except the Four. At the end of the season, the KH Ariel twin was dropped, for the firm were close to some major changes of direction.

There was no immediate sign of these when the 1958 range was announced with no alterations, but the firm had been working and planning for some time on a new future. They made a major decision to design a new radical machine for the next decade, using modern production techniques to reduce costs and keep quality high. Initial market research indicated that a 250 cc twin two-stroke was the engine type to use, but not much else. Engineering sense dictated the use of pressings, mouldings and die-castings as much as possible, while the trend of the time lent towards enclosure.

So Val Page set to work, and the result was announced in July 1958 as the Ariel Leader. It was a sensation, for it not only used the suggested engine, but had a pressed-steel frame with full enclosure, legshields and windscreen, as for a scooter, but on motorcycle-size wire-spoke wheels.

The engine capacity was 247 cc and its two parallel cylinders were inclined well forward and cast in iron. Each had an alloy head with its plug inclined forward. The cylinders went into a single, massive, lower-half casting. This combined the crankcase, inner primary case and gearbox as one, but with space between the two major units.

The full-disc crankshafts went in from each side to be joined in the centre with a keyed taper joint, and the chambers were sealed with a door on each side. The alternator was on the right and the points, plus an external flywheel, were on the left, outboard of the primary drive. The gearbox was a four-speed Burman, and the final drive remained on the left within a chaincase.

Left **The Earles leading-link front forks tried out during 1953, but which never went into production and seen here on a KH twin**

Right **Basic Ariel single in the form of a 346 cc NH during a 1953 road test, when it demonstrated the tough nature of the type**

Right **The Ariel Colt, which owed much to the BSA C11G, but had a 198 cc engine**

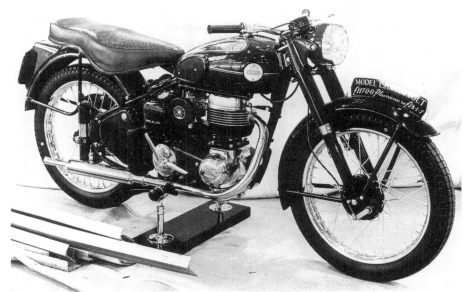

The engine unit was hung from the main frame beam, which was large enough to contain the box-shaped petrol tank. The beam was extended down behind the gearbox to support both the box and the rear fork, and swept up at the front for the headstock. The front suspension was by trailing links, the units and arms being concealed within the fork pressings. There was no top crown as such, so the handlebars were simply clamped to the top of the column. Both wheels had light-alloy, full-width hubs with 6 in. brakes, 16 in. rims and whitewall tyres.

The mechanics of the Leader were then hung with its clothes. A dummy tank, with parcel compartment, went on top of the main frame beam and extended back to form the seat base. The seat itself was hinged and beneath it were the tools and battery. The sides of the machine, beneath the dummy tank, were enclosed by panels and to the rear of these there was a hinged section to blend with the seat base.

At the front there were legshields, which blended into the side panels and continued up to form the base for the windscreen. There was an instrument panel behind it and a cowl for the headlight in front. The front wheel had its own well valanced mudguard, and there was an internal one at the back. A pressing on the bars concealed the pivots and cables.

The machine was conceived to have extras, which included panniers, indicators, clock and many more, rather in the scooter vein. They were available when the machine went on sale and combined with it to make the whole operation very successful. There were minor criticisms, but the machine ran well enough for 1958 and was received favourably by press and public.

Thus encouraged, Ariel decided on the major step of terminating their entire four-stroke range, which caused consternation among enthusiasts for the marque. The first to go was the venerable VB at the beginning of 1959, followed by the competition HT and HS models within a month or two. The remaining Colt, two Hunters, Huntmaster and Square Four went in August that year, although the 650 twin did survive into 1960 as the Cyclone for the USA.

This left the Leader, which was unchanged for 1959, but for 1960 it was joined by the Arrow. This was a sports version, which dispensed with

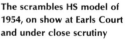

The scrambles HS model of 1954, on show at Earls Court and under close scrutiny

Traditional Ariel single, in pivoted-fork frame, having its finishing touches applied for the late 1954 show at Earls Court

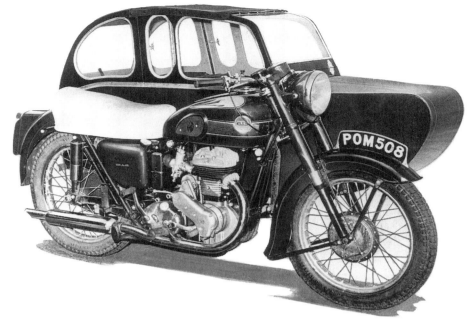

The 1955 Ariel 598 cc VB hitched to a double-adult Watsonian Maxstoke sidecar, and thus carrying out its traditional role

Ariel Leader 247 cc twin-cylinder two-stroke with all its enclosure and forward-looking engineering

most of the enclosure, but kept the basic engine unit, frame beam and forks. To this was added a dummy tank, rear mudguard and revised seat and other details. The hubs were in cast iron, as the alloy ones had shown signs of cracking in a few cases. The machine was an instant success.

Later on, in the 1960s, were to come the Golden Arrow and the smaller 200 cc version, but in 1965 the parent group decided to stop production in a declining market. It was a tragic decision, for the formula could easily have been developed over many years, but it was not to be.

Val Page had other ideas for the Leader, including a 700 cc four-stroke tourer with in-line, four-cylinder engine laid down with the heads pointing to the left – just as the BMW K series of 1983. Sadly, the parent group did not share his vision and let it all fall apart.

BAC

These were the initials of the Bond Aircraft and Engineering Company, which launched a three-wheeler and a light motorcycle in the late 1940s, both rather unusual in design and appearance. Manufacture was taken over by Ellis of Leeds at the end of 1950, and BAC moved on to a pair of lightweight motorcycles that owed nothing to the earlier design.

The BAC models were given the name Lilliput and really were machines in miniature, but in proportion. The engines used were either the 99 cc Villiers 1F with its two-speed gearbox, or the 125 cc JAP with three speeds.

The cycle parts were common and included a single-tube loop frame, which was rigid at the rear and had light telescopic front forks. The tyre size was 2.00 × 20 in., which matched the machine, and the rider was provided with a saddle. The lighting was direct, so the horn was a bulb type, although an electric one was listed as an option. The smaller model weighed in at 89 lb.

The 125 was only offered for 1951, partly because supplies of the JAP engine were not very reliable, but the smaller machine was built for 1952 as well. For that year, it was joined by a new model with rather odd styling. This was the Gazelle scooter with a 122 cc Villiers 10D engine.

The machine was laid out much as any other scooter, with twin frame tubes running down from the headstock and then back to the rear wheel. They were joined under the engine by a box that acted as a silencer, the gases being led out of the ends of the tubes which, thus, became tail pipes. The engine was mounted just ahead of the rear wheel with the saddle above it.

The petrol tank was behind the seat, immediately above the rear mudguard, and the oddest feature was the protective grille round the engine.

This comprised a number of wide steel bars, each of which ran across in front of the engine and back on each side. Their purpose was to keep the rider's clothing away from the hot cylinder without restricting the airflow to it, but they did little for the appearance.

There were telescopic forks at the front, 4.00 × 8 in. tyres on pressed-steel wheels, drum brakes and a typical scooter apron. The lighting was direct, and there was a bulb horn and a speedometer.

At the end of 1952, the 122 cc Gazelle was joined by a model powered by the 1F engine. Otherwise, it was the same, and both were given a triangular toolbox bolted to the rear of the apron and a new seat. This sat on four small springs and was based on a pillion pad with the addition of a little backrest for the rider.

In addition to the new model, BAC also offered a light sidecar, the body of which was fashioned in aluminium sheet. It used the same wheel as the motorcycle, so one spare could replace any in the event of a puncture. However, it seems unlikely that there were many customers who believed in 122 cc sidecar outfits.

The solos also failed to make much of an impact, and by May 1953 the Gazelle had been taken over by Projects and Developments of Blackburn. They moved the fuel tank forward under the seat, and over the hot engine, to leave room for a rear carrier or even a pillion seat. This was optimistically being suggested for the 99 cc version, but sanity must have returned, for no more was heard of the machines at all.

The BAC Gazelle scooter, for 1952, with its 10D Villiers engine and odd enclosing 'cage'

Bantamoto

This was one of the many cycle attachments that came on to the market around 1949 or 1950 and stayed there for a few years until the true moped appeared. They were intended to take the effort out of cycling, which they did, and for a few years were a common sight. All could be attached, in some way, to a standard bicycle, so if all else failed, they could be pedalled home for repair.

The Bantamoto was produced by the Cyc-Auto firm in Acton, West London, and was attached to the cycle on the left side of the rear wheel, which it drove via a train of gears. The engine was a two-stroke with vertical cylinder and featured an alloy head and barrel, plus rotary-valve induction via a sleeve driven by the inboard end of the crank-shaft.

Less modern was the deflector-top piston, while the crankshaft was pressed-up with bobweights and a roller big-end. A Wipac Bantamag rather appropriately went on the left-hand end of the crankshaft to provide ignition. The exhaust and silencer ran from the rear of the cylinder, with the Amal carburettor beneath it and feeding into a cast passage in the crankcase, which led to the rotary valve.

There were three stages of gear pairs from the crankshaft to the wheel to give an overall reduction of 26:1. The first two stages were by normal spur gears, but the third pinion drove an internally-toothed gear ring attached to the rear wheel.

The whole unit was mounted on a spindle which attached to the wheel spindle with a clip and to the lower chainstay with a rubber insulator. Clever design allowed the engine to slide out of mesh if necessary. Lubrication was by oil in the gear case and petroil in a small, separate tank.

It was a neat unit, and the positive drive was preferred by some to the more usual friction-roller on to a tyre. Controls were simply the throttle and decompressor. Running costs were minimal.

The unit came on to the market in 1951 and was offered for two years, but was dropped in favour of Cyc-Auto's more usual range.

The Bantamoto cyclemotor unit, introduced for 1951, had a gear-train drive to the rear wheel and remote petroil tank

Bikotor

This was a short-lived cycle attachment that came and went in 1951. It was designed to drive the rear wheel by friction roller, and had a 47 cc two-stroke engine of all-alloy construction to keep the weight to a minimum.

The engine's cylinder was to the right of the wheel and upright, but inclined back a little. It was cast in one with the crankcase, having hard chrome plating on the bore and a simple alloy head to close it and carry the plug and decompressor. The overhung crankshaft was unusual in being a Meehanite iron casting that was fitted into a second casting. This, in turn, was spigoted into the crankcase. The connecting rod was in light alloy, as was the piston, although this was of the deflector type.

The drive roller went on the centre of the mainshaft, which had the flywheel magneto on the left-hand end. Above and ahead of the engine, a fuel tank was tucked in behind the cycle saddle and fed an automatic carburettor with a ported, cylindrical throttle and a mushroom control valve. Even the silencer was in light alloy and comprised three castings with a cylinder held between two detachable end caps, the top one of which had a flange for bolting to the exhaust port.

It was all very ingenious and well made, but it failed to catch on, so it was another of which no more was heard.

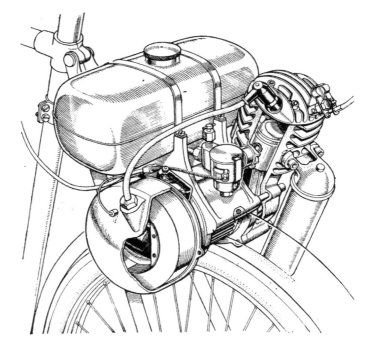

The Bikotor clip-on unit of 1951, which drove the rear wheel with a friction roller and was of all-alloy construction

Bond

Lawrence Bond is best known for the small three-wheeled cars that carry his name, but for 1950 he introduced a motorcycle that was just as unusual.

The new machine was a lightweight using the 99 cc Villiers 1F engine with two-speed gearbox and weighing in at 90 lb, thanks to its unusual all-alloy frame. This was based on a large, tapered, oval-section tube, which ran back from the head-stock. It was rolled from sheet and lap riveted on its underside. At the rear, it was cut away for the wheel, but stiffened by a massive rear mudguard that enclosed more than half the wheel

The engine was hung from the main beam and flanked by footboards with deep legshields. The fuel tank went into the beam, which was closed at the front by an aluminium casting with a plain-bearing steering head. The forks on the prototype were steel strips, but these were replaced by tubes for the initial production run. The front mudguard was as large as the rear, so it also concealed much of the wheel.

There was no springing front or rear, so comfort was provided by the saddle and the 4.00 × 16 in. balloon tyres, which were fitted on split rims. The alloy hubs had 4 in. drum brakes, the rear one being heel operated. The lighting was direct, and there was a bulb horn and a rear carrier.

By July 1950 the forks had become telescopic, and for 1951 the machine was joined by a de luxe version powered by a 125 cc JAP engine with three-speed gearbox. The prototype of this had been seen a year earlier, but no doubt supply problems had kept it back.

Previously, the machines had been built by the Bond Aircraft and Engineering Company in Lancashire, but for 1951 manufacture was taken over by Ellis of Leeds, while the original firm produced another small range under the BAC label (see page 42). The new firm incorporated some minor frame changes, but the models continued with their unique frames and a light-blue polychromatic paint finish.

Both machines ran on in this form for a year or two, but early in 1953 the smaller was dropped and production of the 125 ceased later that year. However, it was not the end of the name, for the three-wheeler continued in production, and the company moved to a new factory in Preston, Lancashire, returning to two wheels in 1958.

The new machine was a scooter listed as the P1 and powered by a fan-cooled, 148 cc Villiers 31C engine with three-speed gearbox and Siba electric start. This sat ahead of the rear wheel and acted as a frame member, with twin tubes running over it and back to support rider, fuel tank and rear fork pivot. At the front, these tubes joined the main frame tube, which ran down from the headstock and back to the engine plates.

The Bond motorcycle with its monocoque main beam and well enclosed wheels in 1951

Above **First of the P-series Bond scooters at the start of the 1959 Isle of Man rally, with a TWN behind it**

Below **Bond P4 of 1960 with 197 cc 9E Villiers engine and improved lines at the front**

At the front there was a single, pivoted leading arm to carry the wheel on a stub axle. The same was used at the rear, with a single suspension unit to control each. The wheels had split rims and carried 4.00 × 10 in. tyres, and rear chain tension was set with an eccentric at the pivot point.

On to this framework went a plastic body in scooter style, with apron, footboard and rear enclosure with detachable side panels. There was a dualseat on top of the body, which was hinged to give access to the top of the engine and the

fuel tank. This last was also moulded in plastic and incorporated the rear mudguard mounting.

At the front there was a good sized mudguard, which turned with the wheel and had a flat nose for a bumper bar. The headlamp was mounted in the apron, which had a fascia panel moulded to its top with a lockable container below and to the rear.

Styling was provided by a two-tone finish and the side panels, which were extended back to form small fins in the American car style. Two small portholes on each side highlighted this aspect.

In the middle of the year the P1 was joined by the P2, which used the 197 cc Villiers 9E engine, still with fan cooling and Siba electric start, but with a four-speed gearbox. Otherwise, it was the same, and both continued for 1959.

They were replaced by the P3 and P4, which retained the same engines, but had them set lower in the frame. The bodywork was amended by dispensing with the rear panels and hinging the entire rear section from the tail. When raised, it gave exceptional access to the mechanics; it was held down by a single knurled nut.

At the front the mudguard became part of the apron moulding and assumed a lighter and more graceful line. Behind the apron, the fascia and stowage compartment remained and, despite the changes, the lines were really much as before, including the twin fins and portholes. The two models continued in production until 1962, after which the firm concentrated on its three-wheelers only.

Bown

This name from the 1920s was revived in 1950 and used by the firm for its autocycle, which replaced the Aberdale they had built previously (see page 13). The machine itself was revised to use the single-speed, 99 cc Villiers 2F engine, rather than the earlier Junior de Luxe, and the frame was modified to suit its mountings.

The new frame was of the cradle type with duplex downtubes, but otherwise the model was cast in the normal autocycle mould. The petroil tank was fitted between the upper and lower downtubes, there was extensive panelling beneath the tank to shield the engine, and pedals were fitted.

Pressed-steel blade girder front forks were provided for the rigid frame, and there was a saddle, rear carrier and rear stand. The lighting was direct and the finish in maroon with gold lining, which gave the machine a smart appearance. It was listed as the Auto Roadster.

For 1951 the autocycle was joined by a small motorcycle, powered by the Villiers 1F engine with two-speed gearbox. This went into a neat cradle frame with duplex downtubes and tubular forks, which retained girder links, spring and movement. There was a saddle, a tubular toolbox

The tank may say Aberdale, but this is the model which became the 1950 Bown autocycle with the 2F Villiers engine

Bown 99 cc motorcycle with the two-speed 1F engine in a nice duplex frame, but still with girder forks

clipped to the seat tube, and the same maroon finish. Two versions were offered, either with direct lighting as standard or with a battery in the de luxe form.

In the middle of 1952 a further model was added to the range as the Tourist Trophy, which used the 122 cc Villiers 10D engine with three-speed gearbox. The cycle parts were much as for the smaller model, but telescopic front forks were fitted and the toolbox was repositioned to clear the carburettor. The finish remained maroon, but with blue-grey tank panels. The model continued the Welsh firm's reputation for well made, sturdy machines.

All four models continued as they were for 1953 and 1954, but in the latter year production ceased. Two years later the firm returned to the market with a moped powered by a 47.6 cc Sachs engine with two-speed gearbox. This went into a pressed-steel and tubular rigid frame with trailing-link front forks and moped styling. The next year it was given plunger rear suspension, but then faded from the scene.

Bradshaw

The name of Granville Bradshaw runs like a thread through the history of the British motorcycle industry, from as far back as 1913 when he designed a flat-twin for ABC. However, he became better known for the machine that appeared just after World War 1. This had a transverse flat-twin engine, unit four-speed gearbox and leaf springs for front and rear suspension.

It was highly innovative, but also very costly to produce, so its price soon cut the extensive waiting lists. Then the early models showed some weaknesses. These were mainly in the valve gear, but by the time they were eradicated, the firm building them was running down motorcycle production and returning to its aviation roots.

Bradshaw's name was next involved with the idea of oil-cooled engines, and his 350 cc single was used by the Dot company in the mid-1920s. From there, he went to P & M to design the 250 cc V-twin Panthette with its unit construction and forged-steel frame backbone. This, too, was not a success, due to a combination of high price and some technical problems.

In 1939 another Bradshaw design exercise appeared in the form of rear suspension for the big Panther models. As on the ABC, and for the Panthette valve gear, he used leaf springs rather than coils, a pair on each side supporting a vertical tube to which the wheel was attached. All was fine until a spring broke on test, making the machine nearly uncontrollable. As a result of this, together with the complicated design, the cost and the outbreak of war, it was dropped.

Around the same time, he also designed an in-line twin with overhead valves and a complex primary drive. Because the crankshafts ran across the machine, the original used a chain wrapped around the sprockets so that they ran in opposite directions. This proved weak and was replaced by helical gears, which were noisy and consumed power, so the project was dropped.

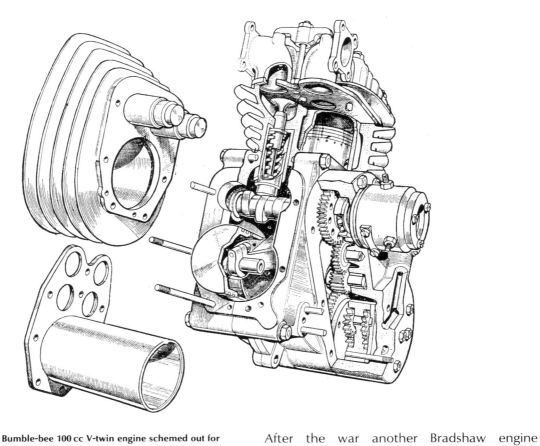

The Bradshaw Bumble-bee 100 cc V-twin engine schemed out for 1946 and very compact

After the war another Bradshaw engine appeared in the form of a 100 cc V-twin with side valves. What might have been prosaic to others, except for the small size, was less so to Granville. The engine was very compact, the valve gear being fully enclosed, and inside were some ingenious features.

Bradshaw Omega engine of 1955 with its oscillating and double-ended pistons, toroidal cylinder and shaft links

One was the liner for each alloy cylinder, which had a flat plate brazed to it that included the valve seats. The liner was only a push fit in its finned muff, which was partly machined away in the bore to allow oil to circulate and assist the cooling. The oil pump was a gear type, driven from the gear train that drove the single, central camshaft. This, in turn, drove an unusual contact breaker and distributor with auto-advance for the coil ignition, but with rollers and contacts in place of the usual points.

Finally, late in 1955, came the Omega engine, which was of a rotary form, ingenious and most unusual. It was difficult to see how it worked at all, but the design was intended to reduce the inertial loadings of the conventional layout.

The design was based on an annular cylinder, formed from two light-alloy castings bolted together. Within these was formed a toroidal chamber, which can be likened to an inner tube or an O-ring, being a ring with a round cross-section.

For the Omega, the working surface was hard chrome plated and within it were four double-ended pistons with rings at each end and a shape to match the toroid. Each opposing pair was joined by a cross-link, and each of these was bolted to one of two concentric shafts. These each had a short arm at the other end, with a connecting rod to join that to a 180-degree, two-throw crankshaft.

As this turned, the links caused the pistons to move some 30 degrees back and forth, so the space between the opposing crowns varied. If this was not enough, the entire cylinder also rotated at half crankshaft speed and was driven from this by helical gears. In its sides were cut inlet and exhaust ports, and the single sparking plug was screwed into the side. Lubrication was by petroil, with a separate system for the crankshaft, and cooling was by fins on the toroid and enclosure to guide the air.

The Omega was the final fling of a man whose ideas were always clever and innovative, but who sadly failed to understand the commercial needs of the business. His designs were novel, but invariably costly and seldom trouble-free, so his long involvement with the industry made news and kept everyone intrigued, rather than producing machines for riding. Without such men, the world would be the poorer.

Britax

This accessory firm moved into the motorcycle field late in 1949 with a 48 cc Ducati Cucciolo engine unit with two-speed gearbox, which they imported. As in its Italian homeland, the engine, the name of which meant 'little pup', was sold as a bicycle attachment, and it was very successful with over a quarter million sold worldwide.

The engine unit was unusual in a number of ways; for a start it was a four-stroke in a two-stroke class. Next were the overhead valves, which were opened by pull-rods moved by rockers at the camshaft. Then there was the two-speed gearbox, which had a preselector control and an all-metal clutch.

Engine construction was actually simple, the crankcase being a major part of the engine and gearbox; the left side formed a lid. Oil for all bearings was carried in the sump. The head and barrel were cast as one in alloy, with inserts for the valves and a sleeve for the piston.

The crankshaft drove the camshaft, which was combined with the input gear shaft. The output shaft carried a gear on the right-hand end, outside the case, and this meshed with an internal gear attached to the right-hand pedal crank. A small sprocket took the drive to the rear wheel, and the whole assembly was clamped to the cycle bottom bracket. The left-hand pedal was also special and acted as the gearchange lever to give either gear or neutral after being positioned appropriately, and the clutch worked.

Britax simply sold the engine unit at first, and owners soon realised that, if they had a three-speed rear hub, they were blessed with a total of six ratios. In addition, the cycle freewheel allowed the engine to tick over on descents, although this meant that there was no engine braking.

In the middle of 1953 the firm moved on to a complete machine, using Royal Enfield bicycle and motorcycle parts. The main frame had a dropped top tube and was constructed of heavy-

The Britax Hurricane road racer, which had a 48 cc ohv Ducati engine under all the panelling. It had a short life in 50 cc racing

gauge tubing in bicycle style. However, the front forks were blade girders with rubber-band suspension and came from the 125 cc motorcycle. The wheels were cycle size, but had 4 in. drum brakes, and the mudguards were heavier than usual. A saddle, rear carrier and fuel tank completed the package, which had direct lighting and a bulb horn. The model was given the name Monarch, but this was soon dispensed with and it became known as the Britax or Cucciolo.

It ran on without change and was joined for 1955 by two further models, one a scooter and the other a road racer. Both had 20 in. wheels and retained the Ducati engine unit, rigid frame and girder forks.

The Scooterette was enclosed with mainly flat panels and had a vast front mudguard, none of which did anything for its looks. Legshields were incorporated, but not a screen, so the rider still became wet in the rain. However, the performance in town was adequate for the time but, despite this and a competitive price, there were very few takers.

The racer was given the name Hurricane and was notable for its aluminium full fairing. This 'dustbin', as all such were called in the 1950s, was joined by further extensive panelling, which

enclosed the tank and ran back to form a seat base and rear mudguard to shield half the rear wheel.

Under all this was the same Ducati engine fitted with stronger valve springs and a megaphone exhaust system. The racing of 50 cc machines was in an embryonic stage in 1955, so the sight of a number of Hurricanes at a Blandford race meeting looked good, even if they failed to win.

There were improvements to the road models for 1956, with enclosure for the valve gear, normal gearchanging with handlebar control and reduced gear whine. The Hurricane was given telescopic front forks and a reverse-cone megaphone, but this would seem to have been for style rather than power. By the end of the season, the Itom had taken over on the race tracks and the Hurricane was dropped.

With it went the other models, for Ducati were moving on to other matters and Britax went back to accessories. Over two decades later they imported a 50 cc Italian fold-up machine for a while, but this was simply as an accessory to a car, caravan, boat or light aircraft.

BSA

Even before their post-war range was announced, BSA were in the news, thanks to a patent for a twin-cylinder engine with overhead valves. This set out how a single camshaft, placed at the rear of the crankcase, could control the valves which were set at an included angle by the use of different length pushrods and rocker arms. The arrangement was to appear in the A7 twin late in 1946.

The patent was announced in March 1945, and three months later was joined by another, which concerned a telescopic centre stand. The idea for this was Edward Turner's, for his name, along with BSA, appeared in the original application, which had been made in 1943 when Turner was technical director at the Small Heath firm.

The stand comprised a tube which slid up into the frame's seat tube and a transverse foot to support the machine at ground level. Inside the tube was a spring to hold it up, and on the outside there was a pawl and ratchet to lock the stand down. Thus, the rider was required to push the stand foot down, where the pawl would hold it, but to raise either wheel from the ground required him to lift the machine while still holding the stand down. Not an easy task with a machine of any real weight.

The pawl had a lever for disengagement, when the stand would spring up and the machine fall over if the rider was not prepared for it. The possibilities of interference by small boys, or the consequences of a spring failure when riding, were best not mulled over.

It was not until August 1945 that BSA announced their post-war range, which comprised just four models. However, these covered the learner, commuter, tourer and sidecar markets quite well, and within a few years the BSA range was to be the largest in the country.

The range offered for those first austere months comprised the 249 cc side-valve C10, the C11 of the same capacity (but with ohv), the side-valve 496 cc M20 and, the only new model, the 348 cc ohv B31. Even this last was not totally new, for it was based on the 1940 B29 and wartime WB30 with a strong bottom half, but it was the one model with telescopic front forks.

The two C-range machines shared cycle parts and many engine details, although the C11 did have 20 in. wheels, unlike the C10, which used

Post-war 1945 BSA C10 249 cc side-valve model for getting to work and still with pre-war girder forks

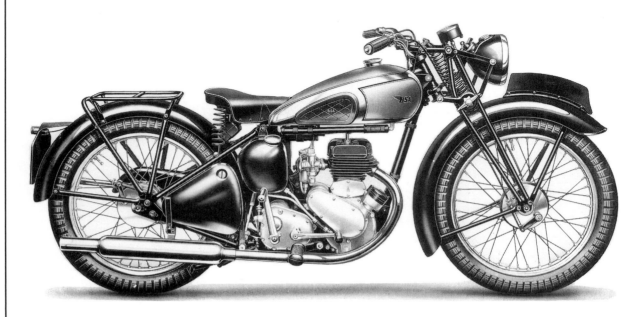

the 19 in. size. The engines were traditionally British with vertically-split crankcase, built-up crankshaft and dry-sump lubrication. The timing gear was of the simplest, with cam followers and then either tappets or pushrods.

In the C11, the pushrods crossed over on their way to the cylinder head, as the rockers lay across the engine, so they and the pushrods had to sit at the valves' included angle. An alloy cover enclosed the top end, but both head and barrel were in iron, as they were for the C10.

The bottom half was completed with a timing cover, which carried the skew-gear-driven points in their external housing. Outboard of this was a chain drive to the dynamo, which was clamped to the rear of the crankcase with an outer cover to enclose it. The oil pump sat low down in the crankcase, where it was driven from the crankshaft.

Both engines drove a three-speed, foot-change gearbox with the primary drive and clutch in a pressed-steel chaincase. The mechanics went into a rigid frame, which had girder front forks that carried the headlamp and speedometer. The oil tank was tucked under the saddle on the right, with the battery to match it on the left, while the toolbox went between the right-hand chainstays. A rear carrier was provided, and a pillion pad and rests were available. The tank was finished in chrome with silver panels, but the rest of the machine was in black for both models.

The M20 was really the same machine that BSA had supplied in large numbers to the army for some six years, and by simply painting the tank silver and the rest of the machine black, another civilian model was available. The sturdy frame and girder foks were ideal for sidecar work, as was the heavy-duty gearbox, while the layout of the detail parts was as for the C-range. A plodder it may have been, but a reliable plodder, for which spares were easily obtained and one that plenty of men were now well acquainted with. At a time when cars were both few in number and expensive to run, machines such as the M20, with the addition of a sidecar, enabled many a family to get out and about without relying on buses or trains.

While the C and M models were all pre-war in design and style, the new B31 represented the early post-war period very well. Its roots lay in the past, but with the new forks and a sprightly performance it blew a breath of fresh air into the range. The machine itself was to seem prosaic enough in later years, but in 1945 it was bright, shining and a rapid means of travel on the twisting roads of the day.

The B31 engine was a combination of light and heavy builds of the past, which gave it a good strong bottom end with less weight than before. In layout and construction, it was very conventional, with an all-iron top half, mag-dyno and all the expected BSA construction methods. About the only uncommon feature was the design of the head studs, which were attached to the crankcase and threaded into the underside of the cylinder head. By this means there were no bolt holes running through the head casting, decreasing the fin area, and no need for spanner access and deep counterbores.

For the rest, the engine drove a four-speed gearbox, similar to that of the M20, with a steel primary chaincase to enclose the chain and clutch. The engine and gearbox went into a rigid diamond frame, so there were no frame tubes under the crankcase. At the front were the new telescopic forks, which had hydraulic damping and supported the headlamp on lugs welded to the upper shrouds.

Both wheels had offset hubs with 7 in. single-leading-shoe brakes and 19 in. rims. Long mudguards kept the weather at bay, and the rest of the equipment was arranged in much the same way as for the other models. One variation occurred with the speedometer, which went in the top of the tank next to the filler cap and well out of the rider's line of sight.

The four models formed the basis of much of the BSA single range for the next decade or so, and before the end of the year were joined by one more machine. This was the M21, which was simply the M20 fitted with a 591 cc engine to provide more grunt for hauling even larger sidecars, packed with ever bigger families.

Within a month the five had become six, with the appearance of the B32 competition version of the B31. This was aimed at both the trials and scrambles rider, despite the lack of rear suspension, and most of it was pure B31. The differences were mainly external, although the gearing was lowered, and a magneto and battery lighting set could be substituted for the usual mag-dyno if the purchaser wished.

In other areas, there was a 21 in. front wheel, 4 in.-section rear tyre and abbreviated, chrome-plated mudguards. The exhaust system was swept up to waist level, and competition tyres fitted, together with a crankcase shield. There was more plating than usual and the result was a cobby mount that allowed many a trials rider a chance to compete at weekends.

In April 1946 the C-range machines received hydraulically-damped, telescopic front forks. At the same time, the speedometer was moved into the tank top, so these models copied the B-range in both these aspects. The headrace adjustment of these forks was by a patented method that the firm was to use for many a year.

In May 1946 a further patent was granted, and this related to the wheel hub. It became known as the 'crinkle' hub, due to the shape of the outer tubular part, which was formed in a 'pie-crust' style to allow the use of straight spokes. The outer tube was riveted to the inner one, which housed the bearings and carried the drive splines to the brake drum and sprocket. These rivets were the only weak point in the design, for they could work loose under heavy sidecar loads and if all failed, so did the drive to the wheel rim.

The new hub made its first appearance on a new twin-cylinder model announced in September 1946. This was the A7, from which an extensive range was to come over the years. The engine was a 360-degree vertical twin, of mainly conventional construction, with an iron head and barrel. The layout utilized the single rear camshaft for all four valves, as patented earlier, and this was gear driven with the train extending on to the rear-mounted magneto. The dynamo was clamped to the front of the engine and had a chain drive, while the oil pump went in the timing case with a worm drive from the crankshaft.

This last part alone was unusual, for it featured a built-up construction that allowed the use of one-piece connecting rods. Each crankpin was forged in one with its outer web and mainshaft, so the rod could be assembled and the pin fitted to the central flywheel. The two outers were held in place by a single through-bolt with a double thread which, thus, slowly, but powerfully, pulled the parts together. The whole assembly then ran in a bush and a ball race.

The bottom half carried a one-piece, cast-iron block, while the cylinder heads were also in one and in iron. They were fed by a single carburettor via a separate manifold. The valve gear was completed by two rocker boxes, which were in alloy and bolted in place. Each carried a pair of rockers, access to their ends being via caps.

The four-speed gearbox was a separate assembly that bolted to the rear of the crankcase, which was formed to suit. The effect was the same as unit construction, and the appearance was enhanced by a handsome, cast, light-alloy chaincase, which enclosed the primary drive and included a tensioner for the chain.

The engine unit went into a loop frame with duplex downtubes that ran back under the engine to the rear wheel. There was no rear suspension, but the standard telescopic forks, as used by the B model, were fitted at the front. The remaining cycle parts were much as for the B31, but adapted to the twin frame, so the oil tank, saddle and toolbox were placed as expected.

The patented stand also appeared on the twin, but failed to inspire much confidence, for the

For more serious work, BSA offered this 499 cc B33 in 1947, and it continued right up to 1960 with its solid and reliable performance

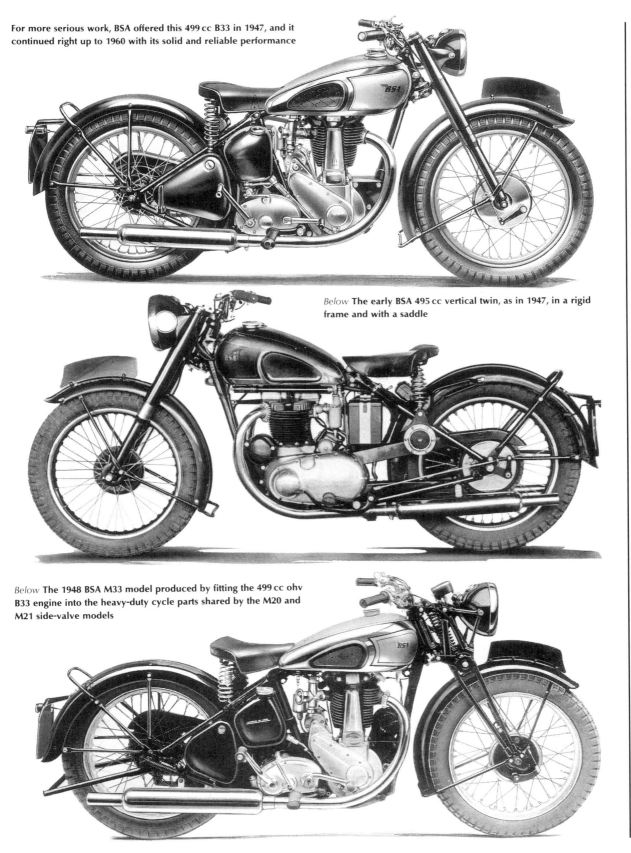

Below **The early BSA 495 cc vertical twin, as in 1947, in a rigid frame and with a saddle**

Below **The 1948 BSA M33 model produced by fitting the 499 cc ohv B33 engine into the heavy-duty cycle parts shared by the M20 and M21 side-valve models**

result seemed unstable. The speedometer went into the top of the tank, which was chrome plated with black or Devon red panels. The rest of the machine was finished in one of those two colours, and was matched by the rims, which were also plated with painted centres.

The rest of the range continued as it was for 1947, and right at the beginning of the year was joined by yet another new model, the B33. This was a 499 cc version of the B31 and was virtually identical, with the exception of an enlarged cylinder bore, higher gearing, greater power and a fatter rear tyre.

By April of that year, it had been joined by a competition version, listed as the B34. This, again, duplicated the smaller model. For 1948 one further single was added by slotting the 499 cc ohv B33 engine into the M20 frame and forks to make the M33. This had a brighter finish as standard and a little more pep for the sidecar driver, for whom it was intended.

There was a de luxe edition of the C11 for 1948 with a nice blue finish and more chrome, while the B-range had their speedometers moved from the tank to the fork top, and the competition versions were given a folding kickstart. The twin copied the B-range with its speedometer also moving, and most models had some detail changes, although production remained paramount in those austere days.

In June 1948 one of the best known of all BSA models made its debut as the 123 cc Bantam. This simple two-stroke was to become their most popular model, and it sold round the world in large numbers. The engine unit had been announced three months before and, in fact, the design was a mirror-image copy of the pre-war DKW RT125.

The engine was built in unit with its three-speed gearbox and was based on a vertically-split crankcase. In this ran the pressed-up crankshaft with roller big-end on three ball races, a steel rod and domed piston. The barrel was cast in iron and the head in alloy, with the plug laid back at an angle. Both parts were secured by nuts on long through-studs.

The Wipac flywheel magneto and generator for the direct lights went on the left, with the contact points outboard and easily accessible. On the right was the primary drive to the very sturdy, three-plate clutch, which drove the cross-over gearbox. The gear pedal and kickstart went on the right on concentric shafts, and the design enabled the machine to be kicked over when in gear, a rare feature in Britain at that time.

The complete unit went into a rigid loop frame with light telescopic front forks. There was a petroil tank, saddle, rear carrier and toolbox, 5 in. drum brakes, and a flat silencer that had a nice

An M33 doing its duty attached to a single-seat sidecar, which it would haul along with little trouble

The first post-war Gold Star was this 1949 B32GS, which set the style for the machine from then on

line to it. The front mudguard was sprung and deeply valanced, the bulb horn worked through the steering column, and the headlamp switch was cable operated from a handlebar lever.

The M-range was also in the news that month, for all three models were fitted with the telescopic front forks used by the A and B models.

By now the BSA empire was really getting into its post-war stride, and 1949 brought more new models and improved features for the existing ones. Foremost among the latter was the option of plunger rear suspension for the twin and the B-range singles. The suspension was undamped, but had load and rebound springs. The gearbox of the heavier models was revised and became common to the B- and M-ranges, and also for the twin, except for the special shell needed to mate it with the engine. Of rather less note was the appearance of an alloy head on the C10 during the year.

The most exciting news for 1949 was the launch of the Gold Star at the show held late in 1948. This revived a name the firm had first used in 1938 for a sporting 500 cc model and which was associated with the gold star awarded for a lap of the Brooklands track at over 100 mph during a race. It was never an easy award to win, but in June 1937 Wal Handley managed a lap at over 107 mph, riding a tuned Empire Star running on alcohol fuel.

The resulting production model was listed for two years, but not 1940, and the new one moved into a new class with a 348 cc engine. It was built in a super-sports style, but based on the B-range

with an all-alloy engine. This had the usual gearbox and was mounted in the plunger frame as standard with mainly stock parts, which included the chrome-plated mudguards from the competition machines.

There was a large range of options listed to suit road use, trials, scrambles or racing, and with the last BSA had their eye on the TT Clubman's races. For this there was an extension pipe to go with an open exhaust – then allowed – provision for a rev-counter, and a racing pad to go with the saddle. During the year the Gold Star, listed as the B32GS, was joined by a larger 499 cc version, which was built to the same specification and with the same options.

The final new model for 1949 was the A7 Star Twin, which was a sports version of the original. It was given a second carburettor and raised compression ratio to perk up the engine, the revised gearbox and the plunger frame being standard. It also had a brighter finish for its tank and wheel rims, making it a very handsome motorcycle.

There were two more models, various options and some detail changes for 1950, the most important being the 646 cc A10 Golden Flash twin. On the surface this was an enlarged A7 but, in fact, the engine had been revised, using the original basic design simply as a starting point. Few parts remained common, and the most obvious change lay in the cylinder head, where the rocker box became a one-piece part and the inlet manifold was cast as part of the head.

That aside, the new engine looked very much like the old one, although there were many internal changes. The gearbox continued as before, being bolted to the back of the crankcase, and there was still the polished alloy chaincase on the left. Both rigid and plunger models were offered, and much of the cycle side was unchanged, although the model did have the benefit of an 8 in. front brake from the start. The finish was new, being golden beige for all painted parts. This gave the machine its name. There was an all-black finish as well, which tended to be used for home-market machines at first, but in time the beige became the norm and was generally preferred.

At the other end of the scale, a competition version of the Bantam appeared. This had a raised saddle, fatter rear tyre, tilted silencer, blade mud-guards and a decompressor. It proved a handy tool, for its light weight made it easy to paddle through sections if things went wrong, which was better than stopping.

There were options that year for the all-alloy or Gold Star engines in the B-range machines, although it is unlikely that these were taken up. Otherwise, changes were minor, the Bantam leading the way with a revised Wipac magneto, and the options of plunger rear suspension for road or competition models, and a Lucas alter-nator and battery lighting system. Either or both options could be taken, although most road models with the Lucas equipment would also have the plunger frame. The Gold Star models were given the 8 in. front brake, except when built for trials or scrambles, while the rest of the range stayed as it was.

The A7 and Star Twin were revised in line with the A10 for 1951, so many components became common to both engine sizes. The capacity of the new version was 497 cc. Both had a single Amal carburettor and, as before, the A7 was in a rigid frame with the plunger version being an option, but standard for the Star Twin.

There were changes for the more prosaic models that year, with options of plunger rear suspension and a four-speed gearbox for the C10 and C11 machines. The plunger option was also made available for the M-range, in which the side-valve models were given light-alloy cylinder heads.

The rigid-frame versions of the A7 and A10 were not continued into 1952, when the only noticeable change was the option of a dualseat for the A-, B- and M-ranges. More happened for 1953 on the home market, with a headlamp cowl for the larger models, a dualseat option for the Bantam and C-ranges, and an 8 in. front brake for the B33.

The Gold Star machines went over to a frame with pivoted-fork, rear suspension, and in this form were known as the BB models, the earlier ones being designated ZB. These letters were to be found as the prefix of the engine number, which also included the letter GS if the motor was genuine.

On the export market there was more news, for the first of the hotter twins appeared as the Super Flash. This used the A10 engine, with its power output raised, and retained the plunger frame, but with sports mudguards and a brighter finish. The power was really too much for the frame, which weaved even in standard A10 form, but on long, straight American roads it was fine.

First of the sports twins was this 1949 Star Twin, which had two carburettors and was supplied in the plunger frame as standard

During 1953 BSA joined the cyclemotor market, which had sprung up a few years before. They made bicycles anyway, so it was a logical move. Their solution was the Winged Wheel, which was fitted in place of the standard rear wheel. The only other part was the fuel tank, which was made as a flat carrier to fit above the wheel.

A simple two-stroke engine with clutch and gears was housed in the hub, its capacity being 35 cc. The horizontal cylinder was on the left and was fed by a small Amal, the mixture being ignited by a flywheel magneto. The gears took the power via the clutch to the hub, which was formed as a full-width type with brake-drum surface.

There were major changes to most of the range for 1954, when the pivoted-fork frame came into more general use. The original user, the BB Gold Star, was joined by the CB model, which had a revised engine with much deeper finning and a swept-back exhaust pipe.

The B31 and B33 followed suit with the frame, although the rigid and plunger models stayed in the range until the ends of 1954 and 1955 respectively. With the new frames came a dual-seat as standard, a one-bolt fixing for the petrol tank, and a slim oil tank tucked into the corner of the subframe on the right side. It was matched on the left by a cover for the toolbox and battery.

The competition B32 and B34 went over to a new rigid frame with duplex downtubes and had the all-alloy engine as standard. They were also listed with the pivoted-fork frame as an option, when they became very similar to the ZB Gold Star.

The new frame and all its matching features was also used by the twins, although the four plunger-frame models continued. The A7, A7ST and A10SF were dropped at the end of the year, but the A10 ran on until 1957 to keep the sidecar buyer happy. The touring twins in the new frame remained the A7 and A10, but the engine and gearbox became separate units, although the internals stayed the same.

The sports models were the A7 Shooting Star and A10 Road Rocket, which had many common parts between them and the tourers, but had light-alloy cylinder heads. They kept to the single carburettor, but differed from the tourers in respect of their finish.

Among the smaller models, the Bantams with Lucas electrics were phased out, but the D1 was still available in rigid or plunger frames, with direct or battery lighting, and in road or competition

Looking over a Bantam in 1955 to see if it would meet their needs if a pillion seat was added

form. It was joined by the 148 cc D3, which was produced by simply boring out the engine, but it also had heavier front forks and a larger front brake. The road model had the plunger frame as standard, but either electric system, while the competition version had the choice of frames.

The C-range, too, was altered from 1954 with a change to alternator electrics. The side-valve model became the C10L, using some Bantam cycle parts, and only came with three speeds and a plunger frame. The ohv machine was the C11G. The rigid-frame version of this came with three speeds, but the plunger one with three or four. In other respects, they carried on as they had from 1945 to provide cheap, reliable transport.

Following all these changes, there was little alteration for 1955, except a change to Monobloc carburettors for most models. There were no competition Bantams in plunger frames, and the C11G gained a 7 in. front brake, but was no longer built in rigid form. The BB and CB versions of the Gold Star continued to be built, but were joined by a DB, which was very similar to the CB.

At the end of the year there was a major reduction in the number of models, along with

news of some new ones, and this simplified the range. Right at the bottom end of the scale, the Winged Wheel was dropped, despite having been offered as a complete machine, for the day of the clip-on was past and the moped was taking over.

Next, out went the rigid and competition Bantams, to leave the D1 in the plunger frame available with direct or battery lighting. These were the forms that buyers liked, and the models continued to run errands for them for the rest of the decade, and a little beyond. For the Bantam purchaser seeking a little more power and comfort, BSA fitted the D3 engine unit into a new frame with pivoted-fork rear suspension. This, too, had the choice of lighting system.

In the 250 class, the C10L acquired a four-speed gearbox and continued with the plunger frame, while the C11G was replaced by the C12. This used the same ohv engine with a four-speed gearbox in a pivoted-fork frame. Both wheels had full-width hubs. The one odd feature was the position of the light switch, on a panel behind the oil tank on the right.

The B31 and B33 also changed to full-width hubs in light alloy with 7 in. brakes that came from the Ariel range, but the plunger-frame versions were no more. It was the same with the rigid competition models, and the B32 and B34 were only listed with the pivoted-fork frame, in which their oil tank was now centrally mounted.

The Gold Star line-up was also simplified, being reduced to the two DB versions, which were joined by the DBD in the 499 cc size only. This

Below **Assembly line of BSA Dandy machines in the Small Heath works around 1957**

The 1956 BSA B31 which retained its 1945 engine with little change, but now had a new frame, tank, seat and wheels

was very similar to the others, except for a tapered front section for the silencer. All three had the option of the 190 mm, full-width front hub and a five-gallon alloy tank added to the list. The Gold Stars were only built in road, scrambles, road-racing and Clubman's forms that year, the first being phased out that season.

The side-valve range lost the M20 and the M33 in rigid form, but the M21 with either frame and the plunger M33 were given the 8 in. front brake. The twins alone stayed much as they were, except for the brakes, which became the full-width type, as used on the road B models.

Two new models were shown at the end of 1955, one being a 70 cc scooterette and the other a 200 cc scooter. The former was called the Dandy and had a moped-style, pressed-steel beam frame with short, leading-link front forks, legshields, a small fuel tank under the saddle, and a pivoted fork for the rear wheel. The engine and gearbox were built as part of this rear fork, and it was this area that was both the clever part and the flaw in the design.

The engine was a two-stroke with overhung crankshaft and arranged so the axis of this lay close to the fork pivot, the cylinder being laid back as part of the right-hand fork leg. The end of this leg was bolted to the cylinder head, while the crankcase extended across to the left, ahead of the wheel.

Along its length were first the flywheel magneto and then the clutch, followed by a two-speed gearbox. From this, a chain on the left drove the

rear wheel. Within this area lay the problems, for the points could only be inspected by taking the engine out of the frame, and the trade knew only too well that this was the second item to check after the plug. The other snag lay in the gear-change, which was a preselector arrangement controlled from the handlebars and much more trouble than the type by then common on continental mopeds.

The scooter was called the Beeza and had a side-valve engine laid across the frame, with the cylinder laying flat and pointing to the left, while the crankshaft was in line with the machine. The mechanics were built as one unit, so the engine drove back to the clutch and then to the all-indirect, four-speed gearbox, all on the right-hand side. A short shaft ran back from the box to the spiral bevel gears and the rear hub.

All this was contained in a series of alloy castings, which were bolted together and pivoted to act as a rear swinging arm. A spring unit controlled it, and the construction allowed for a stub axle at the rear for the 12 in., pressed-steel wheel. At the front were short, leading-link forks, while the works were enclosed in scooter style, but with a noticeable tunnel to conceal them and the frame. Electric starting was standard, and the machine appeared to have potential, but by then the market was used to light, zippy Italian scooters with two-stroke engines, so a side-valve plodder was unlikely to find much favour.

BSA decided not to proceed with the Beeza and put the Dandy on ice for another year, so it

Left **The C10L was the final form of the 249 cc BSA side-valve model**

Below **By 1958 the A10 Golden Flash was only built in pivoted-fork-frame form, even for sidecar use, but it still made a nice outfit**

Left **The first 172 cc Bantam was the 1958 D5, and this example is being made to work for its living by the full load of AA gear it carries**

The DBD34 was the final form of the 499 cc Gold Star and is seen here in its 1958 Clubman build

Below The BSA C15 was based on the Triumph Cub and was to sire a whole range of models in the next decade

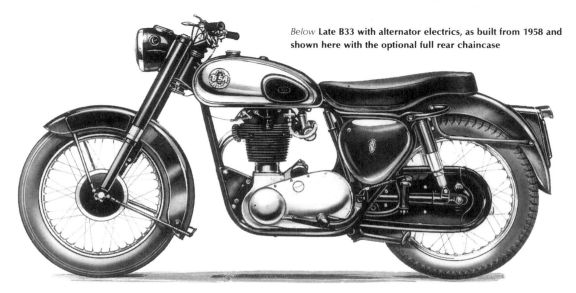

Below Late B33 with alternator electrics, as built from 1958 and shown here with the optional full rear chaincase

did not appear until 1957. It was the only new machine that year, which was a period when the firm was nearing the end of an era and approaching some major changes. This was highlighted at the end of the season by the disappearance of a number of old favourites from the range.

Out went the C10L, for a new 250 cc range was in development, and out went the M33 and plunger A10, to leave only the M21 for the sidecar man. This old stager was now mainly sold to the AA and the services, for there were few private owners left for such machines. The competition B32 and B34 singles were dropped, for the trend was to smaller and lighter machines for trials or scrambles. Out went the DB Gold Stars, so only the DBD remained, and solely in scrambles and Clubman's form as a 500.

The D3 and A10 Road Rocket were replaced by new versions for 1958, and the smaller was enlarged to 172 cc, becoming the D5. As with the D1, which continued, the D5 was listed with a choice of direct or battery lighting. The sports A10 became the Super Rocket and was given new full-width hubs and a nacelle for the headlamp, as well as detail improvements.

The other three twins continued, also with the new hubs and nacelle, and were joined by the 646 cc Rocket Scrambler, which was built in street scrambles form for the USA with open, waist-level exhaust pipes, no lights and off-road cycle parts. Among the singles, the C12 continued as it was, but the M21 lost its headlamp cowl without gaining the nacelle, so it reverted to its earlier style.

The Dandy ran on with some detail changes, while for that year the Gold Star came in DBD form only. Finally, the B31 and B33 went over to alternator electrics and coil ignition, plus the new full-width hubs and headlamp nacelle.

In September 1958 BSA launched the first of a new series of unit-construction singles, which were to run on to the end of the company. The machine was the 247 cc C15, and while presented as new, it was, in truth, a stretched Tiger Cub. It repeated the features of this model, with plain big-end for the pressed-up crankshaft, simple timing gear for the overhead valves, and skew-gear drive to a points housing behind the iron cylinder. The head was in alloy with a separate rocker box, and the pushrods moved in a chrome-plated tube running from the crankcase to the head. An alternator provided the current and was

mounted on the left-hand end of the crankshaft, from where a chain drove the four-speed gearbox. This was the same as in the Cub. A polished alloy cover enclosed the left-hand side.

The engine unit went into a simple loop frame with twin tubes under the engine, and telescopic front and pivoted-fork rear suspension. Full-width drum brakes, similar to the others of the range, were fitted, along with a headlamp nacelle and dualseat. The oil tank and toolbox were blended into one by a central panel, which carried the ignition switch, while the lighting switch went into the headlamp.

With the advent of the C15, the C12 was dropped, and for 1959 the D5 gave way to the D7. This used the same engine unit with an extra cover to streamline the generator, but in a new frame with pivoted rear suspension and new forks. These were based on those used by the Tiger Cub and fitted with the headlamp nacelle.

The two B models continued, although their days were numbered, the B31 leaving the lists at the end of 1959, and the B33 following suit a year later. The M21 was available to special order and only listed in the plunger frame, although some rigid ones were built from stocks for that year alone. The 348 cc DB Gold Star reappeared, but was listed as the 500 cc version fitted with the smaller engine. The larger model was only built in DBD form, and as Clubman's or scrambles models, the latter having a central oil tank.

The twins in A7 and A10 forms continued, as did the Dandy, which was joined by a trio of scooters, but these were sold under the Sunbeam label (see page 168). Once the road C15 was underway, it was joined in the New Year by two competition versions, listed as the C15S for scrambles and C15T for trials. These had minor changes inside the engine, raised exhaust systems and competition wheels and tyres, but retained much from the standard model.

In this form, the BSA range entered the 1960s. The company was flush with success and sure it was set for a long period of prosperity. For this, they revamped the twins in 1962, while introducing the much favoured Rocket Gold Star, expanded the unit-single range, and kept the Bantam, at least in 172 cc form, for many years. It was, however, the beginning of a decline but, regardless of what was to come, BSA could look back on many years of producing some of the best motorcycles for all classes of user.

Cairn

Commander

This machine was built by a Mr Farrow, of Reading, in the Corgi mould (see page 67), but with full enclosure. It was based around a 99 cc Villiers 2F engine, hung from a brazed, steel-tube frame.

There was no suspension front or rear, although this was promised for the future, and disc wheels with 4.00×16 in. tyres were used. The entire frame and engine were hidden by panels, which had louvres to assist cooling. Both the handlebars and saddle were adjustable for height, and there was a rear carrier, luggage grid and twin tail lights as part of the direct lighting system.

The machine performed as well as the Corgi, but had more positive steering. It made a reasonable runabout, but Mr Farrow soon found that, while a one-off is difficult to build, repeating the exercise brings many more problems. No more was heard of the Cairn, which remained an interesting solo endeavour.

This make made a dramatic appearance in the press in October 1952, and certainly existed, for one was given a brief run on the road and they were exhibited at Earls Court. There were three models in the range, all powered by small Villiers engines, but the styling was in total contrast to the pedestrian looks offered by the rest of the industry.

The machines were made by the General Steel Group of Hayes, in Middlesex, and all used the same set of cycle parts. The frame was all-welded, from square-section steel tubing, and of the beam type with pivoted-fork rear suspension. The main part ran from the headstock as two pairs of tubes, one on each side, and these swept back, down and back again as each pair came together near the rear wheel.

From this beam, a loop hung down to carry the engine and also helped to support the rear fork

The Cairn built by Mr Farrow around a Villiers 2F engine in 1950

65

The Commander range on show at Earls Court in late 1952, when the machine's strange styling created great interest

pivot. A subframe ran up for the seat to complete the frame and had cross-members to brace it. The rear fork was also made from square-section tubing, the legs running forward to a cross panel and then down to the pivot. The panel had a compression spring bolted to it, which reacted against a matching frame panel ahead of it to provide the undamped suspension. At the front were short, leading-link forks, for which the suspension medium was a rubber band on each side, working on suitably arranged bobbins and links.

On to this basic structure went the bodywork, which was quite unprecedented for a British model and more relevant to a prototype for the Paris show. As a start, the frame beam was panelled in and its front section housed the petroil tank with a flush fitting cap. The beam line ran to its end and was continued in a stay that ran to the tail of the rear enclosure and number plate.

The enclosure rose from the middle of the beam and ran along under the single seat, or optional dualseat, until it reached the end of the machine. The tail light was at the top of the rear panel, which dropped to the stay, curled forward on the line of the tyre, and then down to the rear wheel centre.

Below and ahead of the beam, the line was

continued in the form of a chrome-plated grille, which enclosed the entire engine unit. The lines of this tied in with the upper part, and only the foot controls lay outside it. The theme was continued with the sprung front mudguard, which extended up into a cowl for the headstock, a cover for the handlebars, and a shaped glass for the headlight.

The finish was ivory for the beam and fork top, with the front mudguard, rear enclosure and grille framework in light blue, dark blue or maroon, depending on model. There was a good deal of chrome plating, and the Commander name was emblazoned on each side of the tail.

Rather sadly, all that was under this exciting styling were the very prosaic Villiers 2F, 1F and 10D engines, in 99 and 122 cc sizes. The models became the Commanders I, II and III, with the same numbers of transmission speeds. The enterprise really deserved something a little better.

Whether this was the reason or not, the make left the market as quickly as it arrived, and no more was heard of it. Traditional riders were pleased at its demise, but it showed an imagination much needed in the industry, the lack of which was to cut the firms down in the years to come.

Corgi

The notion of a small motorcycle that can be folded up for easy transit when not in use has been around for a long time, and the Corgi was such a machine. It was developed from the wartime Welbike, which was built for parachute drops and used a 98 cc Villiers engine to propel its very basic chassis.

The Welbike was made by Excelsior and proved useful in both its original role for the paratroops, and for short-distance duties on camps and airfields around the globe. After the war the design was made more suitable for the civilian market, and the results often confused with the Welbike. The Corgi, as the post-war model was called, used a 98 cc Excelsior Spryt engine, but was made by Brockhouse Engineering of Southport, who also built the engine under licence.

The first news of the machine came in 1946, although it was 1948 before supplies reached the

public. The engine was a two-stroke with horizontal cylinder and was virtually a carbon copy of the Villiers Junior de Luxe, having minor alterations to the barrel. It drove a countershaft with clutch contained in an extension of the crankcase and thence to the rear wheel.

The engine unit went into a duplex cradle frame, the tubes of which ran back from the headstock, turned, came back under the engine and then up to the steering head again. On top went the petroil tank, while the saddle was on a pillar so it could be raised for riding and lowered again for storage.

At the front were rigid forks with handlebars that rose up to match the saddle, but could be swung down when necessary. The wheels had small drum brakes and were originally spoked, but were soon changed to discs. The tyre size was 2.25 × 12.5 in., so the Dunlop tyres were special. The lighting was direct with a small headlamp at the front, and there was no kickstarter, for the rider was expected to push the machine to start the engine.

It was crude, but it was transport, which was all that mattered in those days, so they sold quite

The Corgi, which was developed from the wartime Welbike, but had an Excelsior 98 cc Spryt engine

Corgi with sidecar, which enabled parcels and the shopping to be carried, so it was a useful tool for the time

well for shopping and trips to work. By the middle of 1948, the starting was improved with a kickstart lever, plus a dog-clutch, which disengaged the drive by the output sprocket to provide a neutral. Rather ingeniously, this was linked to the right-hand footrest, so raising this, as was required to give the kickstart lever clearance, put the machine into neutral.

As a further asset, a sidecar platform became available with a steel box and canvas top. This proved very handy for taking parcels to the post or when collecting the shopping.

The original machine was known as the Mark I, and with the dog clutch as the Mark II. In the middle of 1949 both became available with two major options, one a two-speed gearbox and the other telescopic front forks. The box was an Albion with a kickstarter and foot control, while the forks were basic, but included hydraulic damping.

During 1950 an enclosed bodywork was offered for the Corgi by the Jack Olding company, which handled the sales of the marque. This turned it into a miniature scooter, but removed its ability to be folded up, so did not catch on. There was also a banking sidecar for this version, which was intended for carrying loads and not a person.

The enclosure and sidecar continued to be available for 1951, when the machine itself ran on unchanged. It became the Mark IV for 1952, but this was simply the older type fitted with the two-speed gearbox and telescopic forks as standard. A weathershield was added and the headlamp moved to its top, while a luggage grid appeared on the tank top. The Mark II continued to be offered, although it had really been overtaken by time, and in October of that year it was dropped.

The Corgi continued in Mark IV form for 1953 and 1954 without any major change, but the advent of the moped and improvements in standards caused it to come to an end late that year. It had been a useful method of transport, but its day had run.

Cotton

This Gloucester-based firm was best known between the wars for its fully triangulated frame, which gave exceptional handling for its day. Stanley Woods won his first TT on a Cotton in 1923, and for two decades the company built ranges of machines using proprietary engines.

They returned to motorcycles during 1954 with a simple lightweight called the Vulcan. This used the 197 cc Villiers 8E engine in a rigid frame, built on the triangulated principles of the past. At the front were light MP telescopic forks, and both wheels had 19 in. rims and 6 in. drum brakes. There was a dualseat, battery lighting and electric horn to complete a neat, if conventional, machine.

For 1955 the Vulcan was joined by the Cotanza, which used the 242 cc British Anzani engine in a new frame with pivoted-fork rear suspension. The engine was a twin-cylinder two-stroke and unusual in having a horizontally-split crankcase with a plain centre bearing, in which was incorporated a rotary inlet valve. This gave the incoming mixture a rather convoluted path, which

one two-stroke specialist described as strangling it at birth.

The rest of the engine was conventional, with one carburettor, an iron cylinder block and one-piece alloy head. The four-speed gearbox was bolted to the rear of the crankcase, and the primary drive was enclosed by an alloy cover.

The cycle side was conventional, and during 1955 was also used for another version of the Vulcan, but this time fitted with the 9E engine with three-speed gearbox. For 1956 it was also offered with four speeds, and the Cotanza with the 322 cc Anzani twin engine. This was similar to the smaller unit, except that it combined piston-controlled inlet ports with the rotary valve.

One further model for 1956 was the Trials, which used the 9E engine, four-speed gearbox and pivoted-fork frame. The cycle parts were altered to suit its job, with competition tyres, no lights and a saddle.

During 1956 the original Vulcan, with 8E engine and rigid frame, was dropped, and for 1957 the whole range continued with one addition. This was the Villiers Twin model, which had the 2T engine in the Cotanza cycle parts. The complete range then continued for 1958. The one significant change for that year applied to the Vulcan only and comprised the fitting of Armstrong leading-link front forks.

The whole range had these forks for 1959, when it remained unchanged, except for the Villiers Twin. This was renamed the Herald and given a rather crude design of rear enclosure to follow the trend of the times. It emphasized the limited

The 242 cc British Anzani twin engine, with rotary valve, installed in a Cotton Cotanza and fitted with a siamezed exhaust system

Cotton trials model based on an 8E engine, the pivoted-fork frame and leading-link forks. In production, in 1956, the 9E was used

The 1959 Cotton Herald with the 249 cc Villiers 2T engine and rather crude rear enclosure

resources of the small company and their need to produce such parts with the minimum of costly tooling.

They did add another model to the list that year, in the form of the Messenger, which was powered by the 324 cc Villiers 3T twin-cylinder engine. The cycle parts were mainly the same as for the Herald, except that the front rim was of 21 in. diameter and both wheels had 7 in., full-width drum brakes. The rear enclosure of the smaller twin was fitted.

The appearance of the Villiers twin-powered models made the Anzani ones redundant, so for 1960 the Cotanzas were only listed to special order. The other models continued as they were and were joined by a Scrambler, powered by a 246 cc Villiers 33A engine.

From then on, the Cotton range expanded greatly, a sports 249 cc twin – the Double Gloucester – arriving in March 1960, and all manner of road, trials, scrambles and road-racing models during the 1960s.

Cyc-Auto

This machine was the ancestor of the autocycle and, thus, in a way, of the clip-on and moped, which were all aimed at providing transport at minimal cost. It was announced in 1934 and, at first, used its own engine, but later switched to Villiers. Just before the war, it was sold to the Scott concern, who redesigned the power unit, and in post-war years, this alone was used. Its production remained in Yorkshire, although the machine itself was built in Acton, London.

The engine was unusual in that the crankshaft lay along the machine. For the rest, it was a conventional, 98 cc two-stroke with upright iron cylinder which, at first, had an integral head but, from July 1947, had a detachable alloy one.

The carburettor sat in front of the cylinder on an inlet stub, and the flywheel magneto on the front of the crankshaft. This ran straight back to the clutch, and the drive continued on to a worm under the machine's bottom bracket. This contained the worm wheel which, in turn, drove the rear wheel by chain. A shaft ran through the worm wheel centre for the cycle pedals and chain, which complemented the engine. The silencer was bolted straight on to the rear of the barrel and comprised a large, cast alloy box above and around the clutch housing.

The engine went into an open frame, typical of autocycle practice, except for the worm wheel housing at the bottom bracket. There were pressed-steel blade girders at the front, and a cylindrical petroil tank behind the saddle.

The Cyc-Auto continued in this form, and for 1949 was joined by the Carrier model, which was aimed at the delivery market. To this end, it was fitted with strutted forks, which lacked suspension, and a large butcher's-boy-type carrier over the front wheel. The engine was modified for both models for 1950, the carburettor being behind the barrel, which was given twin front exhaust ports, each connected to a long pipe and tubular silencer.

The Cyc-Auto in its 1940 form, which was continued in the early post-war years

Otherwise, the Carrier model continued as it was, but the other became the Superior. This had the petroil tank moved to between the upper and lower frame tubes. It continued with the blade girders, while the Carrier kept its rigid, strutted fork, Both retained their saddle and rear carrier. For 1952 the Carrier was fitted with the blade girders, but from then on the two models continued as they were. They were no longer listed by 1955, but continued in a small way for another three years.

There was one attempt to produce a small motorcycle using the Cyc-Auto mechanics, and this was shown at Earls Court late in 1953. The engine remained as it was, but behind the clutch was a two-speed gearbox installed in unit with the engine. From this, a shaft drove to the rear wheel.

A simple loop frame carried the engine and had plunger rear suspension and telescopics at the front. Motorcycle-size 19 in. wheels with small drum brakes were used, and the equipment included lights, electric horn, saddle, rear carrier and toolbox. The machine was listed as the Scott model, but no more was heard of it.

The Cyclaid cyclemotor unit fitted above the rear wheel, which it drove by belt

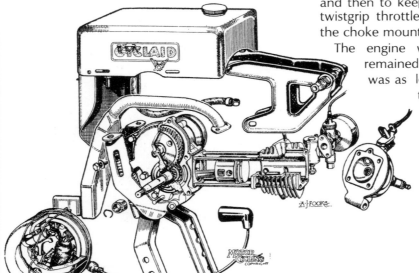

Cyclaid

This was one of a number of cycle attachments that sat over the rear wheel, but differed in that the drive to it was by V-belt. The unit was made by British Salmson at Raynes Park, London, and first appeared during 1950.

The engine was an all-alloy two-stroke of 31 cc with horizontal barrel. All the major parts were die-cast. The cylinder was lined and fed by a small Amal, while the exhaust was to the rear of the assembly. Inside was a built-up crankshaft, with roller big-end, running on ball races. This carried a Wipac flywheel magneto on the right.

A countershaft was fitted above the crankshaft and driven by helical gears, also on the right and inboard of the magneto. The V-belt pulley was on the left to give the second stage in the reduction ratio to the rear wheel.

A petroil tank went above the engine, and at the rear was extended downwards to form the number-plate mounting. Suitable brackets supported the unit, a spring-loaded arrangement being provided to allow the belt to be adjusted and then to keep it in tension. Controls were a twistgrip throttle and lever decompressor, with the choke mounted on the carburettor.

The engine worked well, so the Cyclaid remained in production until 1955, which was as long as most. By then, the day of the clip-on was really past, and riders were moving on to the moped, so the unit was taken out of production.

Cyclemaster

This cycle attachment came as a complete rear wheel, so hardly qualified as a clip-on, although it served the same purpose. It was first seen at the 1950 Utrecht fair, and some of its parts were also used in the Berini unit, which was mounted over the front wheel with friction-roller drive.

The Cyclemaster unit was formally introduced in Britain two months after the fair and was to be made by the giant EMI concern at Hayes, in Middlesex. That same company bought the Rudge firm in the 1930s, so were not unacquainted with two-wheelers, although they stopped production at the end of 1939, as they needed the space. Later, they sold the name to Raleigh.

The Cyclemaster wheel replaced the standard bicycle one and was built with heavier-gauge rim and spokes. These were connected to a large drum, and most of the mechanism was contained within its 13 in. diameter, which was vented to assist engine cooling. The engine was a two-stroke of 25.7 cc with inclined iron barrel, alloy head and vertically-split crankcase. The crankshaft was pressed up with caged needle rollers for the big-end and ball races for the mains.

Induction was controlled by a disc valve, driven by the right-hand end of the crankshaft, and the mixture was fed from a small Amal at the rear of the crankcase through a passage to the valve. A Wipac flywheel magneto was on the left, and inboard of this was the first stage of the chain drive. This ran back to a countershaft, on which the clutch was mounted. This shaft then drove the second-stage chain. This was connected to a sprocket that was riveted to the inside of the drum to complete both the reduction ratio and the drive.

The upper part of the drum was filled by a small petroil tank, while the exhaust pipe ran down to a silencer tucked under the magneto. Suitable covers concealed much of the mechanism, and the complete wheel weighed in at 33 lb. Controls were the clutch and throttle, with a tap to turn the fuel on and a choke built into the air filter attached to the carburettor.

The unit sold well, and for 1952 was bored out to raise the capacity to 32.6 cc, which gave it a little more power. At the same time, lighting coils were added to the flywheel magneto and the paint finish changed from black to grey. By then, at least one bicycle maker, Mercury, was producing a machine especially for the Cyclemaster. This was sturdier than usual and sold without a rear wheel!

This trend continued, and by the middle of 1953, Cyclemaster themselves were offering complete machines. In addition to the Mercury, there was the Pillion which, optimistically, was fitted with a pad and rests for a second person, and the Roundsman. The last made more sense and was built as a delivery bicycle with small front wheel and large carrier. It was ideal for a tradesman to use for local deliveries, especially if the roads were hilly or the wind inclined to blow hard.

The next move came for 1955, when the Cyclemate was created. This was more in the moped image. For this the engine was moved ahead of the bottom bracket and went into a frame built

The Cyclemaster unit, which replaced the bicycle rear wheel, had a disc-valve engine of 25.7 cc at first

for Cyclemaster by the Norman company. It was open, as a woman's cycle, and retained the rigid forks, but did have drum brakes. The petroil tank was fixed to the lower downtube.

It was a good attempt at producing something with minimal tooling costs, but lacked the style of the mopeds then beginning to arrive in Britain.

This was highlighted when the firm revived the Berini connection and began to import their moped for 1956, as this Dutch machine showed how far the trend and styling had moved on.

Despite this, the firm continued to build the Cyclemate and the rear wheel unit, the latter remaining in production until 1958, and the former until 1960. However, by then both were well out of date.

Before that the firm tried another tack with a small scooter of unorthodox construction. It was called the Piatti, after its Italian designer, and the prototype was shown at the 1952 Brussels show. Two years later negotiations were concluded for the rights to build the machine in Britain, and in mid-1956 the model was launched on that market.

In appearance, the machine was low and small, having a monocoque body built up from four steel pressings, which were welded together. This produced an inverted bath-like form, under which went the mechanics and the wheels, while on top was a dualseat mounted on a single saddle pillar. The steering column also rose above the main body, and ahead of it there was an apron, the lower edges of which ran into footboards.

There were two small access panels, but for anything else the machine was simply laid on its side. The body was rigid enough to act as the frame, and the engine unit, complete with transmission and rear wheel, was pivoted to it. A tension spring acted as the suspension medium

Above **Cyclemaster taking the hard work out of riding a bicycle against the wind and on hills, whether carrying a load or not**

The Cyclemate, which appeared in 1955 to combine the Cyclemaster engine with a Norman cycle built for it

A Piatti scooter, as built under licence by Cyclemaster from 1956, but only until 1958

and had three settings to provide a load adjustment. Front suspension was by a leading arm. Thus, both wheels with their 7 in. split rims were quickly detachable.

A wide centre stand went under the body, and this was lowered by pulling a knob beneath the instrument panel, which shrouded the handlebars. The knob was connected by cable to the stand. Once the stand was lowered the machine would readily roll back on to it.

The engine unit assembly pivoted at a point just below the base of the horizontal cylinder. Capacity was 124 cc, and the two-stroke had an iron barrel and alloy head. The carburettor was on the left, and the rectangular silencer on the right, so both items moved with the engine as the suspension worked.

The crankcase was cast in two parts, which made up the case, plus a beam to run back on the right to carry the wheel and the suspension spring attachment. At the front of the case was the crankshaft. This had an overhung big-end and

a mainshaft that extended to the right to the clutch and then the flywheel magneto.

A chain took the drive from the clutch to the three-speed gearbox, which was housed so that one of its shafts also acted as the wheel stub axle. A jockey sprocket dealt with chain adjustment, while the gearbox was controlled by a handlebar twistgrip.

As supplied, the machine came with dualseat, spare wheel and front carrier, while there was an optional windscreen. It was a trifle odd in looks, due to its small size and the vertical louvres in the front of the body, but adequate transport for town use.

For 1958 the original machine became the De Luxe and was joined by a Standard model. This came without the spare wheel, carrier and dualseat, having a saddle in place of the last, and at a reduced price. The missing items were available as options, so could be added when funds allowed.

In this form, the two models continued for another year, but late in 1958 production came to an end. This left the Cyclemate, which was to trickle on, well out of date, until 1960.

Cymota

This 1950 clip-on had a conventional, 45 cc two-stroke engine, which drove the front wheel with a friction-roller. The unit sat above the wheel, ahead of the steering column, and was nicely styled with a cowling, in which a small headlamp was fitted.

The engine was not very sophisticated, even by the standards of that time, for it had a deflector piston, overhung crankshaft and plain bronze bush big-end bearing. The mains were ball races, but crankcase compression was low, due to a nut on the crankpin to keep the rod in place and a bobweight flywheel, which was keyed and bolted to the crankshaft.

A Miller flywheel magneto and generator was on the left-hand end of this, and the friction roller in the middle. The head was alloy and the barrel cast iron. A small Amal supplied the mixture, and there was a drum-shaped silencer on the end of the exhaust pipe.

The engine was mounted on a backplate, with a small petroil tank above it, and could be moved by a lever to bring the drive roller into contact with the tyre. Springs provided a degree of tension, and the arrangement allowed the machine to be used as a bicycle if desired. The cowling completely enclosed the whole unit and was louvred to assist cooling.

The Cymota came and went in two short years, for even by 1951 the clip-on era was beginning to show signs of age. It was very much an early post-war trend and, although it persisted well into the 1950s, buyers were always aware of its shortcomings. As soon as they could, they moved on to something a little better, and the Cymota, along with the rest, was replaced.

The sole concessionaires had been Blue Star Garages, and this, too, must have been a factor in its demise. The profit margins were slim, for the unit sold at 18 guineas, and they must have soon found that their normal car business was more rewarding.

The Cymota clip-on went over the front wheel and had a bonnet that carried a headlight powered by the engine magneto

Dayton

On their fiftieth anniversary as a bicycle maker, in 1955, this firm entered the scooter market with a luxury model they called the Albatross. It was powered by the 224 cc Villiers 1H engine and was larger and heavier than the popular Italian models, so it was also more expensive.

The engine unit, with its four-speed gearbox, was installed in a tubular-steel frame with pivoted-fork rear suspension. At the front were Earles leading-link forks, and both ends were controlled by Girling or Woodhead-Monroe spring units. The wheels had split rims and were shod with 4.00 × 12 in. tyres, while the alloy hubs contained 6 in. brakes with steel liners bonded in place.

The bodywork comprised the usual apron, floor and rear section, with both hinged and detachable panels for access. The dualseat was hinged at the rear to give access to the petroil tank over the engine, and the tail section could also be swung up to let the rear wheel roll out. The body was cut away for the sides of the engine, which also allowed the controls to emerge, and footboards ran along most of the body length.

The tunnel behind the apron was very deep to assist airflow and ran into a shroud enclosing the steering column. At the top of this was a small panel for the instruments and switches, while the headlamp was built into the apron. The front mudguard was separate and well valanced. It turned with the steering, but did not enclose the

Dayton Albatross in 1955 with Villiers 224 cc 1H engine unit

The Albatross for 1956, but still with rather unfortunate front end. The name did nothing to help, either

fork tubes. A screen and luggage grid were listed as options.

The Albatross continued with minor alterations for two years, and early in 1957 was joined by the Albatross Twin. This used the same set of cycle parts, but was fitted with the 249 cc Villiers 2T twin engine, which gave the machine a little more zip.

Both were to continue unchanged for 1958, except for a new front mudguard, which enclosed the fork tubing and improved the looks. However, in March, the twin became the Empire and was joined by the restyled Continental Twin, while the Albatross became the Single. Both continued to bear the Albatross name as a prefix, and this practice remained with the firm, resulting in rather clumsy nomenclature.

The Single was fitted with the 246 cc 2H engine, which derived from the 1H and preceded the better known A-series. It went into a machine with some revised bodywork, which was also used by the new twin. The major change was to the apron. This now included a glove compartment, and there were other changes to the dashboard, footboards and dualseat, all of which enhanced the luxury specification.

Within two months, there were some name

changes and the Empire became available to special order only, remaining so until withdrawn in the middle of 1959. The Single became the Continental Single, while the new twin stayed as it was, but both still retained the Albatross prefix.

The two models continued for 1959, when they were joined by a third, called the Albatross Flamenco. This was lighter in style and concept, having a 174 cc Villiers 2L engine with fan cooling, electric start and three-speed gearbox. The frame and bodywork were new, but were shared with Panther and Sun (see pages 140 and 165) to reduce costs. Each firm tricked out the parts to look a little different.

The frame was still tubular and the forks of the Earles type, but with the suspension units outside the mudguard valance. The bodywork had no tunnel, so the floor was flat behind the apron, which had twin compartments in it and the dashboard panel just above these. The seat remained hinged to the rear body, but a single panel gave access under each side of this. Wheel size was down to 10 in., but they still had split rims.

The Flamenco was far more in the style of the scooter world than the original Albatross, despite a rather heavy appearance to the front mudguard. It continued for 1960, along with the Twin, but the Single became available to special order only. This only lasted to the end of that season, when the make went out of production.

DKR

This scooter was built in Wolverhampton and launched in July 1957 as the Dove. It had a rather heavy appearance, but had to make do with a 147 cc Villiers 30C engine with fan cooling and a three-speed gearbox.

The engine went into a frame comprising a single, large-diameter tube running from the headstock to the pivot for the rear fork. There were long leading-links at the front, 10 in. split-rim wheels, and drum brakes of 5 in. diameter at the front and 6 in. at the rear.

Much of the heavy appearance came from the petroil tank's location in front of the headstock, above the front wheel. It was enclosed by a massive pressing that extended down to form the mudguard and up into the headlamp nacelle. The pressing swept back to the apron, and its top ran back to form an instrument panel on top of a large glove compartment at the back of the apron.

From then on, the looks lightened, with a small tunnel in the floor and a rear body with detachable side panels. The dualseat was hinged, and the various sections of the body could be removed quite easily for maintenance. A neat, oval-section silencer went under the gearbox and could be readily dismantled for cleaning.

The Dove went forward into 1958 as it was, and in February was joined by two more models. Both used the same frame and body, and both had electric starting and a fan-cooled engine. The first was the Pegasus with a 148 cc Villiers 31C engine. This copied the Dove in having a three-speed gearbox. The second was the Defiant, which used the 197 cc 9E unit, but with a four-speed gearbox.

All three went forward for 1959, when they were joined by the Manx, which was powered by the 249 cc Villiers 2T engine. As with the Defiant, it had four speeds, fan cooling and electric start, but also a 70 mph potential. However, it still retained the same size brakes as the other models, which indicated the tight financial constraints under which the firm worked.

At the end of the season, the Dove was replaced by the Dove II, which used the 31C engine, but with kickstart. Early in 1960 the Pegasus was replaced by the Pegasus II with 174 cc 2L engine, while the Defiant and Manx ran on as they were.

The last two continued for another year, but the two smaller models were dropped at the end of 1960, when the firm launched a new model. This was the Capella, which had lighter looks and took the firm on to their end in 1966.

DKR Dove in 1957 with heavy front end due to the forward mounting of the fuel tank

DMW

This firm was briefly associated with the Calthorpe name just after the war, when a small prototype was built, using a twin-port, 122 cc Villiers engine. This went into a rigid loop frame with telescopic forks. Its most noticeable feature was a saddle mounted on a single post, bicycle style, which, thus, was adjustable for height.

It was April 1950 before any more was heard of the Sedgely firm, but then came news of a small range of lightweights. The machines were available with Villiers 1F, 10D or 6E engines, and the two larger with rigid frames or plunger rear suspension. All had MP telescopic forks, which the firm themselves had developed and were to sell to other companies for many years.

The machines retained the post saddle mounting and could have direct or battery lighting, the power source for the latter being housed in a box on the left. This could also act as a toolbox and

was matched by another on the right. The machines were nicely finished in turquoise blue.

The range was revised for 1951, when the smallest model with the 1F engine only stayed in the line-up for a few months. The others became the Standard or De Luxe, depending on whether they were rigid or had plungers, and had direct or battery lighting respectively, although the latter was an option for the Standard models.

Two further De Luxe models were added in 122 and 197 cc capacities, and these had plunger frames constructed from square-section tubing. This was all-welded and gave a weight saving, thanks to the reduction of lugs. The machine was fitted with a dualseat, and the toolbox was formed by a pressing between the seat nose and the frame. Access to the box was by removing the seat, which was held by two wing nuts.

The De Luxe models with round-tube frames were dropped for 1952, to leave four road machines, comprising Standard and De Luxe with 10D or 6E engines. These were joined by competition models using the same engines, again in rigid or plunger frames. In effect, they were the road models with trials tyres and without lights, which remained an option.

During the year, the frame was amended to allow a 4 in. rear tyre to be fitted to the competition models, and for 1953 these were only listed in plunger form. The rigid versions remained as options for a few months, while the 197 cc

The 1952 competition DMW with square-tube frame, plunger rear suspension and Villiers engine

DMW fitted with the French 170 cc ohv AMC four-stroke engine unit and offered for 1954

model became referred to as the 4S. The four road models continued, the 197 cc De Luxe being fitted with a headlamp cowl to match the style of the times. The 122 cc rigid model became the Coronation to mark the event that took place that year. Later in the year, it was tried with some short leading-link front forks, not seen elsewhere.

There was a considerable change to the model line-up for 1954, as DMW established a link with the French AMC engine company. This was Ateliers de Mécanique du Centre, nothing to do with the Plumstead group, who produced a nice line of single-cylinder, four-stroke engines. The largest of these was of 249 cc and had a chain-driven, single overhead camshaft, hairpin valve springs, gear primary drive and unit construction of its four-speed gearbox. The other two engines, of 125 and 170 cc capacity, had overhead valves. All three were well finned and nicely styled.

There was also a new frame, which became known as the P-type. This had the top and downtubes in square-section, but the rear half comprised a series of pressings welded together. Rear

suspension was by pivoted fork, which was located on a movable pivot at the front to provide rear chain adjustment. The pressings were continued to the rear to form the mudguard and number plate, while there were compartments formed in it for the battery and tools. Access to these was by raising the dualseat, which was hinged at the rear.

This frame was used by the Dolomite model, which had the 249 cc AMC engine, the 175P with the 170 cc AMC, and three using Villiers power. Of these, the Cortina had the 224 cc 1H, and the De Luxe the 197 cc 8E, while the Moto Cross used the similar-sized 7E. The plunger frame remained for another 197 De Luxe and the competition 4S. These followed suit and changed to the 8E and 7E engines.

The model with the 125 cc AMC engine failed to get off the ground, but there were two more with French engines that did. One made only a brief appearance during 1954 and used the 170 cc engine in the P-type motocross frame, fitted with Earles front forks. It was an export-only model with a short life.

The other model was a show surprise at Earls Court, late in 1953, and was built purely for road racing in the ultra-lightweight class. It had a twin-overhead-camshaft engine based on the pushrod job, so the bottom half looked much as that of the 170. The camshaft drive was by bevels and vertical shaft, with a train of spur gears in the cambox. Lubrication was much improved to suit, and a well finned oil filter and cooler unit went in the return line from the cambox. The engine unit went into the P-frame with Earles forks and was called the Hornet.

All these models continued for 1955, when they offered the option of the Earles forks in place of the usual telescopics. There was one new machine, which replaced the earlier 125 cc model, and this used the 147 cc Villiers 29C engine in the P-type frame. It was called the Leda and was one of the few to run on into 1956, when all the AMC engines were dropped. As a result, the firm used only Villiers engines.

Also out was the road plunger model, but the competition one continued as the 5S. The other models with the P-frame were given Mark numbers, the 197 cc De Luxe becoming the 200P Mk I. The Moto Cross with the 7E had Mk V added to its name and was joined by a Mk VI, which used the 9E engine. In matching style, there was

a 7E-powered MK VII Trials and, for the road, the 200P Mk IX with a 9E engine. The Cortina simply continued, as did the Earles forks option, except for the Leda and Moto Cross models, which had these as standard.

The Leda, 5S and Mk V were all dropped for 1957, but the Mk I, VI, VII, and IX all continued, as did the Cortina. There were five new models, including two more Mk IXs as the 150P and 175P. These used the usual P-type frame and telescopic front forks, but were fitted with the 148 cc 31C and 174 cc 2L engines respectively. The same cycle parts were also used by the Dolomite II, which was powered by the 249 cc Villiers 2T twin two-stroke. However, the 200 Mk VIII was simpler, having an 8E engine in a tubular loop frame with telescopics, 5 in. brakes and a utility specification.

The final new model was totally different, for it was a scooter that used the 99 cc Villiers 4F engine with two-speed gearbox. It was called the Bambi. The prototype had been seen a year or more earlier at Earls Court, but now the machine was ready for production. The frame was a mono-coque, built up from steel pressings that were welded together in scooter style, with apron, tunnel and rear body. The front forks were of the Earles pattern, but with a stirrup linking the fork arms to a helical spring concealed within the steering column. A well valanced mudguard concealed most of the supporting members.

At the rear, the wheel was carried in a pivoted fork constructed from two major pressings. These

The DMW Bambi scooter launched in 1957 and fitted with a Villiers 4F engine with two-speed gearbox

also supported the engine unit between them, so the whole became a major assembly that was readily detached from the main frame. Both wheels were of the disc type with 2.50 × 15 in. tyres, so they were larger, but narrower, than the norm for a scooter. Together with the body shape, single seat pad and windscreen, they gave the machine a rather unusual line. Access panels and

a hinged seat enabled routine servicing to be carried out.

The range was well thinned out for 1958, only four models remaining, although there was a newcomer. Those left were the Bambi scooter, 200 Mk VIII, 200P Mk IX and Dolomite II, so little of the past remained. New was the Mk X, which was built as either a trials or scrambles machine, fitted

Left **The basic DMW 200 Mk VIII with Villiers 8E engine in tubular frame, as listed for 1957**

Below **The Dolomite II with 249 cc 2T engine in the DMW P-type frame with pressed-steel rear section**

Trials version of the Mk X with 2T engine, Earles forks and increased ground clearance

with, of all things, the 2T engine. The frame members were cut short to increase ground clearance, and high-level pipes, suitable tyres, and wide or close gear ratios to suit the intended competition were fitted.

The Mk VIII did not continue into 1959, but the other models did, and in the middle of the year the Dolomite IIA was produced by fitting the 324 cc 3T twin engine in the Dolomite II frame. Late that year, a competition Mk XII appeared, which was much as the Mk X, but fitted with a 246 cc 32A engine for trials, or a 33A for scrambles.

These two were revised a little with alloy hubs and Girling brakes, and for 1960 were joined by two more with 9E engines. Otherwise, the range was as before and was to continue with a variety of road and competition models until 1967. These included the unique Deemster, which was part scooter and part motorcycle.

Dot

Dot were mainly a competition company, and one of the oldest in the business, for they began building their machines in 1903 — the founder, Harry Reed, won a TT in 1908. They continued with motorcycles until 1932, but from then on only built a tradesman's three-wheeler until 1949.

They then decided to return to motorcycles, and initial plans were for 125 and 200 cc road models, but only the larger machine was built. It used the Villiers 6E engine in a rigid loop frame with blade girder forks. Equipment included a battery, saddle and centre stand, making a neat machine.

For 1950 two versions were offered with direct or battery lighting, and for 1951 these were fitted with telescopic front forks. They were joined by the Scrambler model, which had alloy mudguards, trials tyres and a waist-level exhaust system. It was supplied with lights, which could be easily removed, and a silencer.

During 1951 the firm introduced a road-going 250, which used the 248 cc Brockhouse side-valve engine in the road cycle parts. The engine was made by the Lancashire firm because they had an involvement with the American Indian company, as well as making the Corgi (see page 67). It was of unit construction with a three-speed gearbox, an iron barrel and alloy head. Its oil was carried in the sump. To suit the USA, the gear pedal and kickstart were on the left, which put the final drive on the right, but Dot fitted it into their cycle parts without much trouble.

The range began to take the shape it was to keep for the rest of the decade in 1952 with a variety of models, which used the same basic

Dot Mancunian with 9E engine, which was one of the few road models built by this competition-oriented firm

85

A Dot 246 cc scrambler of 1960 with the inevitable Villiers A-series engine

parts. From these, a series of competition machines was introduced by varying the basic specification. The two road models remained, as did the Scrambler, which became the S and had road equipment, but no lights. With direct lighting added, it became the SD, while stripped for action it was the SC. In a similar manner, the trials machines were the T and TD, with direct lighting only fitted to the latter.

They all continued for 1953, when they were joined by a range with a new frame with pivoted-fork rear suspension. These models had the letter H added to their type, so the two road machines became the DH and RH. The three scrambles and two trials models followed suit, and the latter were joined by two more. These were the THX and TDHX, which had a further change to a 21 in. front wheel.

This massive range was much reduced for 1954 by deleting the road models, including the 250, and the rigid-framed scramblers. All that remained went over to the 8E engine, with the option of the four-speed gearbox, while all models had telescopics as standard. An Earles-type leading-link fork was offered as an option.

The T and TD remained alone with the rigid frame and were accompanied by the sprung trials models with 21 in. front wheel, but not the TH or

TDH. The scramblers were in the three forms as before, with or without lights and stripped for racing.

The rigid trials machines were dropped for 1955, when the TH and TDH returned, so there remained three scrambles and four trials models in the range. They were dropped again for 1956, as all trials riders wanted the larger-diameter wheel, so there were five competition machines. Their front fork option became short leading links controlled by long external units. The range was joined by a road model once more, which used the Villiers 9E engine and the leading-link forks. It was called the Mancunian and displayed an attempt to cowl the headlamp and enclose the area beneath the dualseat nose. Colours were British Racing green or Continental red.

For 1957 there was talk of offering the 31C and 2L engines to special order, as the 10D had been in the past. Nothing came of this, but the range was given a new engine in the form of the 9E. The five competition models were joined by one more called the Works Replica Trials Special, which had detail changes to improve its trials capability. All models were fitted with the leading-link forks as standard.

Early in 1957 the firm began to import the Italian Vivi machines, produced by Viberti of Turin. All those brought in were of 50 cc with a two-stroke engine and two-speed gearbox. They were built as moped, racer and scooterette and helped to augment the company's cash flow.

The whole range continued as it was for 1958, at the end of which the Mancunian was withdrawn. The other models ran on, and the range was extended by offering all of them with a 246 cc Villiers A-series engine in place of the 9E. Otherwise, the machines were the same, and for scrambles were fitted with the 31A, or for trials the 32A.

There were also three new models with twin-cylinder engines, two being built for scrambles and the third for the road. The first competition model used the 249 cc Villiers 2T and was much as the single-cylinder version, except for the twin open pipes. These had no expansion box and were simply cut-off short. The machine was listed as the SCH Twin.

The second scrambles model had the same name, but differed in having a 349 cc RCA engine. This unit was of advanced construction, with horizontally-split crankcase and full flywheels, twin Amals and a four-speed gearbox. The block was in iron, with side exhausts feeding alloy adaptors to the pipes, while separate alloy heads were fitted. The cycle parts were as for the Villiers twin model.

The third twin was a road machine, named the Sportsman's Roadster. It also used the RCA engine and had leading-link front and pivoted-fork rear suspension. Its specification included dual 6 in. front brakes and polished aluminium mudguards and petroil tank.

The range still included the Vivi machines, and the firm continued with these for 1960, along with some motorcycles from the Guazzoni range. Otherwise, the 1960 range was as 1959, except that the 2T-engined scrambler was dropped. This happened to nearly all the Dot range at the end of that year, and from then on they offered a much reduced selection of models until 1968, after which they were forced to use foreign engine units.

Douglas

Douglas were building flat-twins before World War 1 and continued to do so throughout their commercial life. There were other models along the way, but they were few in number, and while the company went through many financial ups and downs, they remained true to that original concept.

So it was no surprise to learn that their post-war model had a flat-twin engine when it was first described in September 1945. What was nearly new was that it was mounted transversely, as they had only done that once in pre-war days, while the 348 cc capacity and overhead valves had not been seen on a Douglas since 1932.

The machine was totally new, with unit construction of the engine and gearbox, but with chain final drive. The engine dimensions were near square, and the crankshaft built up with roller big-end bearings. There were twin camshafts beneath the crankshaft, and the valve gear was totally enclosed.

Both heads and barrels were in cast iron, but the rockers were concealed by a polished alloy cover, and there was an Amal for each side. The exhaust pipes curled under the cylinder, and both ran to a cast alloy silencer box under the gearbox. The timing gears were at the front of the engine, under a large polished cover, and the drive was extended up to a Lucas mag-dyno mounted on top of the alloy crankcase. This item was extended downwards to form the sump for the oil system.

The drive was taken via a single-plate, dry clutch with Ferodo linings to the four-speed gearbox. This was controlled by a pedal on the right, while its output shaft drove a bevel-gear pair. This, in turn, passed the drive to the rear wheel by chain. The kickstart lever was also on the right and swung in line with the machine, so a further pair of bevels was used to enable it to turn the layshaft and, thus, the engine.

Left **The post-war 348 cc flat-twin Douglas T35, as first seen in 1946 with its leading-link forks and torsion-bar rear suspension**

Right **The T350, or Mk III, road tested during 1948, when the superb suspension was greatly and rightly praised**

The engine and gearbox unit was mounted in a duplex frame with pivoted-fork rear suspension and short leading links at the front. Both were unusual in that the suspension medium was torsion bars, and the rear ones ran along inside the lower frame tubes. The front end was locked with an arm splined to the bars, while a lever at the rear connected to the fork with a short link.

The front suspension in the original design used torsion bars running up the main fork tubes and secured at their upper ends. At the bottom were the short leading links, which were connected to the bars to provide the suspension. For production, this arrangement was altered to what Douglas called their Radiadraulic fork, which kept the short leading links, but connected these to compression springs within the fork legs. The springs were taper ground to give a variable-rate action over a total 6 in. of movement, and hydraulic damping was incorporated in the fork legs.

Both wheels had 19 in. rims and 7 in. drum brakes in offset hubs. A deep rear mudguard was supported by a subframe, and the machine came with full electrical equipment, a saddle and a centre stand. A large toolbox was tucked under the saddle in the frame bend. In this form, the machine was known as the T35, or Mk I, and eventually reached production in 1947.

For 1948 the cylinder head was revamped by Freddie Dixon and the frame improved, as there had been breakages. The engine work improved the performance, and the manner in which it was achieved, and in this form the machine was called the Mk III. In the middle of the year it was joined by a second model, listed as the Sports, and this was styled to suit, with upswept exhaust pipes and a tubular Burgess silencer on each side. The mudguards were slimmer, and a small toolbox appeared above each silencer, which left the original space over the gearbox available for an air filter if the owner wished.

The two models continued in Mk III form for 1949, but the range was expanded for 1950 with three new machines, while the existing ones were modified to a Mk IV form. For this, they had the subframe altered to carry a large triangular toolbox on each side and to provide support for the pillion footrests, which had previously been mounted on the pivoted fork.

The front mudguard was no longer sprung, so followed the wheel more closely, which meant that it had to be attached to the brake backplate on one side and the hub spindle on the other. The result was rather messy and not carried out particularly well. The exhaust system of the standard model varied, with either the silencer box of the early machines being used or separate low-

level pipes and tubular silencers, which were raised by an upward kink in the pipes.

Of greater interest to the enthusiast were the 80 Plus and 90 Plus models, which were built as sports machines, although the second could be obtained in Clubman's form, stripped for racing. The engines had deeper finning and were well worked on inside to raise the power output. They were bench tested and anything over 25 bhp became a 90 Plus, while the failures were used for the 80 Plus.

On the cycle side, both models were much as the Mk IV, except that the exhausts ran straight back to the silencers, the front brake was a massive 9 in. diameter, and its hub was spoked into a 21 in. rim. The finish was maroon for the 80 Plus and gold for the 90 Plus, which made them stand out.

The 1948 Sports model Douglas introduced during that year

When supplied for competition, the 90 Plus came with racing magneto and tyres, close-ratio gears, rev-counter, alloy guards and a dualseat of most uncomfortable appearance. A further option was the fitting of alloy heads and barrels, but their only advantage was weight reduction. Cooling was no problem once the big finned exhaust nuts were removed from the air flow, but the different expansion rate of the steel hold-down studs could pull them out of the crankcase. The Douglas solution was slack head nuts when the engine was cold, but this caused leaks, so the all-alloy engine was soon abandoned.

The final new 1950 machine was the Competition model, which was built for trials use. The engine and gearbox were standard items, but the frame was new and rigid. Its ground clearance was increased and an undershield added to protect the crankcase, but the forks were stock and a 21 in. front wheel was used. At the rear was a 4.00 in.-section tyre, and the gearing was lowered to suit the intended use. The exhaust pipes were swept up, the left one crossing over above the gearbox to a single silencer high on the right. A raised saddle and light-alloy mudguards were fitted, the front one being sprung and well clear of the tyre. An air cleaner went above the gearbox, and the machine had the option of lights, dualseat and alloy cylinder heads. It was a nice machine, but the engine width soon became a major problem, both in and between sections, while a small twin was not the easiest to ride in the trials of the day.

The standard and Sports models became a single model for 1951, listed as the Mk V, which was very much as the year before, except for the Plus-type exhaust pipes and a ribbed front mudguard. The early box silencer remained available as an option, along with crash bars, a dualseat and a steering damper. The Plus models continued much as before, but with alloy heads, while the Competition model could still have the all-alloy engine.

Of equal importance to the firm was the launch of the Douglas Vespa scooter for 1951, following an earlier showing at Earls Court. At that time, scooters were viewed disparagingly by the British industry in general, but Douglas had the good sense to see which way the tide was running. They came to an arrangement with the Italian Piaggio firm of Genoa to make the Vespa under licence, and the official launch took place in March 1951.

The design was brilliant, the concept of a monocoque frame with a compact engine and gearbox unit running on for many years. There was no frame in the accepted sense, for the Vespa followed car practice and combined this with the body panels to save weight, while retaining rigidity. Thus, the apron and floor were one pressing, to which a bracing section was welded and which carried the rear suspension arm with its single right leg. A rear body was welded to the main section to form the seat mounting, enclose the petrol tank and act as a rear mudguard. Large blister cowlings on each side gave a balanced appearance; the right-hand one enclosed the engine, while that on the left was used to conceal the battery and tools. The fuel cap was set in the top between the saddle and the rear carrier, which could have a mounting for a spare wheel added to it. The cables and wiring harness were all located within the body shell, which made replacement awkward.

The front suspension was by a single trailing arm, pivoted at the lower end of the steering column, which was cranked round the wheel. A compression spring provided the suspension medium, as it did at the rear, where there was a hydraulic damper, a fitting the front end lacked. The front mudguard was mounted on the steering column, so it was sprung and turned with the

Left **First signs of the Vespa came at the late 1949 Earls Court show, where this early model with mudguard-mounted headlamp was shown**

Right **The production Vespa differed in the headlamp location and is seen here in 1951, outside Victoria bus station in London**

bars. In Italy it had the headlight mounted on top of it, as on the 1945 Piaggio original, but this was too low for the British height regulations, so it was moved up and on to the apron. Below it went the electric horn, the fitting of which doubled as an access hole when dealing with the cables.

Both wheels were of the split-rim type with small 3.50 × 8 in. tyres, and they were inter-changeable, so the spare was a real asset. There were drum brakes in the hubs and studs for the wheel mounting.

The engine and gearbox were built as a very compact unit, which was mounted to the rear pivoted arm. Thus, it was very easy to detach the wiring, controls and rear unit, pull out the arm's pivot bolt and wheel the whole assembly to the bench for maintenance.

The engine was a simple 125 cc two-stroke with alloy head and horizontal iron barrel. A deflector piston was used, along with a built-up crankshaft with roller big-end and bobweight flywheels. The flywheel magneto, with its lighting coils and cooling fan, went on the right, to the outside, and the clutch on the left. This drove back to the all-indirect, three-speed gearbox, which was carried within the extended crankcase castings.

The gearbox had all three input gears locked as one on their shaft and selected by engaging the output gears to their shaft with a drawbar

device. This was controlled by rotating the left handlebar twistgrip, complete with clutch lever, and the connection between them was by rods. Thus, the model is referred to as the 'rod type' more often than by its formal 2L2 designation. The output shaft extended from the gearbox to the rear wheel, so the drive was very direct. It was supported by two ball races, which were housed in an extension of the left-hand crankcase casting, as this, in turn, was clamped into the end of the cast alloy rear pivot arm.

Thanks to the compact design and need for a minimum number of bearings and seals, the Vespa was always a lively performer, which usually had the edge over the rival Italian Lambretta. The snag was that, as many parts had more than one job to do, once they wore, the effect could be dramatic. For all that, the machines proved very popular and, in their green finish, were soon selling well. As they were made in the Douglas Bristol works, they featured British components from Amal, BTH, Lucas and others. There were plenty of options to catch the scoot-erist's fancy. The machine had a centre stand that was easy to use, and the offset engine weight did not seem to worry riders.

The Douglas Competition model was dropped at the end of 1951, to leave the three flat twins and the Vespa with little change. At the show, there was a 489 cc prototype that was based on the existing design, but had the mag-dyno enclosed by a finned cover, which extended back to include the air cleaner. It went into a frame with sidecar lugs and was exhibited with a chair attached.

The production twins had an external Vokes oil filter added for 1953, at the end of which the 80 Plus was dropped. The other two twins continued for 1954 without change, but the Vespa became the model G, the gearchange being controlled by twin cables instead of the complicated rod system.

It was all change for 1955, as a new flat-twin replaced the earlier models and the Vespa had a revamped engine. The twin was first called the Dart, but in production became the Dragonfly. It represented a major update of the original design, especially with regard to the frame and suspension.

The engine was basically as before, but most components were revised in some way or other. The crankcase and crankshaft were stiffer, the iron barrels recessed deeper, but the heads remained iron and the timing gear unchanged. The magneto was replaced by a points and distributor unit under a cover, and the dynamo by a Miller alternator on the crankshaft nose. There was only one Amal carburettor, which fed an inlet tract cast into the clutch housing. This emerged

on each side, where a curved and plated tube took the mixture to the cylinder. The exhaust ran down and back to a silencer on each side. The transmission was as before, with four speeds and chain final drive.

The frame was duplex with a single top tube and conventional, pivoted rear fork controlled by Girling hydraulically-damped suspension units. At the front were Earles-type leading-link forks with more Girlings, while both wheels had 19 in. rims and 7 in. drum brakes. The mudguards were deeply valanced, and the model had a dualseat fitted as standard with a large toolbox under its nose. This could accommodate the optional air filter, if required, but not the battery, which was low down on the left, just behind the cylinder. The most distinctive feature of the model was the headlamp mounting, which was flared back to the fuel tank, so the lamp did not turn with the bars. The tank itself held over five gallons of petrol, so the model was a true tourer in that respect.

The Vespa became the GL2 with revised engine

Right **A Douglas Vespa on tour in Glencoe, Scotland, and highlighting something of what two-wheeled transport is about**

Below **The Douglas Dragonfly, which kept the essence of the past in a new frame and forks with an unusual fuel tank**

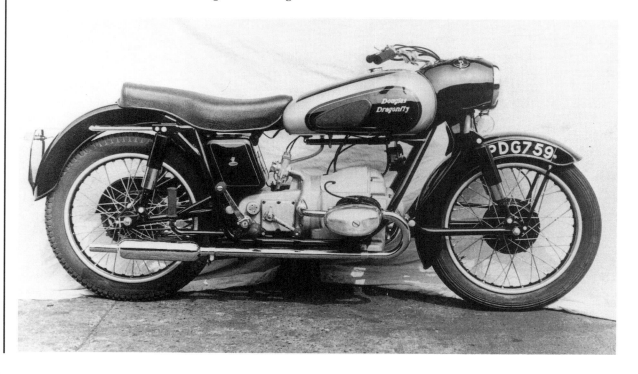

dimensions, full flywheels and a new head and barrel. The last now had two transfers. Outside the engine were other alterations to the cycle parts, including the option of a dualseat. The model had a very short life, for early in 1955 it was replaced by the 42L2 and joined by the 145 cc GS. The 42L2 differed from its predecessor in having the headlamp mounted on the handlebars, instead of the apron, where it was joined by the speedometer, which had also been apron-mounted up to then. The front suspension gained a hydraulic damper, and the engine blister was cleaned up with louvres in place of a cut-away section for cooling.

The GS, or Gran Sport, had a four-speed gearbox, as well as the extra capacity, and was an import built entirely in Italy. It continued with the 42L2 and the Dragonfly for 1956 without change, and on into 1957. For that year, the 42L2 became the Vespa Standard and was joined by the Magna and Ultra models, which had different levels of equipment.

Unfortunately, time ran out for Douglas and they were unable to develop the Dragonfly, which had become known as being too slow for sports riding and too noisy and fussy for touring. Sales were poor, and late in 1956 the company was taken over by Westinghouse Brake and Signal. By March 1957 production at Bristol had ceased and the flat-twins were no more. The Vespa continued as an import, of course, but to devotees of the marque, it was the end. Only the old sales slogan remained: 'A twin is best, and Douglas is the best twin'.

Dunelt

Dunkley

This company had first appeared in 1919 and became best known between the wars for a two-stroke engine design with a double-diameter piston. They continued with proprietary engines until 1935 and then left the industry.

Dunelt returned for the briefest of spells in 1957, when the name was revived for a 50 cc moped. This had a two-stroke engine with two-speed gearbox and twistgrip change. The frame had front and rear suspension by telescopic and pivoted forks respectively, the wheels had small drum brakes in full-width hubs, and there was direct lighting.

It came and went in months, with virtually no record nor any impact on the market. At that time, there were scores of continental mopeds of all styles, so there was little call for yet another marque.

This make came and went in three short years, leaving barely a mark on the industry but, for all that, represented a good attempt to break into the market. The models often had continental lines, but were mainly made at Hounslow on the outskirts of West London.

They came on to the market early in 1957 with the Whippet 60 Scooterette, which had a 61 cc ohv engine with inclined alloy barrel and parallel valves in an alloy head. These were arranged across the engine, so the carburettor was mounted to an inlet tract on the right, and the exhaust emerged from the left. The camshaft lay behind the cylinder, where it was gear driven, lubrication was wet sump, and ignition was provided by a Wipac flywheel magneto. A two-speed gearbox was built in unit with the engine and controlled by a left-hand twistgrip.

The Dunelt 50 cc moped, which made the briefest of appearances on the market in 1957

The engine unit went into a spine frame with telescopic front and pivoted rear suspension. There were 4 in. drum brakes in wheels with 23 in. rims, a short dualseat and direct lighting.

Later in the year, the Scooterette was joined by the Super Sports 65. This had an engine with a slightly longer stroke, to increase the capacity to 64 cc, and a raised compression ratio. The two-speed gearbox remained, but the frame took on a very continental look and was made from two pressings in spine form. The suspension systems were as before, as were the full-width hubs. The dualseat, as well as the rear legs, came from Italy.

For 1958 these two models were joined by the S65 Scooter, which retained the 64 cc engine in a new set of cycle parts. The frame had a single, large tube which ran from the headstock, under the engine, to a vertical member. This supported the fuel tank, the bodywork and the pivot for the rear suspension fork.

The body, including the apron, was a single assembly, which was hinged from the top of the apron to give access to the engine and rear wheel. A deep mudguard enveloped the front wheel, while both had 15 in. rims with the same full-width hubs and 4 in. drum brakes as the other models. The front suspension differed from these, being by short leading links. The scooter came with a dualseat and footboards on each side of the deep engine tunnel.

For 1959 the Super Sports 65 became the Whippet Sports and the other two models ran on with two new ones. These were very similar and listed as the 49.6 cc Popular Scooter and 64 cc Popular Major Scooter. They had a common rigid frame with telescopic front forks and the 15 in. wheels. The engine was set well back and was fan-cooled so that the apron could lead to a flat floor ahead of the rear bodywork. This simply enclosed the engine unit, with a further rear mud-guard enclosure extending to the number plate. There was a simple saddle. The result was some-what stark, but functional.

The two models used similar engines, the larger being the same as that used by the other models, and the smaller having reduced bore and stroke. The larger-capacity machine had some additional trim to enable it to carry a de luxe tag, but otherwise they were the same.

At the end of 1959 the firm dropped the entire range, and the marque vanished as quickly as it had come. Maybe they had a premonition about the next decade.

EMC

Josef Ehrlich came to Britain in 1937, and by 1939 had an engine of his own manufacture installed in an old Francis-Barnett for road and track testing. He was Austrian, so it was hardly surprising that his interest lay in two-strokes and that these were of the split-single type, favoured by Puch and the German DKW.

The 1939 engine was of this type, with two 44 mm bore cylinders sharing a common 79 mm stroke to give 240 cc capacity. The cylinders sat one behind the other, with a side inlet and rear exhaust for the back one, while the transfer port was in the front one. The two were joined at the top under the single combustion chamber. The connecting rod was of Y-shape and joined to both pistons, having a slotted small-end for one of them to compensate for the movement of the parts.

After the war, Ehrlich set up in business to produce his EMC machines, which were launched in 1947. The engine had grown to 345 cc, but otherwise was laid out as before. However, it had a master connecting rod and a slave rod. Its appearance was odd, and this was accentuated by the fins on the cast-iron block, for they were rectangular in outline and alternated in depth. Due to this, a casual glance suggested few fins, widely spaced.

The head was in alloy, as was the crankcase. Lubrication was by petroil for the model T tourer and by a Pilgrim oil pump, driven from the magneto sprocket, for the sports model S. This item sat behind the engine and above the Burman four-speed gearbox, the drive of which was enclosed by a cast alloy case.

The engine and gearbox went into a rigid duplex frame with a forged bronze backbone and steering head. This had twin tubes formed into loops bolted to it at each end, and these completed the structure. The front forks were Dowty oleo-pneumatics, which combined air suspension with

The machine Joe Ehrlich was showing to the press in 1939 with its 240 cc split-single engine

The post-war 345 cc EMC split-single engine installed in a rigid frame with Dowty Oleomatic forks

The EMC exhibited at the 1952 show with a 125 cc JAP engine, spine frame and downtube suspension unit

hydraulic damping. Both wheels had 7 in. drum brakes, but the front had one on each side, its hub being fitted into a 20 in. rim.

The machine was highly geared, and Ehrlich claimed over 100 mpg in advertising, which was an important point in those days of petrol rationing. Owners, however, found it difficult to achieve half that figure and spoke of vibration at the

70 mph top speed. It was also expensive, so most buyers opted for AMC, Ariel or BSA, which they knew and understood.

For 1948 there was talk of a second model in a plunger frame, which came to nothing, but the backbone forging was changed to a light alloy. The oil pump was modified so its output could be varied by a cable connected to the throttle, and conical hubs with 7 in. brakes were adopted for both wheels.

There was also mention of a road-racing model, which had a phasing piston, despite the ban on supercharging. Ehrlich held that it would become admissible and that the engine was all his, but it looked remarkably like the pre-war blown DKW. It was installed with a Burman gearbox in a frame with Dowty suspension front and rear, and a 250 cc version won the Hutchinson 100 race late in 1947. This was not Ehrlich's first involvement in post-war racing, for he had been in a dispute at the 1946 Manx with claims regarding patents and demands for the two DKWs entered to be run as EMCs. Once the daily paper correspondents had filed their stories, with suitably sensational head-lines, no more was heard of the matter.

In the early 1950s Ehrlich became linked with the Puch firm, and one outcome was a neat 125 cc racing model. This used the split-single Puch engine with its unit-construction, four-speed gearbox, twin carburettors and twin exhaust pipes and megaphones. The engine went into a simple loop frame with telescopic forks and a Puch rear fork constructed from pressings welded together. They performed quite well and were on offer for two or three years.

A 500 cc split-single was also spoken of, and a 125 cc road model with a JAP engine. The latter was shown at Earls Court and had an unusual frame. It looked conventional at first, but was of the spine type with pivoted rear fork. This fork also extended ahead of its pivot and carried the engine and three-speed gearbox unit in one. What looked like a normal downtube was, in fact, a lengthy suspension unit, and the pivoted fork tubes also doubled as exhaust pipes. The weight of the unsprung parts was thus considerable, and only the prototype was seen.

There was a move to sell the Puch 250 cc road model with EMC badges, but this did not last for long, for the firm was wound up in 1953. Puch later set up their own organization, while Joe Ehrlich went on to fresh pastures, but remained with motorcycle racing for a good few years.

Excelsior

This company dates back to before the dawn of the industry, for they began with penny-farthing bicycles in 1874 and took to power in 1896. They had their ups and downs and built just about anything, from TT winners to utility models.

The 1939 range reflected this, with models from 98 to 496 cc, and with two-stroke, ohv and ohc engines. During the war, they built the Welbike, from which the Corgi sprang (see page 67), but after that, restricted themselves to lightweight models.

There were just two of these for 1946; one was the Autobyk with a 98 cc Villiers Junior De Luxe engine, and the other the Universal model O with a 122 cc 9D unit and three-speed gearbox. The latter was a neat machine with rigid loop frame and blade girder forks, but its oddest feature was the hand gearchange. This worked in a gate set in the top of the petroil tank, which had a slot in it for the linkage to pass down to the box.

It continued in this form until the end of 1948, while for 1947 the Autobyke became the model VI. It was joined by the Super Autobyk G2, which was fitted with an Excelsior 98 cc Goblin engine with two-speed gearbox. This was not unlike the Villiers JDL and retained the near horizontal incli-nation for the iron barrel with its alloy head. An overhung crankshaft was used, with the flywheel magneto on the right, outboard of the chain drive to the clutch and simple gearbox, which had the output sprocket on the left.

This engine unit went into the same simple autocycle frame as before, with light blade girders, petroil tank between the frame tubes, engine covers, saddle and rear carrier. Before the year began, however, the forks were altered to tubular girders and their suspension medium from a com-pression spring to rubber bands working on cross-bars.

Within a few months, it was joined by the Autobyk de luxe model S1, which used the single-

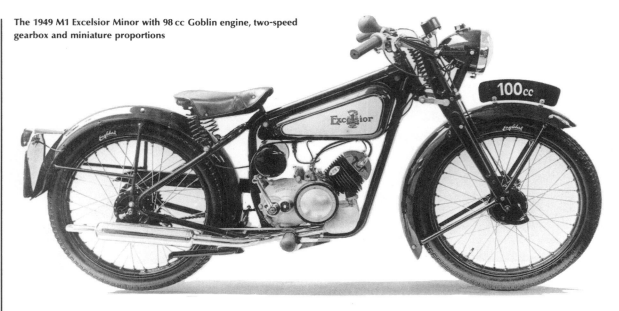

The 1949 M1 Excelsior Minor with 98 cc Goblin engine, two-speed gearbox and miniature proportions

speed, 98 cc Excelsior Spryt engine. This was much as the Goblin, but with a single shaft for the clutch and output sprocket in place of the two speeds. All three autocycles continued with the model O for 1948.

There were changes for 1949, but not to the autocycles. The Universal became the model LO and was fitted with the 122 cc Villiers 10D engine with three-speed gearbox. During the year, it gained telescopic front forks to become the U1, which had direct lighting, and was joined by the U2, which had a battery and rectifier. With these two machines came the R1 and R2 Roadmaster models, which were the same, except for a 197 cc Villiers 6E engine. Two further machines were added to the list, both with the name Minor, and coded M1 and M2. They were miniature

motorcycles with loop frame and blade girders, but with a wedge-shaped tank hung beneath the top tube. Both models had Excelsior engines, the M1 using the 98 cc Goblin, and the M2 a bored-out, 123 cc version. Both kept the two-speed gearbox.

This design only lasted for the year, and when the two models were dropped, the V1 Autobyk with the JDL engine went with them. This left the S1 and G2 autocycles and the Universal and Roadmaster models, which were all given plunger rear suspension for 1950. There was one further model introduced that year, and this was, perhaps, the best known post-war Excelsior – the Talisman Twin.

For this, the firm built their own 243 cc, twin-cylinder two-stroke engine. It was of conventional

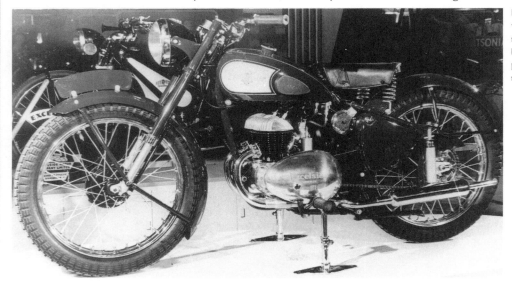

Early Talisman Twin with its 243 cc two-stroke engine and Excelsior form of plunger rear suspension

One of the two Excelsior autocycles in 1951, both of which had their own make of 98 cc engine with one or two speeds

The 1957 Excelsior Consort F4 with 99 cc engine, two speeds and girder forks to provide minimal transport

The Excelsior Skutabyk, as it appeared in 1957 based on a Consort with enclosure panels

form, the crankcase being divided vertically into three sections, and the two crankshafts keyed together and held by a nut on one mainshaft. The cast-iron cylinders were separate with alloy heads, and an alloy manifold carried the single Amal that supplied the mixture. A flywheel magneto went on the right and the primary drive to the four-speed Albion gearbox on the left.

This engine unit went into the same loop frame, with plunger rear suspension and telescopic front forks, as used by the other motorcycles. The fittings were either common or similar, and there was a saddle. However, there were two toolboxes instead of only one on the left, and there was a battery in front of the right one. The twin exhaust pipes were connected to a single silencer on the left, and the machine had full lighting and an electric horn.

The whole range went forward unchanged for 1951 and 1952, when it was joined by a Sports version of the twin. This was listed as the STT1, which had twin Amal carburettors and a strange dualseat with side pads below the rider's part to act as kneegrips for the passenger.

The 1953 range showed some change, for the Universal models became export-only machines, being replaced on the home market by the C2 Courier. This had a 147 cc Excelsior engine, which was very much in the Villiers mould, other than the Wipac generator and Amal carburettor. One further difference was that it was mated to a Burman three-speed gearbox, rather than the usual Albion. The cycle parts were as before, and as still used by the Roadmaster models, while the Courier had battery lighting and a rectifier as standard.

The two Autobyks were still going strong, so with the twins this made a useful range. It was expanded in April 1953 with the F4 Consort, which was a small motorcycle fitted with the 99 cc Villiers 4F engine with two-speed gearbox. This went into a simple, rigid loop frame with light girder forks, 19 in. wheels and small drum brakes. The equipment included a saddle and cylindrical toolbox beneath it, bulb horn and direct lighting.

The whole range continued for 1954, with a change to the 8E engine for the Roadmaster models and a direct-lighting C1 version of the Courier. There were also five new machines, four in a new frame with pivoted-fork rear suspension. With this came a dualseat. The first two models were the R3 and R4 Roadmaster with the 8E engine and direct or battery lighting respectively. The

other two were twins, the TT2 being the Talisman and the STT2 the Sports version.

The final new model was the D12 Condor, which was effectively the Consort fitted with a 122 cc Villiers 13D engine, but still with the rigid frame and girder forks. It was only built for 1954 and was dropped at the end of the year, along with the plunger-framed C1 and C2 Courier, R1 and R2 Roadmaster, TT1 and STT1 twins, and U1 and U2 Universal, which were no longer even available for export.

The direct-lighting R3 was also phased out, but the R4 continued, as did the Consort and two twins, this line-up being joined by five new models in a new frame for 1955. The smallest of these was the C3 Courier with a 147 cc Excelsior engine and three-speed gearbox, while its frame was simpler than before, having a single tube loop under the engine unit.

The same frame was used for the R5 and R6 Roadmaster models, which had direct or battery lighting, and for two more twins. One was listed as the Popular Talisman, or TT3, and was distinguished by oval toolboxes, as well as the new frame. The second was the Special Equipment Sports Talisman Twin, or SE-STT2, which had full-width alloy hubs.

There were more revisions and new models for 1956, when the Consort changed to the 6F engine and was joined by the F4S Consort, which was much the same, but with plunger rear suspension. Of the Roadmaster models, only the R6 continued, but it was joined by the A9 Autocrat, which was powered by the 9E Villiers engine with four-speed gearbox. Also new was the C1 Condex with 147 cc Villiers 30C engine and three-speed gearbox, which used the Consort spring frame with telescopic front forks.

Among the twins, the Special was dropped, along with the TT2, to leave the TT3 and the Sports model in STT4 form with twin pipes and silencers. That year, the firm also moved into the scooter and moped market by importing the Heinkel products, which served them for a few years.

The C3 Courier was joined by the C4 Convoy in April 1956 and, like the C3, this used the 147 cc Excelsior engine. It was very similar, but had had a few economies made to reduce the price. It replaced the C3 for 1957, when there were finally no Autobyks as both went, along with the R6, C1 and A9, although the last did remain for export only for a short while.

The Excelsior scooter, which was launched in 1959 in two forms, both powered by the firm's 147 cc engine. It shared body pressings with DKR

The two Consort models continued for 1957, but with the sprung one listed as the F6S, along with the TT3 and the Sports Twin, which became the STT5 with deeper fins and revised porting. New was the Skutabyk which, in a sense, replaced the Autobyk. It was based on an F6S Consort, but to this was added extensive exclosure panels, which ran on each side from the downtube to the rear plunger. At the front, legshields were formed and footboards ran back from these to the rear of the machine. The panels had louvres to assist cooling and access holes, while the machine was finished with a dualseat with a suggestion of the pillion kneegrips of the past.

The Consorts, as such, were dropped at the end of the year, although the Skutabyk continued and a new Consort CA8 joined it. This had a pivoted-fork frame with telescopic forks, in which to accommodate the 6F engine, while the rider was provided with a dualseat. A new Universal model, coded UB and fitted with a 147 cc Villiers 30C engine, replaced the Convoy and had a similar specification. The Talisman became the TT4 and the Sports version the STT6, but of more

Excelsior Roadmaster R10, of 1959, with Villiers 9E engine in conventional cycle parts

interest to enthusiasts of the marque was the appearance of the larger 328 cc S8 Super Talisman. This was much as the Sports Twin, with twin carburettors and the same set of cycle parts, including 6 in. brakes in full-width hubs.

The S8 engine had been developed to suit the light three-wheelers then on the market, and late that year this idea was taken one step further. The result was a 491 cc, three-cylinder engine with Siba electric start and suitable Albion gearbox.

Most of the range continued for 1959 with minor changes. The Consort became the CA9, and the Universal the U9 and UR9 with battery and rectifier. The Skutabyk, Talisman and Super Talisman also ran on, but not the Sports Twin model. In its place, there was a new Special Talisman, the S9, but this used the 328 cc engine, with twin carburettors, and was distinguished by full enclosure of the rear end down to wheel-spindle level. It was also unusual in having a tool compartment set in the tank top, the filler neck being inside this with its cap part of the toolbox lid.

The early form of the Consort reappeared in April 1959 as the F4F, complete with rigid frame and girder forks, as in the past. The 6F engine with foot-change was used, but otherwise the fixtures and fittings were as before.

A week later, the firm announced a two-model scooter range, achieving this by dint of using the DKR cycle and body parts (see page 79) fitted with their own 147 cc engine. The models were given the name Monarch, and were designated KS with kickstarter, and EL with an electric one. The body kept the large front section of the DKR, because the fuel tank remained in place ahead of the headstock and above the front wheel, so it was hard to tell the two makes apart, except by the badges fitted to them.

The scooters became the MK1 and ME1 for 1960, when the Roadmaster model returned as the R10 with 9E engine and four-speed gearbox.. It used a frame based on that of the twins, of which the Talisman became the TT6, the S9 ran on as it was and the S8 was dropped. Among the smaller models, the Skutabyk was no longer listed, while the Consorts became the C10 and the utility F10. The Universal had its engine changed to the 148 cc Villiers 31C to become the U10.

In this way, the long established firm entered the 1960s, but soon began to flag. After 1962 the range was down to just two models, and the last of these went in 1965 to remove one more famous name from the role of British manufacturers.

FLM

This was Frank Leach Manufacturing of Leeds, who entered the lightweight market in 1951 with a machine that looked like many others, but differed a good deal. Unlike most, they used the 125 cc JAP engine with three-speed gearbox, installing it in a frame with pivoted-fork rear suspension.

The frame differed further from the norm in being constructed from channel-section steel, while control of the rear fork was by four springs located beneath the engine unit. These were linked to the fork and allowed it some 5 in. of undamped wheel movement.

At the front were telescopic forks, and both 19 in. wheels had 5 in. drum brakes and well valanced mudguards. The machine had a dualseat and was called the Glideride, while a Utility model with rigid frame was also spoken of, but not seen. Only the Glideride was offered for 1952, but during the year a second machine was seen in prototype form.

This was larger with a 197 cc Villiers 6E engine installed in a neat tubular loop frame, which retained the unusual rear suspension of the 125. It failed to reach production, so there was still just the one model for 1953, although it was then offered with a choice of colour schemes and either direct or battery lighting.

Production of this model was totally dependent on supplies of the JAP engine, and as these began to dry up the firm decided to stop production. Perhaps they could have continued with a Villiers engine, but FLM preferred to leave the market.

Francis-Barnett

A famous firm, best known for its lightweight models and a between-the-wars frame built from lengths of straight tube bolted together. The first machine produced by Gordon Francis and Arthur Barnett appeared in 1920, and soon they had a good range. After the war, they returned to the market with just two models for 1946, one being an autocycle and the other a light motorcycle.

The former was the model 50 Powerbike, which was built much as others of that type, with a 98 cc Villiers JDL engine. This went into a drop frame with blade girder forks, saddle, rear carrier and the usual extensive side-shields around the engine. The other was the model 51 Merlin with 122 cc Villiers 9D engine and three-speed hand-change gearbox. The frame was a simple rigid loop with tubular girder forks, and both wheels had 19 in. rims and 5 in. drum brakes. The machine came with a saddle and rear carrier, while the toolbox between the right-hand chainstays was matched by an oil tank on the left. This had a tap and the fuel tank cap a measure, so mixing the petroil was an easy task.

In 1947 the firm became part of the AMC group, but it was some time before this had any great effect. Meanwhile, the two models continued, the Powerbike changing to tubular girders with rubber-band springing for 1948. These were further braced for 1949, when the original Merlin was replaced by two models with a 10D engine and joined by two more with the 197 cc 6E engine and the name Falcon.

All four new models used the same rigid frame, which was much as before, but with telescopic front forks. The saddle, carrier and oil tank continued, as did the wheels. The Merlin models were the 52 with direct lighting, and the 53 with a battery on the right, under the saddle. The equivalent Falcons were the 54 and 55, all four having a quickly detachable rear number plate to assist wheel removal.

During 1949 a new version of the Powerbike appeared as the model 56, which used the 99 cc Villiers 2F engine in a new loop frame. The front forks continued to be tubular girders with rubber-band suspension, while the remainder of the machine stayed in the autocycle style with saddle, carrier and engine enclosure. These five models continued for the next two years with no real alteration, except that for 1951 the motorcycles were offered in an azure blue finish as an option. Quite a change for a utility range.

At the end of 1951 the Powerbike was dropped, and for 1952 the four motorcycles were joined by four more. Two of these had a new frame with pivoted-fork rear suspension, using a system of rubber bushes as the pivot point. The hydraulically-damped rear units were made by the firm, and there was a rubber rebound stop on the frame beneath the fork.

To suit the new frame, there was a centre stand, rather than one at the rear, and a single toolbox on the left with battery and electric horn on the right. The facility of an easily-removed rear number plate remained, as did the saddle. With the 10D engine, the machine was the Merlin 57, and with the 6E, it became the Falcon 58.

The same names and engines were used by the models 59 and 60, but these had rigid frames and were built for competition use with the cycle parts suitably altered. These two were replaced by four more purpose-built models for 1953, the Merlin 61 and Falcon 62 being for trials and the Merlin 63 and Falcon 64 for scrambles. The two types no longer used the same cycle parts, for the trials models kept the rigid frame, but the scramblers went into the pivoted-fork version.

The Merlins used the competition 10D engine, but the Falcon 62 and 64 changed to the 7E unit to match the 54, 55 and 58, which went over to the 8E. Otherwise, the four rigid and two pivoted-fork models ran on, still with the optional blue finish, and were joined by one further machine.

This was the Overseas Falcon 65, which fell between the road and trials models and was effectively a trail bike. Thus, it had the 8E engine in the pivoted-fork frame, but with narrow sprung mudguards – the front one with massive clearance – stiffer forks and a 21 in. front wheel.

The rigid road models did not continue for 1954, and neither did any of the Merlins. The Falcon 58 became the 67, much as before, and the models 62, 64 and 65 continued as they were. New was the Kestrel 66, which had the 122 cc

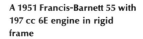

A 1951 Francis-Barnett 55 with 197 cc 6E engine in rigid frame

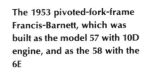

The 1953 pivoted-fork-frame Francis-Barnett, which was built as the model 57 with 10D engine, and as the 58 with the 6E

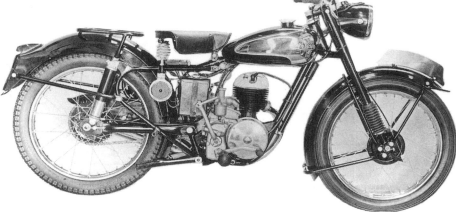

The export Falcon 65 Francis-Barnett with 8E engine, an early trail machine

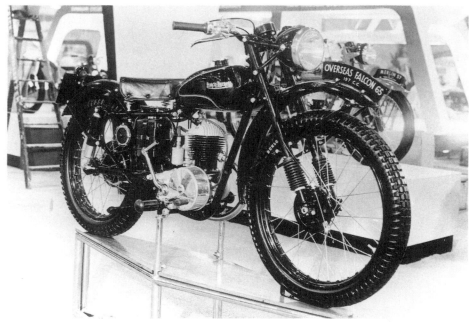

The Francis-Barnett Cruiser 68 with 224 cc Villiers 1H engine in a built-up frame

Villiers 13D engine with three-speed gearbox fitted into a simple loop frame. This had plunger rear suspension and telescopic forks. The equipment included a saddle and direct lighting, while the finish was in azure blue. The machine offered low-cost transport to the commuter.

Shortly after the main range was announced, Francis-Barnett reintroduced a pre-war name for another new model. This was the Cruiser 68, which used the 224 cc Villiers 1H engine with its four-speed gearbox. The machine's frame was built up from a massive, tapered down-member, to which were bolted tube loops with a fabricated pressing in the area beneath the dualseat that extended down to form the rear engine plates. This then formed a stowage space for the battery, rectifier and tools, and gave the model a very neat appearance. Telescopic front and pivoted-fork rear suspensions were used, along with 19 in. wheels and 6 in. drum brakes. The mudguards were deeply valanced, and the finish was in a very nice dark green, set off with gold tank lining.

There were only five models for 1955, all of them having a new front fork with hydraulic damping. The road Falcon was also given a new pivoted-fork frame to become the model 70, while the Cruiser became the 71 with full-width hubs, and the scrambles model the 72. The last, and the trials 62, now had four-speed gearboxes with suitable ratios as standard, while the 62 still kept to its rigid frame.

The one new model was the Kestrel 69, which replaced the 66, had full-width hubs and the new forks, but kept the plunger frame. Into this went a 147 cc Villiers 30C engine with three-speed gearbox to give the cheapest model of the range

a touch more power.

All the models had their numbers changed for 1956, the smallest becoming the Plover 73. It retained the 30C engine, but this went into a new frame with tubular front, but pressed-steel rear sections. The pressing supported the pivoted rear fork, concealed its rear suspension units, and housed the tools, battery and electrics, with a single seat for the rider. There were oil-damped telescopics at the front, full-width hubs and a cast alloy expansion box beneath the gearbox with twin outlet pipes.

The other road models became the Falcon 74, with 18 in. wheels, and the Cruiser 75, which had this change for the front only. On the competition front, the trials model became the Falcon 76, and the scrambles machine the Falcon 77. Both had a new frame and a specification to suit their intended use.

The only model to have its number changed for 1957 was the Plover, which became the 78 and gained a dualseat. It also had its silencing arrangements altered, the expansion box becoming a pressed-steel, welded assembly with a single outlet, to which a further silencer was attached. The range was joined by the Cruiser 80, which was the first Francis-Barnett to be fitted with the unhappy AMC two-stroke engine.

The 80 used the 249 cc version, which was the first to appear and presented a smooth shape to the world. Smooth would also seem to apply to the Italian designer, who accepted his brief and fee, but departed for home before his work was either developed or fully tested.

The engine was laid out much as the Villiers 1H, with the four-speed gearbox being bolted to the rear of the crankcase, the castings blended together and full-length covers on each side. The right-hand one concealed a Wipac generator and had a points cover set in it, while the Amal carburettor was enclosed by a further cover. The main odd feature of the engine was the head, barrel and piston assembly, for there were no transfer ports, only depressions in the cylinder walls. To guide the mixture, the long piston had ports in its skirt and a tall crown shaped to match the head. This was different from most in having sunburst radial fins and internal downward projections to match the piston.

In use, this design was to prove poor in oper-ation and reliability, while weak gear-selector parts and poor electrics did nothing to enhance its reputation. In keeping with their traditions, AMC never took the obvious way out with a new top half, but persevered with their troublesome design well into the 1960s, until their empire collapsed from this and other similar ailments.

For the Cruiser 80, this engine was fitted into the 75 frame, with minor alterations, which included Girling rear units. The rear wheel size came down to match the front, at 18 in., and the wiring and switches were amended to suit the Wipac circuits. The filler cap was set flush with the tank top and was hinged to swing up in use.

Early Francis-Barnett scrambler with the 249 cc AMC single engine, which led to the model 82, but no real success

Cut-away show model of the Francis-Barnett Cruiser 84, of 1959, with 249 cc AMC engine and normally fully enclosed with panels

The older Cruiser was dropped for 1958, to leave the AMC-engined 80, which continued with the Plover 78. For the 200 cc class, the Falcon became the 81 with the more streamlined, 197 cc Villiers 10E engine, but with three-speed gearbox, while the cycle side remained as it was. The trials and scrambles Falcons were both dropped, for AMC had fully committed themselves to their new engine, but it was April before a new competition machine appeared.

This was the Scrambler 82, which used a tuned version of the 249 cc AMC engine in a very nice frame with Norton front forks. There were Girlings to control the rear end, and the whole package was very neat, except for the engine. The heart of the problem was the strange piston design and its poor ring sealing, but this was aggravated by the Wipac energy-transfer ignition system.

A month after the Scrambler, the second road model appeared with the AMC engine. This was the 171 cc Light Cruiser 79. The engine was simply a smaller edition of the 249 cc version and the cycle side was similar to the Cruiser. The centre-section enclosure was even larger, extending forward to the carburettor and along the subframe down to footrest level.

All the models continued for 1959, when the Trials 83 with the 249 cc AMC engine joined them. This used the same frame and forks as the Scrambler, but had a long silencer tucked inside the right-hand subframe tube and rear unit. Also new was the Cruiser 84, which created great interest due to its extensive enclosure and legshields fitted as standard. It was based on the 80, so had the 249 cc AMC engine, but was fully enclosed from the cylinder to the rear number plate, and down well below wheel spindle height. It made an impressive machine.

The two Cruiser models ran on for 1960, along with the Light Cruiser and the two competition machines, of which the Trials version became the 85. The last two machines with Villiers engines were changed to AMC units to make the Plover 86 and Falcon 87, but in later years the company had to eat its words and ask Villiers for both engines and technical assistance.

As it was, the 1960 range ran on into the new decade, minus the model 79, and, with later changes, on to the company's end in 1966. It was a sad fate for a firm that had lived through some hard times by building good reliable machines, and from them gaining a reputation of producing some of the better utility motorcycles.

Greeves

Bert Greeves came into the motorcycle industry because his cousin, Derry Preston Cobb, was paralysed from birth. Bert made him more mobile by fitting a small engine to his wheelchair, and this led to the foundation of Invacar to build powered invalid carriages.

Derry joined in this enterprise as salesman and buyer for the Southend-based firm and, despite his handicap, often travelled about the country, either selling or attending sports meetings once the Greeves name was established. At a later date, his invalid car was powered by a hot Starmaker engine, which must have surprised a few people.

Invacar built up a good business after the war, serving the needs of the disabled, and in 1951 began their move into motorcycles. Unlike most of the industry, they set out on a development programme, which was long enough to sort out most of the problems. Part of this work was done by running a machine in scrambles, which also helped, as the public became used to the machine and its odd appearance and specification.

This centred on the suspension system, which used rubber bushes in torsion as the springing medium. The design was taken from the invalid carriage, so they had experience of it, but it did make for an odd machine. This was especially so at the front, where trailing links were used with the bushes located at the pivot point. The links were joined by a tube that ran round in front of the wheel, while a brake torque stay ran down from the fork leg to the backplate.

At the back there was a conventional pivoted fork, but the rubber bushes were sited above this and at the rear end of the top tube. Each had a short lever arm which was connected to the fork ends by a link on each side. There were no dampers at either end.

For the rest, there was a tubular loop frame with duplex downtubes, a 197 cc Villiers engine tuned for scrambles, offset hubs with drum brakes, and a dualseat. Development work continued on this and other models until late 1953, when the marque was finally launched on to the market.

There were four machines at first, and all used the 197 cc Villiers 8E engine. If this was a feature common to most British lightweights, the Greeves frame and forks were unique. The frame was part tubular, but included a cast alloy beam that ran down from the headstock to the front of the engine. The casting was poured round the welded tubular section which, consequently, was totally locked to it for all time.

Further deep alloy sections ran under the engine unit and were bolted to the main beam and to the rear end of the top tube. The frame loops carried the lugs for the rear fork pivot and the housings for the rubber torsion bushes, which had friction dampers incorporated into them. At the front, there was a leading-link fork which, again, used the rubber bushes at the pivots and had the dampers incorporated with them. The links were joined by a tubular loop behind the wheel, so they did not have to rely on the wheel spindle for their rigidity.

The road models were the 20R with three speeds and the de luxe 20D with four. Both had battery lighting and an electric horn, which sat just ahead of a cylindrical toolbox beneath the dualseat. The headlamp was held by four thin stays, and the entire rear mudguard and seat assembly was easily removed to give access to the rear wheel. Both wheels had 6 in. drum brakes in offset hubs and 19 in. rims.

The competition models were the 20T trials and 20S scrambles, which had special hubs with plain bearings that had proved successful during development. The trials model alone had a 21 in. front wheel, while the cycle parts of both models were altered, or dispensed with, to suit the machine's purpose.

A further model was added to the range for 1954 and differed from the others in using the 242 cc British Anzani twin two-stroke engine with four-speed gearbox. It was listed as the 25D Fleetwing and used the same cycle parts as the Villiers-powered road models with an exhaust system on each side.

For 1955 it was joined by the 25R Standard Twin, which used the same engine in a tubular frame. For this there was a front section, comprising top and downtubes, which were well supported in the headstock, the downtube being extended under the engine unit and up to the rear fork pivot. In this way, it was a direct replacement for the composite tube and alloy frame, was cheaper and nearly as strong. Unlike the earlier models, it used normal rear suspension units, rather than the rubber ones, and these went on to the scrambler as well.

The tubular frame with rear suspension units was also used by the 20R3 and 20R4 Standard models with three- or four-speed gearboxes, which replaced the 20R, but retained the 8E engine. Both had 5 in. brakes in both wheels, unlike the other models. The 20D ran on as it was, as did the two competition models, except that

The 1957 Greeves Fleetmaster with 322 cc British Anzani twin engine in standard frame with revised forks

they now had wheel hubs with ball race bearings in place of the previous year's plain ones.

One new model joined the range that year as the 32D Fleetmaster Twin, which used the 322 cc British Anzani engine in the cast alloy frame. It differed from the smaller twin in having dual 6 in. brakes at the front and a 7 in. one at the rear, but was otherwise very similar. Neither twin was very speedy, and contemporary tests recorded 61 and 73 mph for the two sizes, at a time when the 197 cc model was good for 60 mph.

Perhaps that was why the 25D was not listed for 1956, although the other two twins remained. All models now had hydraulically-damped rear suspension units, so the original linkage was seen

no more, although the friction dampers remained at the front. Of the singles, the 20R3 continued with its 8E engine, but the 20R4 was dropped and the 20D, 20S and 20T had their engines changed for the 9E unit, all with the four-speed gearbox.

For all road models, the cylindrical toolbox was replaced by a tray under the left rear of the dualseat, but it remained for the trials model with its saddle. The change did little for the line of the road machines, which always seemed ungainly to some extent, in sharp contrast to the competition machines. These had a very purposeful air to them

Left **Greeves 20D road model, from 1955, with 8E engine and four-speed gearbox in original frame with rubber suspension at both ends**

Below **Greeves trials model 20T with 9E engine, as in 1957, with saddle and tilted silencer**

Fleetwing 25D Greeves with 2T Villiers twin engine, as in 1958

and always looked the business – which they were.

The whole range ran on for 1957 with one addition in the form of the 25D. This was a new Fleetwing, powered by a 249 cc Villiers 2T twin engine with four-speed gearbox, which went into the cast alloy frame. It had the dual 6 in. front brakes, but a 6 in. brake at the rear, not the 7 in. version. The Fleetwing retained the rubber bushes at the front, but their movement was damped by a slim Girling unit concealed in each fork leg. The same fork also went on the 32D and the two competition models.

During the year, the 20R4 reappeared, but with a 7E engine and four-speed gearbox in the 20R3 cycle parts. Both models were dropped at the end of the season, along with most of the rest of the range, other than the 20D and 25D. There were four other models for 1958, all for competition, and the 197 cc ones were updates of the previous machines. They continued with the 9E engine and four speeds as the 20TA Scottish Trials and 20SA Hawkstone Scrambler models. Their frame was new, but retained the cast alloy beam, and there were a number of detail changes to improve both models to suit their function.

The other new models were the 25TA Scottish Trials 25 and 25SA Hawkstone 25, which used the Villiers 2T engine unit, suitably modified for the

intended use. Both were to special order only and used the cycle parts from the appropriate 197 cc machine. They were dropped at the end of the year, as riders knew as well as Greeves did that the single-cylinder engines were best.

The 20TA continued as it was for 1959, but otherwise there were changes and additions on the competition front. The basic trials model was joined by the 20TAS Scottish Trials Special, which had a 9E engine with a special, extra-heavy flywheel to aid low-speed pulling. The scrambler became the 20SAS Hawkstone Special, and two further models were created by fitting the 246 cc Villiers 31A engine in place of the 9E to give the 24TAS and 24SAS. For road use, the model with the 2T engine became the 25DB and was joined by the 24DB, which had the 31A engine in the same set of cycle parts.

For 1960 there was little change for the trials models, which became the 20TC, 20TCS and 24TCS, but the last had its engine changed to the 32A unit. The scramblers were given a new frame, so the two competition types no longer shared, having become more specialized. The coding changed to 20SCS and 24SCS, with a 33A engine for the latter, while the two road models ran on. The single also had its engine changed to a 32A. During the year, the 25DB was joined by the 32DB, which used the 324 cc Villiers 3T engine in the same set of cycle parts.

With this range, Greeves ran into the 1960s to more success, road racing and their own engine.

GYS

This was another of the cyclemotor attachments that gave one of the cheapest means of powered transport. It was mounted over the front wheel, which it drove by roller with a 50 cc two-stroke engine, and was made in Bournemouth.

The engine was nearly all alloy, with the crankcase cast in one with the cylinder. The head was separate and the sides of the crankcase were closed with circular doors, the left-hand one of which was extended to carry the main bearings and housed the drive roller. The crankshaft had an overhung roller big-end and a Wipac flywheel magneto on its left-hand end. The silencer was bolted directly to the barrel and was cast in alloy, as was the petroil tank. Carburation was by a small Amal, and its lever control was linked to the decompressor for simplicity. The whole unit was mounted so that the roller was held in spring-loaded contact with the tyre, or could be raised clear of it.

The unit was first sold as the GYS in June 1949, and by the end of the year a firm in Lancashire was making them under licence. Distribution was

by the Cairns Cycle firm, who sold bicycles complete with the GYS attachment.

In 1951 a kit became available from Cobli, a London firm, which mounted the engine below the saddle to drive the rear wheel. The kit replaced the normal rear seat stays, so the roller could be engaged or held clear of the tyre. The unit remained offset to the right of the wheel.

The GYS became the Motomite for 1951, but then changed its name again to become the Mocyc for 1952. It kept this name until 1955, when it was withdrawn from the market.

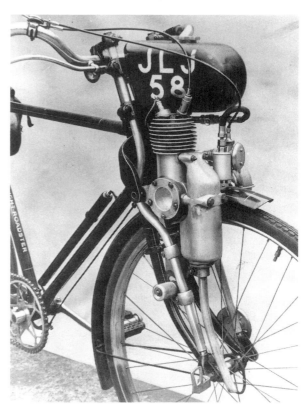

The 1949 GYS clip-on with all-alloy engine, silencer and fuel tank, which was later sold as the Mocyc

Harper

Some makes never really got off the ground, and this was one of them. The intention was to build an all-British scooter at the Harper Aircraft works at Exeter Airport, and the prototype was first seen in March 1954. It had low, wide lines, so both rider and passenger sat in the bodywork, rather than on the machine, and this style was accentuated by the twin headlamps used.

The basis of the scooter was a rather hefty frame that ran low down along each side, behind the rear wheel and up to the headstock at the front. Further tubes ran from the rear, over the engine area, to take the rider's weight, and were braced by more tubing. This also provided a pivot for the rear suspension fork, which was controlled by a torsion bar.

At the front the headstock was bolted to the frame so it could be easily removed, together with the telescopic forks. Both wheels were 12 in. with drum brakes, and the power unit proposed was either a 122 or 197 cc Villiers with three-speed gearbox. This was fan-cooled, so it had a cowling over it. A starter motor was mounted ahead of the engine and drove the flywheel magneto with a V-belt. The engine was installed just ahead of the rear wheel, and the petroil tank went behind it, over the wheel.

The Harper scooter, of 1954, with its futuristic lines, which enclosed the inevitable Villiers engine and was a good try

It was the bodywork that set the Harper apart. This was in fibreglass, the front section being formed rather like a full racing fairing to enclose most of the front wheel and extend back to the rider's legs. In it were set the two headlights, with a nose between them and the number plate below, which resulted in an odd facial look.

The top of the apron was formed as a fascia behind a deep, curved windscreen and then ran down to the footboards and a good sized tunnel. The body widened out behind the passenger's legs to match the width of the front section, so it did not conform to the normal scooter style. It then ran back to the number plate with provision for two rear lamps, reflectors and turn signals, the last being a rarity then. The style was of the period, but without the excesses of fin seen on some American cars of the time.

Development continued during 1954 after the initial press coverage, and the machine was shown at Earls Court that year, although with only the 197 cc engine. A year later, work was still in progress, so for 1956 there were various alterations, but very few machines indeed.

Then, in 1957, the name began to be used by a Surrey-based firm making a well-styled invalid carriage, and that was the end of the Harper scooter.

Hercules

This was an all-British moped, built by one of the largest bicycle firms in the country and launched at the Earls Court show late in 1955. It was a true moped, with pedals and a 49 cc, two-stroke engine, and was sold as the Grey Wolf. Its finish matched its name.

The engine was made by the JAP company and, like the Cyc-Auto, had its crankshaft set along the machine. The crankshaft was pressed up with

bobweights and a roller big-end. It carried a Miller flywheel magneto at its front end and a drive tongue at the rear. The top half was conventional, with iron barrel, alloy head, small Amal to the rear, and long exhaust pipe to a good sized silencer on the left. An extension casting was bolted to the rear of the crankcase, and behind this was a further housing for the clutch and two-speed gearbox, which were driven by a shaft mated to the crankshaft tongue. The rear casting also housed a bevel-gear pair and the output shaft, which connected the drive to the rear wheel by chain.

This unit was hung by lugs in the rear casting from a spine frame, the main member of which was a pair of D-section tubes. These ran down from the headstock, over the engine, and then divided to form the chain stays. A bracket pro-

The Her-cu-motor, as sold for 1957 and fitted with a small in-line JAP engine with two-speed gearbox

The Hercules Corvette in 1960, but really an imported French Lavelette given new tank transfers

vided the engine mountings and carried the pedalling gear, while another supported the seat tube, which had a toolbox clamped between it and the rear mudguard.

At the rear, there was no suspension, other than the saddle, but the front forks had short leading links. These used rubber in shear as the suspension medium, the units being housed in small drums. Both wheels had small drum brakes and 2 × 23 in. tyres with an offset front hub. At the rear, a ribbed alloy cover gave a full-width effect.

The fuel tank was pear-shaped and mounted above the frame tube, just behind the headstock, while a rear carrier, centre stand and electric horn were provided. Control was easy, with a throttle on the right bar and twistgrip gearchange, which incorporated the clutch lever, on the left. The gearchange was connected by cable and pulled

the selector into first against a spring, which returned it to neutral and then second.

The Grey Wolf name was soon dropped, and the machine became the Her-cu-motor. It ran well and was best cruised at 25 mph, as the exhaust intruded a little at 30. The main problems were electrical, a contemporary report mentioning a faint horn note and a number of short circuits.

The model was listed as a Mk II for 1958, but around that time production came to a halt when the JAP engine supply dried up. The firm continued, however, and in 1960 introduced another moped as the Corvette, but it used a 49 cc French Lavalette engine. This had a V-belt primary drive and automatic clutch for its single speed, and went into a simple rigid moped frame with telescopic forks. Its appearance was similar to the earlier machine, but it was short-lived, for it was withdrawn at the end of 1961.

HJH

H. J. Hulsman gave his initials to this small Welsh firm, which was based at Neath, in Glamorgan. There, in 1954, he began production of a conventional lightweight, which was called the Dragon, for all its prosaic Villiers 8E engine and three speeds.

The frame, at least, was individual, to the point of using square-section tubing, but was otherwise a loop type with plunger rear and telescopic front suspension. Equipment included a dualseat and twin toolboxes, while the machine was nicely finished in maroon and silver with chrome-plated tank and mudguards.

For 1955 the Dragon was joined by four other models to create a range of engine sizes and suspension systems. Thus, the Super Dragon kept the 8E engine and plunger frame, but had Earles leading-link forks. The Dragon Major used the 224 cc Villiers 1H engine with four speeds, but in a frame with pivoted-fork rear suspension and the Earles front forks, while the Dragonette had the 147 cc 30C engine, a rigid frame and telescopic forks. The fourth new model was the Trials, which had a 7E engine, rigid frame and Earles forks. It had four speeds as standard and a small light tank, so was well thought out and constructed.

There were changes and more new models for 1956, but not the Super Dragon, which was dropped. The Dragon went into a rigid frame and was joined by the Sports Dragon with three-speed 8E, telescopic front and pivoted rear forks. This model was also offered in Super Sports form with the Earles forks, and in a de luxe version of this with four speeds and rectified lighting.

The Dragon Major and Dragonette continued as they were, the latter being joined by a sports version with pivoted-fork frame. The Trials model was also given this type of rear suspension and was joined by a Scrambles model, which was much the same, but had its 7E engine tuned and close gears in its four-speed box.

This extensive programme was altogether too much for a small firm, and financial problems arose during 1956. Some were to do with the purchase tax, which was then levied on sales and for which the firm had to account. There were other difficulties of lack of capital and obtaining local skilled labour, so by June, production had ceased, and in October, Henry William James John Granville Hulsman admitted a deficit of £5800 at a bankruptcy hearing. The HJH era was over.

Indian

This was an American make which had a number of different links with British firms in the post-war era. These included Royal Enfield, AMC and Velocette at different times, but the first on the scene were Brockhouse.

This Southport, Lancashire, firm was already producing the Corgi (see page 67) when it became involved with Indian in the early post-war years. Between them, they decided they needed a model to fit between the tiny Corgi and the heavy V-twins, and the outcome was the 248 cc Indian Brave.

The machine was built on British lines as far as the cycle parts went, but this was less true of the engine. For a start, this was in unit with the three-speed Albion gearbox and employed wet-sump lubrication, the oil being carried in the base chamber formed in the crankcase castings.

The engine was a side-valve type with a cast-iron barrel set vertically on the crankcase. It was closed with an alloy head, and the valves went in a chest on the right with a cover to enclose them. The timing gear comprised one crankshaft gear, two cam wheels which meshed with it, and tappets and adjusters.

The primary drive went outboard of the timing gear in its own chamber with chain drive to a three-plate clutch. The gearbox was typically British, so the final drive sprocket remained inboard of the clutch, but on the right-hand side of the machine. The gear pedal and kickstart lever were on concentric spindles, but on the left to suit the American market. The gearchange mechanism was also on the left in its own compartment and separate from the Lucas alternator, which was ahead of it on the left-hand end of the crankshaft. The contact breaker went outboard of it, with access via a small cover in the main one, and coil ignition was used. Carburation was by Amal, equipped with an air filter, and the oil was circulated by a submerged pump driven from the timing gears.

The engine unit went into a simple rigid loop frame with undamped telescopic front forks. The wheels had 18 in. rims and offset hubs with 5 in. drum brakes, and were protected by ample mudguards. There was a saddle for the rider, a toolbox under it on the right, and a battery beside this. Only a prop-stand was provided for parking and, thus, there was no means of holding the machine up to deal with a puncture.

Indian Brave in rigid form with its left-hand-side pedals, wet sump, and side-valve engine

The later model S Indian Brave with spring frame, but otherwise little altered

In some ways, the machine had an advanced specification for 1950, the year it was first seen. It was built for export only, with a price of 345 dollars and a finish in red, blue, green, yellow or black. In later years, it was looked on as slow, but the 56 mph recorded by both British magazines in 1950 was not unusual for the times. It was about par for lightweights with a 197 cc Villiers engine and the LE Velocette, while its direct competitor, the BSA C10, recorded the same 56 mph in 1953, a little down on its 1938 performance.

The real problem for the Brave was poor assembly and a lack of reliability. It failed to make any real impact in the USA, and by 1952 became available in the sterling area, although still not in its home country.

This situation finally changed in 1954, when a second model was introduced with rear suspension. The engine unit remained the same, but the frame gained a pivoted rear fork with tapered bronze bushes, which were adjusted with lock nuts. The rear fork ends hooked into place, where they were held by shouldered nuts. The design failed to impress much, even in 1954.

The springer model S was also given 6 in. brakes, a centre stand and a dualseat, but its other details were as for the rigid model R, which continued. Only red or black colours were available for the home market for either model. The two British magazines managed to squeeze 58 or 59 mph from the springer.

The price of the rigid model was reduced for 1955, when both models had the handlebars cleaned up with fixed pivot blocks, but this did nothing to enliven sales. At the end of the year, production ceased, and within two years Indian were selling Royal Enfields with their name on the tank.

The Brave slipped out of sight, but the Indian name kept reappearing until the 1970s.

James

In later years, this make became part of the AMC group, and the amalgamation brought them ever closer to Francis-Barnett. This led to badge engineering, which began in the mid-1950s, but in the early post-war years the Greet factory followed its own path. It had done this since its first motorcycle in 1902, and at one time was well known for its pleasing machines with V-twin engines. However, from the mid-1930s, the company concentrated on the utility market and stuck with this from then on.

During the war, they had built large numbers of their Military Lightweight, or ML, model, which used a 9D Villiers engine in a simple rigid frame with girder forks. It was intended for paratroops, so was light enough to lift over obstacles, and was known as the Clockwork Mouse. Post-war, it

formed one half of their programme as the ML, which had a maroon and silver tank finish and the addition of a rear carrier.

The ML was joined by the Superlux autocycle, which used the Villiers JDL engine in a typical machine of the type with pedals, engine shields, girder forks, saddle and carrier. It was a minimal range, but met the urgent needs of the times for transport of any sort. Both machines continued in production until the end of 1948.

The autocycle ran on into 1949, but the ML was replaced by a small range of machines in three capacities. Smallest was the Comet, built in standard or de luxe form, the latter being fitted with a battery and rectifier. Both used the new 99 cc Villiers 1F engine with two-speed gearbox controlled by a handlebar lever, and this went into a simple rigid loop frame. At the front were girder forks with single tubes on each side to give the appearance, at least, of telescopics, and both wheels had small drum brakes. There was a saddle for the rider and a cylindrical toolbox beneath this on the standard model, but the battery was in this position on the de luxe, with a toolbox between the right-hand-side chainstays.

Next in size were standard and de luxe Cadet models, which used the 122 cc Villiers 10D engine in similar cycle parts. The electrical variation between the two models was as for the Comet,

Left **James Superlux autocycle of 1948 powered by the Villiers 98 cc JDL engine installed in typical frame with girder forks**

Right **The 1951 James Cadet with 122 cc Villiers 10D engine in a rigid frame with light telescopic forks**

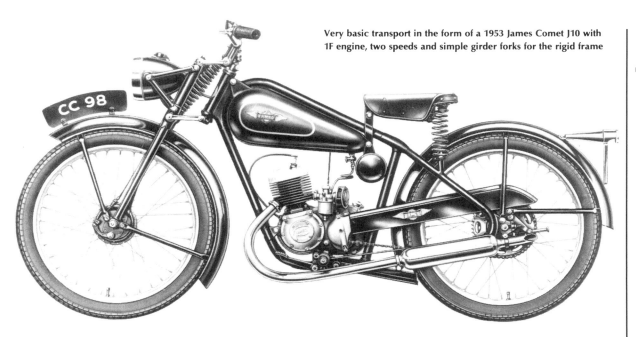

Very basic transport in the form of a 1953 James Comet J10 with 1F engine, two speeds and simple girder forks for the rigid frame

but the larger machines had a rear carrier and the battery and toolbox as on the smaller de luxe machine.

Finally, for the road, there was the de luxe Captain with 197 cc Villiers 6E engine in the Cadet cycle parts, and with battery lighting as standard. Unlisted, but built in small numbers, were competition models using either the 10D or 6E engine with suitably modified frame, forks and wheels.

During March 1949 the autocycle was redesigned to use the 99 cc Villiers 2F single-speed engine unit, but retained its Superlux name. The same month saw telescopic front forks appearing for the 122 and 197 cc road models. These used Dunlop rubber cushions as the suspension medium.

In general, the range continued as it was for 1950, with the autocycle, two each of the Comet and Cadet, plus the Captain, which took the listing

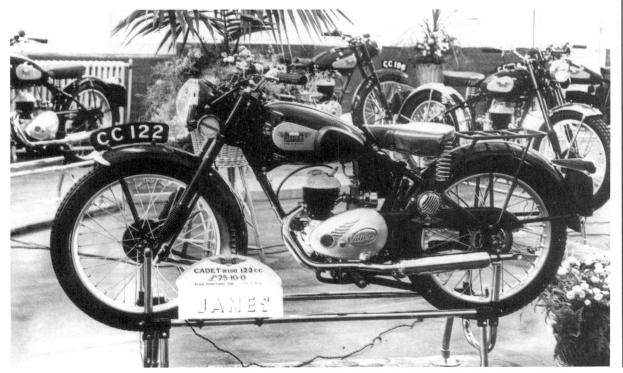

J8. In time, all the James models would have a similar code, but this did not become general practice until 1953. A second version of the J8 was listed with plunger rear suspension, which became an option for the 122 cc competition model. The 197 cc size of this machine was listed in rigid (/D suffix) and plunger (/RS suffix) forms for riders to make their own choice. All models, other than the autocycle, now had the telescopic front forks.

There was little change for 1951, but the rigid J8 became the Captain standard J7 and there was one new model. This was the 99 cc Commodore, which was really a Comet, with 1F engine and enclosure panels. These ran from the downtube to the rear axle, and up from the footrest to the cylinder head, with legshields at the front. The whole range continued for 1952, the 197 cc competition machines being replaced by a single model with rigid frame as the Colonel Competition.

Things changed more for 1953, although the autocycle continued as before as the Superlux, but with a code of J1. The Commodore became the J4, and the standard Comet the Mark II or J10, while the de luxe version became the J3 and was fitted with the 4F engine.

In the 122 cc class, the standard Cadet and competition models were dropped and the de luxe Cadet became the J6. It was joined by the J5, which used the 13D engine with three speeds in a new frame with plunger rear suspension. The J7 and J8 models remained, but with coil spring forks, also used on the 122 cc models, and the competition version became the J9 Commando. This kept the rigid frame, but had a 7E engine and telescopic forks with two-way hydraulic damping.

During 1953 a telescopic fork conversion kit was made available for all the older Comet models. These forks were fitted as standard to the J11, which took over for 1954. This Comet used the 4F engine and a frame with plunger rear suspension and was the only 99 cc model left in the range, except the J1 autocycle. Only one 122 cc model continued, as the J5, while the J9 was joined by a new 197 cc Captain, the K7 with an 8E engine in a pivoted-fork frame. This model had a dualseat with neat toolboxes under its nose, so was much more modern in its appearance.

Similar cycle parts were also used by the K12 Colonel, which was powered by the 224 cc Villiers 1H engine. This had four speeds, and the machine larger brakes, but otherwise the style was the same. Finally, there was the K7C Cotswold scrambler with 7E engine, four speeds, pivoted-fork frame and suitable wheels and tyres.

The autocycle was dropped during the year, but most of the range ran on for 1955. New was the J15 Cadet, which replaced the J5 and had a 147 cc Villiers 30C engine in place of the 13D. The plunger frame remained, along with the saddle, but there were full-width hubs for all models that year.

The Cadet had a major change for 1956, when it became the L15. It kept the 30C engine, but this went into a completely new frame with pressed-steel rear section and pivoted rear fork. This was controlled by coil springs, set far enough forward to be concealed by the very deep valance of the rear guard, which was formed as part of the pressing. Light telescopic forks went at the front, and there was a short dualseat for just one person.

Also new was the L1 Comet, which used the new Cadet frame and forks to house the 4F engine, and the K7T Commando, which replaced the J9. This kept the 7E engine, but it was housed in the pivoted-fork frame from the K7C, which continued. Both the K7 and K12 ran on with 18 in. wheels in place of the earlier 19 in. ones.

The range continued as it was for 1957 with two additions. One was simply the option of the 6F engine in the L1 Comet, in place of the 4F, which remained available. The model kept its single seat, but a dualseat became an option for the Cadet. The second model was a more major addition and was the 249 cc Commodore with AMC engine.

This machine, coded the L25, was the first to use the engine, which was the same as that used by Francis-Barnett (see page 103). It followed the Cadet in the design of its frame. Thus, the front section was tubular, but the centre section was built up from pressings. It carried the pivoted fork and housed the electrics, while the deep rear mudguard, the same part as used by the Comet and Cadet, was bolted to it. The machine had stylish side covers, a deeply valanced front mudguard and a dualseat.

The firm switched more to the AMC engines for 1958, when the Commodore was joined by the 171 cc Cavalier L17. This was much in the manner of the Comet and Cadet, which both continued, as did the Captain, although that was fitted with a 10E engine in place of the older 8E. There were no competition models listed at all at first, but the K7T made a brief reappearance during

Above **Despite the lights and silencer, this is a James K7C Cotswold scrambler fitted with a 7E engine. It was sold in this form for 1954, but in a more suitable style for the next year**

Below **James Commodore, fitted with the 249 cc AMC engine, during a 1958 road test**

the year, when it, too, was fitted with a 10E engine. Otherwise, it was much as before, with pivoted-fork frame and suitable equipment for trials use. It was only listed for a few months.

For 1959 the Comet, Cadet, Cavalier, Captain and Commodore ran on and were joined by two new competition models. Both were powered by the 249 cc AMC engine, modified to suit the intended use. The pivoted-fork frame was common to both, but the L25T trials model used James forks, whereas the L25S scrambler had AMC Teledraulic forks. The fixtures and fittings were to suit each machine's respective role.

During that last year of the decade, James made even greater use of the AMC engine by fitting it in the Flying Cadet L15A model, which used the 149 cc version in the L15 cycle parts. For 1960 only the Comet kept to Villiers power, now with the 6F as standard, and the other models were dropped. This left the roadster and two competition models, with the 249 cc AMC engine, and the Flying Cadet, but not the Cavalier, which had also gone. For the 200 cc class, there was a new Captain L20 with the 199 cc AMC engine in cycle parts that followed the style of the Commodore. On this note, James entered the new decade. That year, they added a scooter to their list, and later came twins and a return to Villiers power for other models, after the trials and tribulations of the AMC units.

Lohmann

This was a German make of clip-on engine, but is included because it was handled in the United Kingdom by Britax and because of its sheer novelty. It was a mere 18 cc in capacity, but even more unusual was the fact that it was a compression-ignition two-stroke with variable compression ratio.

The engine, therefore, was much like a large-scale model aircraft unit, but designed to clamp under the bottom bracket of a standard bicycle. Consequently, it was very narrow, as it had to fit between the pedal cranks. It had a horizontal cylinder with the fins extending above and below

it to some extent, but not to the sides to any degree. The cylinder head contained a twistgrip-controlled moving sleeve, which varied both the ratio and some of the port timings, while the mixture was supplied by a simple carburettor. This avoided the complications of the fuel-injection system of a true diesel.

Due to the small engine size, the crankshaft was geared to a countershaft, which carried a drive roller. This had a means of engaging and releasing it from contact with the tyre, as was usual with the clip-on engine type.

The engine was first seen in 1949, but it was late 1952 before it reached the Britax lists. It proved able to generate enough power to push a cycle along at 15 mph on the flat and to deal well with steep hills. However, it was rather late in the day for a new clip-on and buyers looked for a little more performance, preferring an engine type they understood better, even if it brought them a flywheel magneto to struggle with.

Thus, the Lohmann disappeared from the lists as quickly as it had arrived, and no more was heard of it.

The tiny Lohmann diesel engine fitted to a cycle in 1950, before it was imported into the UK by Britax

Mercury

This firm of bicycle makers decided to enter the powered two-wheeler world in 1956, and for this offered two models. Both were a little unusual, for one was a moped, but with an ohv engine, while the other was a small scooter with motorcycle-size wheels.

The moped was the Mercette, which carried its four-stroke engine ahead of the frame bottom bracket, with the cylinder inclined to match the downtube. It was of 48 cc, built in unit with a two-speed gearbox, and had the ports on the sides of the cylinder head, with consequent effect on the inlet and exhaust pipes. The frame was rigid with light telescopic forks, small drum brakes and a fuel tank perched on the top tube, which ran from the headstock to the rear wheel spindle. The machine had direct lighting and, as standard, was fitted with a pillion seat and rests.

The scooter was called the Hermes and used a 49 cc ILO two-stroke engine with two-speed gearbox to propel it. The engine was fan-cooled with a hand-pull starter and went into a rigid frame with telescopic front forks. The wheels were 20 in. diameter, with small drum brakes, and the rear chain was fully enclosed.

The scooter bodywork suggested that the machine had rear suspension, for the deeply valanced rear mudguard was painted a contrasting grey to the general maroon. This colour applied to the main apron panel, which ran back as the floor and rear cover for the engine unit.

These two models were joined by three more for 1957, two of which used 99 cc Villiers engines with two-speed gearboxes. One was the Grey Streak motorcycle, which used the 6F unit with foot-change in a simple frame. This had telescopic front and pivoted-fork rear suspension, full-width hubs and a dualseat. The other was the Dolphin scooter with 4F engine, and this followed the lines of the Hermes. The third newcomer was the Whippet 60, which was an enlarged version of the Mercette with the same features.

The Mercette and Grey Streak continued alone for 1958, but the two scooters were replaced by one new one, the Pippin, which continued to use the 4F engine. The frame was still rigid, but the wheelbase was shorter and 15 in. wheels were fitted. The body, especially at the rear, was more conventional, and the rear section was easily lifted clear as one part. It carried a dualseat. On test, the machine proved to have an adequate performance.

Despite this, the firm found limited demand for its products, and during the year ceased production of its powered models.

Mini-Motor

This was perhaps the best known of the British clip-on engines and, although of Italian origin, when it appeared in 1949, it was built in Croydon. There was nothing exceptional about the unit, but it was well made and available at a time when anything was better than nothing.

The engine sat above the bicycle rear wheel, which it drove with a friction-roller on the left-hand end of the crankshaft. On the right, there was a Wipac flywheel magneto, and between this and the roller, a crankcase with bobweight flywheels and a horizontal iron barrel. An alloy head closed this, and the capacity was 49.9 cc for the conventional two-stroke unit. The petroil tank went over the engine, with the number plate at its rear. A means of lifting the roller clear of the tyre was provided.

The unit could drive a bicycle at 30 mph, which was as fast as most wished to go on a rigid machine with narrow tyres. Thousands found them ideal for short trips, whether to station, office or shops, and they were soon seen about in large numbers. Some were even fitted to tandems, where they proved equal to the task of hauling two people along at 20 mph.

There were minor improvements for 1951, and during that year, a decompressor was added to the cylinder head to aid both starting and stopping. In this form, the unit ran on until 1955, but by then the moped was taking over and the Mini-Motor was no more.

Mini-Motor at the end of the 1953 National Rally at Weston-super-Mare – a long ride for owner D. J. Anderson

New Hudson

This firm built motorcycles for 30 years from 1903 but, during the 1930s, turned to the manufacture of Girling brakes. Early in 1940 they returned to two wheels with an autocycle, and it was this that they first produced after the war. By then, they were part of the BSA group.

Their 1946 model was the same as the one built six years before, with 98 cc Villiers JDL engine in a typical autocycle frame, having pedals and a rigid front fork. At that time, there were no engine shields, but a rear carrier and centre stand were provided, along with direct lighting.

For 1948 the machine was fitted with pressed-steel blade girder forks, plus engine shields and other detail improvements. It received a new frame and engine for 1949, when the JDL unit was replaced by a 99 cc 2F, which required a major frame change to carry it. The appearance remained much as before, however, as the alterations were concealed by the engine shields. The rest of the cycle parts continued unchanged. In this form, the machine ran on for some years, the centre stand being strengthened for 1952, but otherwise there was little change.

It was May 1956 when the machine was revamped, and on this occasion only the 2F engine remained as before. The frame was amended to make it easier for the rider to mount, and the forks became tubular, although they kept the girder action. The tank shape, and that of the side panels, was new and much more modern, while the chains were well enclosed. Both leg-shields and a windscreen were available as options, while the saddle, centre stand and rear carrier remained as of old.

It was a good attempt to update an old design, but by then the moped was taking over from the autocycle, offering similar performance for a lower running cost and better styling. The machine continued to be listed until 1958, but that year saw the end of the 2F engine, so the New Hudson also left the market.

The 1950 New Hudson autocycle with Villiers 2F single-speed engine unit in rigid frame with blade girder forks

Norman

This company was based in Ashford, Kent, and for 1946 picked up their pre-war models more or less where they had left off. Then, they had built for both themselves and the Rudge company, but post-war simply offered an Autocycle and a Motorcycle.

The former used the 98 cc Villiers JDL engine in a rigid frame with fixtures and fittings that were typical of the type. The latter was equally simple, but used the 122 cc 9D engine with three-speed gearbox, although still in an austere rigid frame.

These two models comprised the Norman range until late 1948, when they were replaced by more modern machines. The Autocycle became the model C with a 99 cc 2F single-speed engine unit. This was mounted in a frame to suit and had the usual engine enclosure panels that were common to the type. The frame remained

rigid and had light girder forks at the front, while the lighting was direct and the finish in maroon.

The other models were the B1 and B2 in standard and de luxe forms, the latter with rectifier and battery lighting. Engines were the 122 cc 10D and 197 cc 6E respectively, and the cycle parts were common, with rigid frame and telescopic forks. The whole range was little altered for 1950, when it was joined by the model D, which mirrored the others, having standard or de luxe forms, but used the 99 cc two-speed 1F engine unit. The frame for these models stayed rigid, but the forks were tubular girders, which were changed to telescopics for 1951.

Otherwise, the range ran on, as it did for 1952, but in February of that year, a pivoted-fork rear suspension system was announced. This differed from most in that the spring units were positioned as upper chainstays, so were laid well down, while the rear subframe was formed to run around them.

It was not until late in the year that the new frame reached production and was offered on the B1S and B2S, again in standard and de luxe forms. The larger machine kept to the 6E engine, but the smaller one used the 13D, while the existing B1 models were replaced by the E models. These

Norman model C autocycle with 2F Villiers 99 cc engine enclosed by rather bulbous shields

were economy jobs, but kept the 10D engine in a very simple set of cycle parts, albeit still in standard or de luxe forms with direct or battery lighting.

At the lower end of the scale, the C and D models continued for 1953, as did the two B2 models, while a competition model was added as the B2C. This used a 197 cc engine, altered to suit trials work, in a rigid frame with telescopic forks, 21 in. front wheel and 4 in.-section rear tyre. These latter features were nearly unheard of on a lightweight at that time, but helped the small company achieve some good results.

Although the model numbers stayed as before, there were a good few changes for 1954. Alone, the autocycle ran on as it was, but the model D machines were given the 4F engine. The B1S machines continued, but the model E was dropped early in the year. The 197 cc road models all switched to the 8E engine, and the B2C to the 7E with the option of a four-speed gearbox. The rigid B2 models were dropped during the year, while the sprung B2S machines had their frame revised to use normal, upright Armstrong units.

There were more changes for 1955, the engine of the B1S models becoming the 147 cc 30C unit. The range lost the B2 models, but gained a twin

Norman B1S with 122 cc 10D engine unit and their laid-down rear units, as still used on this 1954 example

in the form of the TS model, which used the 242 cc British Anzani engine. This model and the B2S were both fitted with Armstrong leading-link front forks, which were an option for the competition B2C. The 99 cc models were little changed, and at the end of the year the model D was dropped.

The autocycle continued for 1956, along with the B1, now with the leading-link forks, the B2 with a further version fitted with a 9E engine, and the TS. The competition model became the B2CS with a spring frame and leading-link forks, while its engine could be the 7E with three speeds, or 9E with four.

New was a moped named the Nippy, which was based on a continental design and powered by a 47.6 cc Sachs engine with two-speed gearbox. This unit went into a pressed-steel beam frame, rigid at the rear and with leading-link forks at the front. It was a smart machine, and the firm intended to gradually increase their own production of parts in place of buying them in.

The autocycle entered its last year in 1957, when the two 147 cc B1 models were joined by another de luxe one, fitted with the 148 cc 31C engine unit. The three B2 machines ran on, two with 8E engines and one with the 9E, as did the TS and the B2CS. All but the first and last had a degree of rear enclosure, which had been developed from prototype designs seen two years earlier. It incorporated toolboxes and mountings

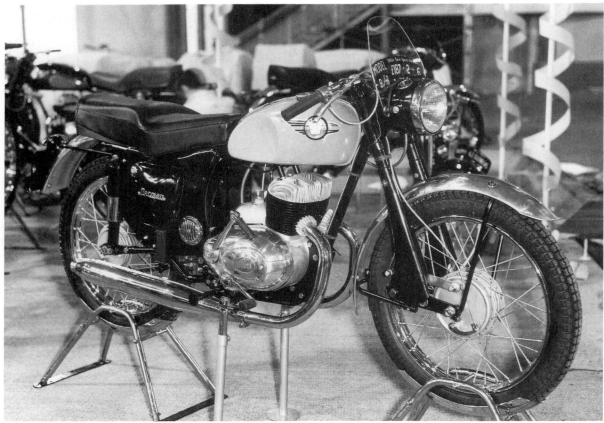

Left **Showtime late in 1955 at Earls Court for the Norman model TS fitted with the 242 cc British Anzani twin engine**

Right **Norman Lido moped of 1959 fitted with the Villiers 3K engine unit with styled enclosure**

Below left **The B3 Sports Norman with 2T engine, leading-link forks, low bars and small screen**

for the electrical equipment, so tidied the machine up nicely. The Nippy continued, but in a plunger frame.

There was no autocycle for 1958, as the moped had taken over its duties and the 2F engine was no longer available. The B1 and B2 models continued with their variety of engines, as did the competition model, which now only used the 9E engine unit. The TS remained in the list when the models were announced, but early in the year it was replaced by the B3, which used the 249 cc Villiers 2T engine.

For 1959 this model was joined by the B3 Sports, which had dropped bars, alloy mudguards, plastic flyscreen and knee recesses in the fuel tank. The same cycle parts were used by the B2S Sports with 9E engine, which also joined the range, while the 8E units were dropped to leave a single 197 cc roadster. The three B1 models remained, along with the competition model, and the Nippy was joined by two more mopeds.

Both had a 49.9 cc Villiers 3K engine with two-speed gearbox, and the Nippy II used the same

cycle parts as the Sachs-powered model. The Lido differed in having pivoted-fork suspension and styled enclosure for the engine unit, which extended back to the rear wheel.

That brought the small firm to the end of the decade, when they dropped their B1 models, but continued with the B2S, B3 and B2CS into the 1960s. All the mopeds were altered and the Nippy IV was alone in keeping the 3K engine, but this now went into a frame with pivoted-fork rear suspension and leading links at the front. The Nippy III looked similar, but had a 47.6 cc, single-speed, Italian Mi-Val engine in a frame that looked like it had suspension, but was, in fact, rigid. The remaining moped was the Super Lido, which kept to the Sachs engine, but in cycle parts based on the earlier Lido model.

The next year, the firm was taken over by Raleigh, so the motorcycles were soon dropped, while the mopeds went no further. Thus, another firm disappeared after some good years and nice, well finished machines.

Norton

On the face of it, all Norton had to do to produce civilian machines after the war was to change the paint colour in their spray guns from khaki to black. In practice, they did rather more to both engine and frame of the 490 cc, side-valve 16H model and added the same size overhead-valve model 18.

Both machines were based on the firm's 1939 engine, so the 16H had enclosed valves unlike the service model, which was based on the 1937 unit. Up to the crankcase mouth, both engines were essentially the same and had a distinctive Norton line that ran back closely to 1931, and could be traced even to the first 1907 single.

Construction was traditionally British and very conservative, for the firm seldom changed much without very good cause. Thus, the crankshaft was built up with a roller big-end, ran in ball and roller mains in a vertically-split crankcase, and had its simple timing gears on the right. One drove the mag-dyno by chain, and a crankshaft worm meshed with the duplex-gear oil pump of the dry-sump system.

Followers above the cams were formed to suit the valve gear, with tappets for the 16H and long pushrods for the 18. The former had a simple cast-iron barrel with valve chest, plus cover. The head was also in iron, as were the head and barrel of the 18, which had an alloy rocker box with side access cover.

The rest of both machines was the same, except for the gearing, where the ohv model had two more teeth on the engine sprocket. The primary drive was enclosed within the Norton pressed-steel case, which remained oil-tight until the single fixing nut was over-tightened. Within it, the very good Norton clutch drove a four-speed Norton gearbox. All of these parts had their origins in pre-war times. The gearbox was one of the best, even though the gear pedal was not positioned very well and had an excessive movement. The only

concession to the post-war period was a new outer cover that enclosed the clutch worm and its cable.

The engine and gearbox went into a rigid cradle frame, rather than the pre-war open type, and kept the Norton girders with their check springs at the front. Both wheels had offset hubs with good 7 in. drum brakes, and were quickly detachable. They could also be interchanged. For the rest, the oil tank was under the saddle on the right, with the battery matching it on the left, the toolbox went between the right chainstays, and there was no tank-top instrument panel, as pre-war. The finish was black, the petrol and oil tanks and wheel rims being chrome plated before painting and lining.

The two models were announced in August 1945 and continued as they were through most of the following year. During 1946 a few road-racing machines were built and supplied in time for the Manx Grand Prix. These were in full racing form and based on the pre-war models. They were the first to carry the simple Manx Norton name and were listed as the 348 cc model 40M and 498 cc model 30M.

Both had single-overhead-camshaft engines, in the familiar Carroll mould, with shaft-and-bevel drive up to the cambox. The design dated from 1930, and the format was altered little in over 30 years, so the post-war engines looked like the pre-war ones. A massive alloy head with separate cambox went on top of the alloy barrel, but the piston gave a rather low ratio in deference to the pool petrol then in use. Compression plates allowed for some variation should anything better come to hand.

The bottom half continued with the massive, well-ribbed crankcase cast in magnesium alloy, and the camshaft drive and oil pump side by side on the right, the racing magneto being chain driven from the latter. The usual oil pipe ran up from the crankcase to the cambox, and the valves were closed by hairpin springs. Carburation was by a remote-needle Amal, and the exhaust terminated in an open megaphone.

An open primary chain and dry clutch connected the engine to the four-speed, close-ratio gearbox, which naturally dispensed with a kick-starter. Both units went into a cradle frame with plunger rear suspension, much as pre-war, but it was fitted with the famous Norton Roadholder telescopic front forks. The frame became known as the 'garden gate', but the forks had hydraulic damping, so were an improvement on the pre-war works type.

Both wheels had conical hubs, the front one containing an 8 in. brake with an air scoop on its alloy backplate. The wheels were 21 in. front and 20 in. rear, fitted with racing rubber and shielded by short guards. The petrol tank was massive and still of the bolt-through type, while the oil tank carried a full imperial gallon of lubricant.

The machines came with a full set of racing details, so had saddle, rear pad, racing plates, flyscreen, chin pad, rev-counter and quick-action filler caps on both tanks. Their finish remained traditional, the tanks being in silver with red and black lining, while the rest of the machine was in black.

The rest of the range for 1947 was announced soon after the Manx had been run, and was expanded a good deal from the two basic 1945 models. They were still there, but with the Road-holder front forks and the speedometer mounted in the fork bridge. They were joined by two similar road models, the first of which was the Big 4 fitted with a 634 cc side-valve engine. This, again, was a pre-war model revived for the sidecar market and much as the 16H, with rigid cradle frame and the new front forks. The second machine was the ES2, which was as the 18 with the 490 cc ohv engine, but with plunger rear suspension, as on the ohc models.

There were two more of these, the models 40 and 30 International, which had all-iron engines with the single overhead camshaft in 348 and 490 cc sizes. The cams were designed to run best on an open pipe, which was to be allowed in the 1947 Clubman TT. The cycle parts were as the ES2 with the plunger frame and Roadholder telescopic forks, but the tanks were larger with wing-nut filler caps.

To complete the range, there were 350 and 500 Trials models, but these were really based on the wartime 16H frame fitted with either capacity ohv engines, telescopic forks and raised exhaust, but full lighting equipment. Competition tyres were provided, but the model was totally unsuitable, even for the events of the time. Some owners changed to girder forks to reduce the wheelbase, and discarded as many heavy items as possible, but it was still a lump for trials work.

The 490 cc side- and overhead-valve engines were modified for 1948, having a new timing case and direct-action tappets in place of the followers. The side-valve engine was given an alloy head and an alloy casting to enclose the valves, while the ohv unit gained a one-piece rocker box. The Big 4 followed the 16H in respect of the engine changes, but also had the bore and stroke revised and the capacity reduced to 597 cc. The ohc models continued as they were, while the Trials ones were dropped, but there was news of their replacement early in the year.

This was listed for 1949 as the 500T and was much lighter, thanks to an all-alloy engine, a short-ened version of the diamond 16H frame and other measures. Special fork yokes helped to reduce the wheelbase, and various means were used to lower the weight. A nice slim petrol tank was fitted, along with alloy mudguards and high-tensile steel rims, while the lighting was optional. The result worked well for many private owners.

Nice 'Garden Gate' Norton with the ohc engine and all the racing goodies of the late 1940s

The major news from Nortons for 1949 was the launch of their model 7 Dominator twin, the engine of which was designed by Bert Hopwood. It was a conventional vertical twin with overhead valves and both head and barrel in iron. The camshaft ran across the front of the crankcase, where it was driven by chain and gear, with a further gear drive on to the dynamo. The magneto went behind the crankcase and was chain driven with auto-advance.

The valve gear was laid out within the integral rocker box to splay the exhaust ports well out for better cooling. The tappets ran in the block, and the crankshaft was built up with a cast-iron flywheel. It ran in ball and roller mains, in a vertically-split alloy crankcase, and drove a typical duplex-gear Norton oil pump.

This engine went into the ES2 cycle parts with plunger frame and telescopic forks, but the gearbox had to be modified to suit the shape of the new engine. In effect, the positive-stop mechanism was moved from above the box to ahead of it, to place the pedal in a much better position and reduce its travel. The box became known as the laid-down type, but the internals were very much as before, although the shell mountings were improved.

The rest of the range ran on with little alteration that year, except that the Manx models supplied to riders in the TT had twin overhead camshafts and alloy tanks and wheel rims. For 1950 all the side- and overhead-valve road models changed to the laid-down gearbox, but not the 500T, the short frame of which could not accommodate it. The ohc machines for both road and track stayed as they were.

Norton fortunes had taken a real upturn in 1950, thanks to the advent of the famous Featherbed frame for the works racers, coupled with the skills of Geoff Duke and Artie Bell. The frame was the result of eight years of work by Rex McCandless and was deceptively simple, with its duplex tubular loops welded to the headstock with a cross-over arrangement. The subframe was bolted in place, and the petrol tank sat on the top rails with a strap to retain it. It was a design that was to accommodate both Norton and many other makes of engine over the years.

For 1951 the production Manx Norton was built with the Featherbed frame and was also given the laid-down gearbox and 19 in. wheels. It was an immediate success. The other singles and the twin stayed as they were, except for a cast alloy front

brake backplate, which had been used by the 500T from the beginning.

The singles and model 7 remained the same for 1952, but the twin was joined by the machine many riders had been asking for since the Featherbed frame had first appeared. It was a marriage of the new frame and the twin engine, and for 1952 it became available, but for export only, as the model 88 Dominator.

The twin engine sat easily in the frame with its usual gearbox, and the model used short Roadholder forks and the road wheels and brakes. A deeply valanced, sprung front mudguard was fitted that first year, along with a strap-held fuel tank, dualseat and long, pear-shaped silencers. The finish was grey for all painted parts, and the result a very smart, fast and well handling motorcycle.

Another new frame appeared for 1953 and, like the Featherbed, this had a pivoted rear fork, but was based on the cradle frame. This was modified to provide the fork pivot and a subframe to support the dualseat, which took over from the saddle. The frame was used by both the model 7 Dominator and the ES2, and both models also adopted the pear-shaped silencer.

The model 88 ran on with just a change to a neater, unsprung front mudguard, while the two side-valve machines and the 18 were given a dualseat, despite remaining in rigid frames. There were, in fact, some side-valve models built with the plunger frame, but these were made in small numbers only.

The Manx was unaltered for 1953, but the Internationals received their last real changes. The engines became all-alloy and went into the Featherbed frame with the laid-down gearbox and pear-shaped silencer. They had become, in effect, a model 88 with an ohc engine. The one difference lay with the front brake, which was increased to 8 in. for the Inter.

The bigger brake was adopted by the rest of the range for 1954, except for the 500T, which kept the 7 in. version. Otherwise, the road singles and both twins remained as they were, while the Manx underwent more extensive engine changes. The strokes of both were shortened and there were a good number of detail alterations, plus a welded subframe for the chassis and a twin-leading-shoe front brake to stop the machine.

At the end of the year, the two side-valve machines, the model 18 and the 500T were dropped, but in their place appeared two new

One of the nicest trials models of the period was the Norton 500T introduced in 1949 and built for just five years

First of the many Norton twins was this 1949 model 7, which had a plunger frame and new laid-down gearbox

A rather special Manx Norton with Featherbed frame, for this is Geoff Duke's 1951 Junior TT winner

The ES2 Norton in its new pivoted-fork frame for 1953. Note the pear-shaped silencer

The Norton model 88 Featherbed twin, as it was in 1957 and one of the best machines of the decade

The 1958 Norton Nomad 99, which used the larger twin engine in off-road cycle parts to make an export model

134

singles with 597 cc ohv engines. These were the 19R in a rigid frame, and 19S in a pivoted-fork frame, so really they were simply enlarged versions of the 18 and ES2. The engine had an alloy head, which also went on the ES2, along with a Monobloc carburettor and various detail improvements. The twins were also given an alloy head and the Monobloc, while the 88 received the welded subframe, introduced on the Manx the year before, and full-width hubs. These two features also went on the International, but the Manx itself continued as it was.

The model 7 went at the end of the year, along with the rigid-frame 19R, but the ES2 and the 19S ran on for 1956 with another similar single. This was the 348 cc model 50, which was as the others, except in capacity, so was stuck with the weight penalty all such machines have to suffer. These three models were fitted with full-width hubs and had many detail changes, but otherwise remained rather prosaic singles with adequate, but unexciting, performance.

Not that the International models offered much more when fitted with the standard, restrictive silencer; these were now only produced in small numbers and to special order. The Manx models had numerous minor changes, but were really very close to the limit of their development and proving the point of diminishing returns.

The 88 had its battery enclosed for 1956 and lost its fork-top instrument panel, as the contents were transferred to a deeper headlamp shell. It was joined by a larger 596 cc version, which used the same cycle parts and was listed as the model 99. The same engine was used for a further model for 1957, this being the 77, which was intended for sidecar work and had the frame from the later model 7.

This model 77, along with all the road machines, changed to a revised gearbox in May 1956, the new type being known as the AMC. It was much as before within the shell, but had a new, more compact change mechanism and revised clutch-lift mechanism. It was also used on AJS and Matchless machines, and continued in service for over 20 years.

The twins, Manx and Inters were little altered for 1957, but the three ohv engines had new cylinder heads with integral pushrod tunnels and many detail changes. There were more changes for 1958, when the twins went over to alternator electrics, except for the 77, had twin carburettors listed for them during the year, and were joined

by the 99 Nomad. This was an export enduro model, which used the 596 cc engine, model 77 frame, an alternator, magneto and off-road cycle parts. Its finish was bright red and chrome, and it had twin carburettors for performance.

The singles had few changes for 1958, and at the end of the year, the International models and the 19S were dropped. For 1959 the ES2 and 50 were considerably revised, with alternator electrics and the Featherbed frame. This was to prove a great blessing to Triton builders, as in later years, more often than not, the donor frame was to come from the underpowered model 50.

The Manx engines had the bevel drive modified, so they lost the lower bevel housing, and this was really the final form for the Carroll engine. Further changes were to play little part in its development, and the better engines became the ones assembled with care by such Manx experts as Bill Lacey or Ray Petty. The twins had no real alteration, but the 77 was dropped, so only the 88, 99 and 99 Nomad continued. They were, however, joined by a new model, which was to sire a further small group.

The new twin was the 249 cc Jubilee, which differed in concept from the Dominator series in most areas. Again, the engine was from Bert Hopwood and originally had each head and barrel cast as one in alloy, but the firm did not allow him to keep this radical feature.

The end result was a conventional, parallel twin engine, built in unit with its four-speed gearbox. It had a short stroke, nodular iron crankshaft, separate iron barrels and alloy heads. Two gear-driven camshafts were employed, with tappets and short pushrods in front of and behind the barrels, the rockers being concealed by domed covers. The points went on the end of the inlet camshaft, and the oil pump in the timing cover.

Complete with gearbox, it made a compact unit and was installed in a frame built up from tubes and pressings. This was similar to a Francis-Barnett design and had a pivoted rear fork and telescopics from the AMC lightweight range. Both wheels had full-width hubs with 6 in. brakes and 18 in. rims, the front one being shielded by a deeply valanced mudguard. The enclosure was more extensive at the rear, with a deep tail unit, which combined with massive side panels that ran forward to conceal the single Monobloc carburettor.

The Jubilee style of rear enclosure was adopted by the larger twins for 1960, and in this form they

Above **Norton 99 de luxe for 1960 with slimline frame and rear enclosure, but little change to engine or gearbox**

Right **The 249 cc Norton Jubilee twin in 1959 with its extensive enclosure and AMC detail parts**

became the 88 and 99 de luxe models. To suit the panels, the frame was modified by pulling in the top rails, which also enabled riders to tuck in their knees more easily. In its new form, the frame soon became known as the slimline, so, inevitably, the earlier type became the wideline.

The new frame was also used by the twins without rear enclosure, and these became the standard 88 and 99. The Jubilee ran on as it was, while the 99 Nomad was joined by a 497 cc

version. For the singles, the new decade brought numerous detail changes for the Manx racers, but little alteration to the road models.

On this note, the firm continued into the 1960s with much more to happen to it. There was to be a move from the traditional Bracebridge Street to London, the end of the Manx, bigger twins and finally the Commando range. Then, with the late 1980s, came a revival of the marque with a rotary engine.

OEC

In pre-war days, the Osborne Engineering Company, of Portsmouth, were well known for their strange motorcycles, which often had a novel duplex steering system and, in some cases a very low, feet-forward riding position. Despite these odd adventures, they survived until 1940, but when they started in business again, in 1949, their machines were totally conventional.

The new models were lightweights, much like other manufacturers', for they used 10D and 6E Villiers engines in rigid frames with telescopic forks. The two machines listed were both called Atlanta, and this name was to continue to apply to all the firm's two-strokes. Model codes were S1 for the smaller, and S2 for the larger, both being supplied as standard with battery lighting.

These two road models were joined by the D1 and D2 for 1950, and these duplicated the first pair, except in having direct lighting. At the same time, C1 and C2 competition machines were introduced, but these differed little from the road ones. They were given the benefit of competition tyres, with a slightly fatter rear one, together with lower gearing, but otherwise remained with the

Press test OEC model ST2 with 6E Villiers engine leaving watering hole for rider in 1953

The OEC Apollo with Brockhouse 248 cc side-valve engine in rigid frame form in 1953

stock cycle parts. The exhaust was raised to waist level on the left and protected at the front by an added plate.

The range continued for 1951 with the addition of further models with pivoted-fork rear suspension. They were available in both sizes and with either lighting system, so this action brought in four new model codes; SS1, SD1, SS2 and SD2. This brought the list up to ten machines, which stayed as they were for 1952, when they were joined by one further model.

This was listed at first as both the Atlanta and the Apollo, but the latter name became normal within a short time. The machine itself hardly lived up to its name, for it was powered by the same 248 cc, side-valve Brockhouse engine unit as the Indian. It retained the wet sump, coil ignition and three-speed gearbox with the change on the left, and was no great performer. For that first year, it went into the rigid frame, but for 1953 it was also available in a pivoted-fork one.

All the other road models ran on, but the competition pair was replaced by a single 197 cc machine. This was the ST3, which had a pivoted-fork frame and an unusual two-stage final drive.

For this, there was a sleeve, which ran on the rear fork pivot centre, with a sprocket at each end. That on the left was driven by a short chain from the gearbox, while the right-hand one drove the rear wheel. All this was in aid of constant chain tension, but the effect was to lengthen the wheelbase, which was not helpful for trials work.

There was a changeover of models during the early part of 1953, with new ones taking over from the old. Thus, all, except the S2 and D2, were dropped, but in their place came the D55 and ST2. The first was little altered from the D1 and retained the rigid frame, while the second was as the SS2 with rear suspension and battery lighting. During the year, they were joined by the D55RS, which had rear suspension.

For 1954 the two 122 cc models continued, along with the ST2 and ST3. These had their engines changed to the 8E and 7E respectively, while the rigid- and sprung-frame Apollo models stayed as they were. In this manner, the range ran to late 1954, when motorcycle production ceased.

Oscar

This all-British scooter was sprung on an unsuspecting motorcycle world late in 1953, with full descriptions in the press and exhibits at shows in Frankfurt and London. Not a lot more happened, but the prototypes did exist, and one, at least, continued running for several years doing development work for the Siba importers based in Surrey.

The scooter presented bulbous lines with its two-section bodywork, which was fabricated in fibreglass, so the manufacturers in Blackburn were in the vanguard of the use of this material. The front section comprised mudguard, apron and footboards, while the rear enclosed the engine unit and was hinged for access.

Underneath the skin went a duplex tubular frame with pivoted-fork rear suspension. This differed from most in that the fork legs were malleable castings, clamped and pinned to the spindle. The suspension medium was a Spencer-Moulton Flexitor bonded-rubber unit, and the preload could be adjusted. There was also a rubber loop on each leg, which assisted when a passenger was carried. The front suspension was formed as leading links in a similar manner, using the same construction and medium. The wheels were pressed-steel discs shod with 12 in. tyres and mounted on hubs with 5 in. brakes. They were both quickly detachable and interchangeable.

The power units were rather less exciting, being either the 122 or 197 cc Villiers with fan cooling and a three-speed gearbox. Less usual was the engine mounting, which used rubber to insulate any vibration, the unit being able to pivot a little on its rear mounting, but restrained by rubber blocks in shear.

The machine was finished off with a dualseat and could have a spare wheel, but following the first announcement all went quiet. Aside from acknowledging its use by Siba five years later, no more was heard of this make.

The Oscar scooter launched late in 1953 with bonded-rubber suspension units and basic Villiers engine

Panther

Panthers were built at Cleckheaton, in Yorkshire, and had their roots in the dawn of motorcycling. They became famous for manufacturing very sturdy machines, including the extremely cheap Red Panther of the 1930s, and for their use of the engine as the frame downtube.

During the war, they made aircraft parts, but late in 1945 came news of their simple post-war range. This ignored the excursions into upright engines and spring frames that had been scheduled for 1940, and kept to their well tried, inclined engine formula. There were three models, listed as the 60, 70 and 100, all with ohv, but with capacities of 249, 348 and 594 cc. They kept their proven oil system with the lubricant carried in a separate chamber cast within the sump.

The engines differed in their method of ignition, for the two smaller machines had a coil with the points set in the timing cover, while the 100 kept to a magneto. On this model, an auto-advance was incorporated into the drive and, as in the past, this extended on to the separate dynamo. Transmissions also varied, the 60 having three speeds and the two larger models four, but in other respects, the 60 and 70 were the same.

All models had rigid frames and girder forks, the smaller ones having a downtube. The 100 alone had a twin-port cylinder head and, thus, two exhaust systems, while it also had a good roll-on rear stand. The other two used centre stands.

It was a good, solid range for the times, so Panther stuck to it for a while, but with a change to telescopic front forks for 1947. These were Dowty Oleomatic, which relied on air for suspension and oil for damping and lubrication. Dowty had extensive experience of such designs in the aircraft industry, and with its progressive rise in effective spring rate, it offered an improvement over conventional springs. Of course, it also offered disaster if the seals failed, and both Panther

and Dowty were to find out that using aircraft-quality components, serviced to commercial standards, could give problems.

One useful feature of the new forks was that the wheel spindle axis was offset from the fork leg. Thus, they were able to arrange that the leg could be used either way round, thanks to common mudguard lugs, giving solo or sidecar trail according to position. This was an asset for the owner, and for Panther, with most model 100s hauling sidecars, as they only needed the one assembly for either condition.

The range was continued for 1948, and during the year, the firm began to compete in trials, using one each of the smaller models. These differed from the road machines in that the cylinder was set vertically, but were otherwise little altered in their essentials. Naturally, there were alloy guards, a 21 in. front wheel, competition tyres and a high-level exhaust, but the main parts were based on the road model.

The use of an engine with vertical cylinder spread to the two smaller road models for 1949, and these took the numbers 65 and 75 to replace the older ones. Both were much in the mould of the past using the same engine dimensions — which made the 250 a real long-stroke — the enclosed ohv arrangement and the separate crankcase sump for the oil. Both had a Lucas dynamo clamped to the front of the crankcase, but differed in ignition. The 75 had a rear-mounted magneto, but the 65 kept to a coil with a points housing, incorporating an auto-advance, in the same mounting position.

Otherwise, the models seemed as before, although the frame was new and the 75 had the roll-on rear stand. The model 100 simply stayed as it was. The works competition models led to a further pair of machines which were based on them and listed as the Stroud in either capacity. They were much as the works machines, but came complete with full lighting equipment and no great weight reduction.

For 1950 a 65 de luxe was added. This had a four-speed gearbox and improved finish, but was otherwise as the standard machine. There was little other alteration, except to manual ignition control for the 100. All six models ran on for 1951, with many detail changes. For the Strouds, this included a low-level exhaust pipe with tilted silencer. It was the same again for 1952, but at the end of that year the 65 was dropped and there were some more major changes.

Early post-war Panther single 60 or 70 from the 1947–8 period, when the inclined engine was used with the Dowty forks

This Panther 100 ran in the 1949 ISDT, but retired on the fifth day with sidecar chassis trouble

Panther Stroud 348 cc model from 1952 with vertical cylinder and odd exhaust-pipe run

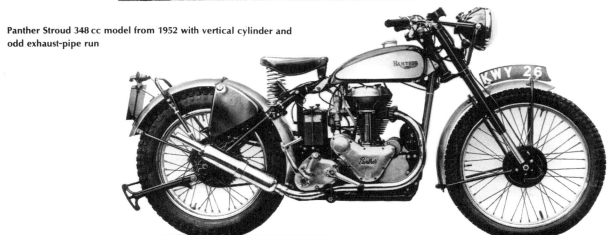

The 1958 model 75 Panther in pivoted-fork frame

Foremost were those to the suspension, for a frame with pivoted-fork rear suspension appeared for the 65 and 75, and with it a new telescopic fork with springs. The Dowtys continued on the rigid models, and the competition Stroud engines were given a light alloy head and barrel. There was also the option of magneto ignition for the 65 de luxe.

At the end of the season, the Stroud models were withdrawn, but the others ran on for 1954, when they were joined by a version of the 100 in a pivoted-fork frame. This, too, used the Panther telescopic forks with springs, which became standard wear, and all models had the option of a dualseat.

The rigid 75 was dropped at the end of the year, so for 1955 there were three sprung models and only two rigid ones, these being the 65 de luxe and 100. The 75 had full-width hubs fitted as standard, these being an option for either 65, and all models had a new headlamp with the speedometer, ammeter and light switch set in it.

Right **The Panther Princess scooter of 1960 with 174 cc Villiers 2L engine under the body panels it shared with Dayton and Sun**

Panther twin model 45 from 1959 with 324 cc 3T engine and Earles leading-link forks

The 65 de luxe was dropped that year, so only the 100 remained in its rigid frame to suit the die-hard sidecar man.

The three sprung models continued with it for 1956, when full-width hubs appeared on the model 100 and were offered as an option for the rigid version. Two entirely new machines were also added to the range, both having 197 cc Villiers engines.

These new lightweights were the models 10/3 with three-speed 8E unit, and the 10/4 with four-speed 9E engine. Otherwise, they were the same and had a loop frame, pivoted-fork rear suspension and Earles leading links at the front. The last were well disguised to appear as telescopics at a casual inspection. The front mudguard was unsprung. Both models had a dualseat, and the area below this was enclosed by panels with spaces for the tools, battery and electrics.

The range was extended for 1957 with further two-stroke models, while the four-strokes kept going with one addition. There was a further 197 cc machine in the form of the 10/3A, which had the 9E engine and three-speed gearbox. The

cycle parts were unchanged and were also used by the model 25, which had a 246 cc 2H Villiers single, and the model 35 with a 249 cc 2T twin. The first was never a successful engine unit and was short lived, as was the Panther 25.

The new four-stroke was a de luxe version of the sprung 100, which kept the full-width hubs, while the original became the Standard 100 without them. The final addition to the Panther line-up was a 125 cc Terrot scooter, which failed to match the Vespa or Lambretta in style or much else.

As well as the 25, the rigid 100 was finally dropped at the end of the year, but all the others continued for 1958. They were joined by a 35 Sports model, which had a tuned engine and revised finish to distinguish it from the basic 35. It retained the same cycle parts, and this policy ran on into 1959, when two more twins were added as the models 45 and 50 Sports, using the larger 3T Villiers engine.

The four-strokes also had a new model in the form of the 120, which was a 645 cc version of the big single. It shared cycle parts with the de luxe 100, and both models still used the archaic twin-port head, unlike the standard 100. The Terrot scooter activity continued, but there was news, late in the year, of a Panther scooter, although it was not to reach the market until 1960.

This it did, along with the rest of the range, which continued much as before, although the lightweight twins were fitted with telescopic forks. The scooter was called the Princess and powered by the 174 cc 2L engine in kickstart or electric-start forms. Both had fan cooling and went into a conventional scooter frame with pivoted-arm suspension at front and rear. This made wheel changing much easier. The wheels themselves were 10 in. split-rim types on alloy hubs. The bodywork had a better line than that of the Terrot and was produced in conjunction with Dayton and Sun (see pages 77 and 165) to reduce costs. It was built up from panels in the usual manner, those at the sides being detachable for access.

On this note, Panther entered the 1960s, but times were soon to become harder for them, and few models survived more than three years. A couple did for a while longer, but with a receiver at the company's helm and built from the stock bins.

Many survivors still demonstrate how tough they built them in Yorkshire.

Phillips

This famous cycle firm moved into powered two-wheelers in 1954, when they exhibited a clip-on model at the Earls Court show as a complete machine. For this, they took a conventional cycle, but shaped the rear end of the top tube so that it curved down to lower the seat, and added bracing struts to the front forks. The front wheel was given a drum brake, and the rear one a coaster hub, so in this area, the machine had an edge on basic clip-on cycles.

The engine was a 49.2 cc two-stroke with alloy head and barrel, and had a clutch built into the assembly. It was mounted above the bottom bracket and drove the rear wheel by chain on the left, while the standard cycle pedals and chain remained as usual. A silencer ran parallel to the downtube, and the engine provided direct lighting.

For 1956 the machine was given telescopic front forks and was joined by the P39 Gadabout. This was much more in the moped image and used a 49.6 cc Rex engine with two-speed gearbox hung from a rigid spine frame with telescopic

forks. The result was much as any other mid-1950s moped and the performance adequate. This meant 35 mph if you could stand the ride and vibration, and 25 mph as the practical speed over any distance.

The original model continued until late 1957, and the P39 into 1959, but for that year it was joined by others. The first to appear was the P40 Panda, which had a single-speed, 49.2 cc Rex engine, which went into a simple frame similar to that used for a woman's bicycle. The engine had a light-alloy head and barrel, while the cycle side was basic with no suspension, other than the saddle.

A little later, the P39 was joined by the P50 Gadabout de luxe, which was similar to the cheaper machine, but with three speeds. A month later, the P45 Gadabout was added. This was as the P50, except that the power unit was a 49.9 cc Villiers 3K unit with the two-speed gearbox.

By the end of 1959 the P39 had gone, but the other three models continued and were joined during 1960 by the P49 Panda Plus. This was much as the P40, but had telescopic forks and well valanced mudguards, although it retained the single-speed Rex engine.

During 1960 the P40 was dropped, but the other three mopeds ran into the new decade and were joined by others, before the name, which was one of the Raleigh group of companies, was dropped. By late 1964 the models were no more.

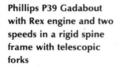

Phillips P39 Gadabout with Rex engine and two speeds in a rigid spine frame with telescopic forks

Phoenix

Ernie Barrett went racing in the 1950s by building a trio of frames and fitting various sizes of JAP engine into them, so when he turned to scooters, it was not surprising that he adopted the same principle. He used the name of the mythical bird that arose from its ashes for his products, which were built in Tottenham, London.

All models used Villiers engines, and the prototype of 1956 had a 147 cc 30C. When the production model was launched later that year, it kept the same engine, which was fitted into a typical tubular scooter frame. This had pivoted-fork front and rear suspension with an 8 in. wheel size. The frame carried a scooter form of body, although this lacked any great style.

A year later, the range was expanded for 1958 with Standard and De Luxe versions of the 147 cc model, which had been tidied up a little by extending the fixed front mudguard cowl upwards to carry the headlamp. This improved the front end, although it remained rather large and heavy in appearance, but the rear body kept its single-curvature forward panel and an enormous fretwork-type Phoenix badge.

In May 1958 the style improved further, as four new models launched had a fibreglass moulding for the rear enclosure. It was held in place by three car-bonnet catches of the period, so was easy to remove for major work. For refuelling, the dualseat swung upwards, which also gave access to the plug.

The new models included two in the 150 class, but with different engines. The 150 Super de Luxe kept to the 30C with kickstart, but the S150 used the 148 cc 31C engine with electric start. Both were fan-cooled, as were the other two models, which used the 197 cc 9E engine for the S200, and the 249 cc 2T twin for the T250. Both had electric start, and the last also had 10 in. wheels.

The range grew further for 1959, although the De Luxe model with the 30C was dropped, but this still left three machines for that class. The two larger ones were listed in solo and sidecar form,

The Phoenix 150 model with 31C Villiers engine under a body shared with the whole range

Phoenix T250 scooter with stowage compartment in rear of apron and fascia above

while the extra model was the T325, which used the larger 3T twin engine. It, too, had fan-cooling and electric start, and was available for solo or sidecar use. It was fitted with the 10 in. wheels, which became an option for all models.

For 1960 the 150 Super de Luxe was fitted with the 31C engine, and a Standard 200 model appeared with kickstart. Two further new models were the Standard 175 and S175. These had the 174 cc 2L engine and specifications as for the 200. The Standard machines were alone in fitting the 8 in. wheels, but the 10 in. ones remained an option for them and a standard fit for the rest.

Thus, the Phoenix range continued into the 1960s, now with far more style, but only until 1964, when production ceased. Once more, the declining market took its toll.

Power Pak

This was one of the many clip-on units on the market around 1950, which functioned by driving the bicycle tyre with a crankshaft-mounted roller. In this case, the rear wheel was used, the unit being mounted above it with the cylinder of its two-stroke engine inverted and on the right-hand side of the machine.

This arrangement allowed the fuel tank to sit neatly over the crankcase, which extended across the machine, with the flywheel magneto on the left. Inside, there was a deflector piston and overhung crankshaft, while outside were hung the carburettor and a tubular silencer. The unit was clamped to the cycle saddle stays with a strut on the right, and a lever was provided to bring the drive roller into contact with the tyre.

Control was by a single lever, which activated the decompressor when moved one way, and the throttle when moved in the other. In a year or two, this was altered, as the engine had gained a clutch and a twistgrip, which disengaged it when turned to its stop. Thus, opening the throttle first allowed the clutch to engage and then lifted the carburettor slide.

The unit remained on the market until 1956, but by then the world had moved on to mopeds, so the firm endeavoured to follow suit. The result was rather odd, for they retained the friction-roller drive to the rear tyre, but positioned the engine unit beneath the model's bottom bracket.

The frame was much as for a woman's cycle, but the downtubes were replaced by a beam, which also acted as a fuel tank. At the front were light blade girder forks, by then very dated, but on top of the handlebars went a fascia panel. This carried a speedometer, ignition key and switches for both lights and direction indicators, the last being a rare feature on two wheels then. Leather panniers were fitted on each side of the rear wheel.

Nothing further was heard of this design, and it is likely that the firm had a good look at an NSU Quickly and realized they would be wasting their time. Of course, they should have done this before building their prototype.

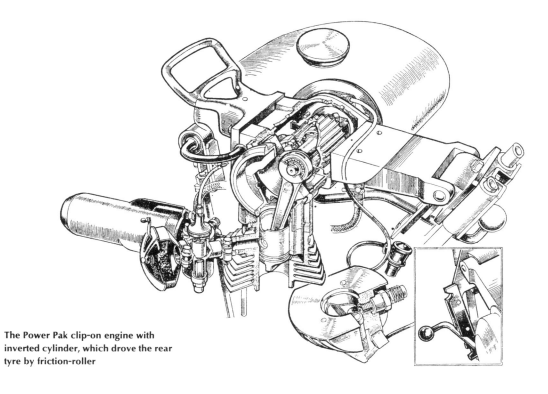

The Power Pak clip-on engine with inverted cylinder, which drove the rear tyre by friction-roller

Powerwheel

Cyril Pullin won the 1914 Senior TT and after World War I produced some interesting motorcycle designs in the form of the Pullin Groom and Ascot Pullin. Both were advanced and innovative, but neither sold in any numbers.

Late in 1951 his name appeared once more as the designer of the Powerwheel, which was to be made and marketed by Tube Investments. It was

aimed at the clip-on market but, like the Cyclemaster and Winged Wheel, sought to build the motive power into a wheel, which could be exchanged for the normal cycle one. This was usually the rear wheel, although the front was equally feasible, as was one at each end.

The engine was a 40 cc two-stroke, but what made it nearly unique was that it was a rotary. Thus, the crankshaft stayed still and the internal workings forced the cylinder and crankcase to rotate about it, along with the piston and connecting rod. Detail arrangements were made to achieve balance, while the intake was along the hollow crankshaft mainshaft, which had the carburettor attached to its outer end. A disc valve between the flywheels controlled the ingoing mixture, which then passed through twin transfers in the iron barrel.

The exhaust was by two opposed ports, each with an alloy silencer, which discharged into an

The complex Powerwheel, which appeared in 1951 as a prototype, but never made it into production. This exploded diagram shows the many parts involved, from the carburettor on the left to the magneto on the right

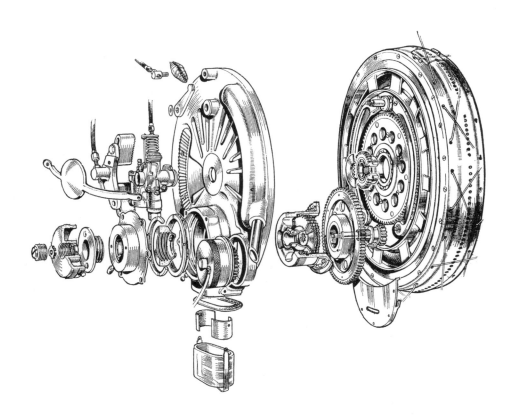

annulus and then to an external chamber. Ignition was by flywheel magneto, the points of which were opened by a face cam, and the compression-release valve was held open by a light spring, until centrifugal force shut it as the engine spun.

In addition to this ingenuity and complication, there was also a transmission with a gear train to give the necessary reduction to the wheel itself. Into this was built a clutch and also a drive to a small dynamo for the lights. The whole was housed within the wheel hub, which also contained a 7 in. drum brake with link operation of the shoes from the single cam.

All told, it was very clever and worked well enough in prototype form on the road. However, although it ran smoothly, thanks to its rotating inertia, it was a complex solution to a simple problem. Most likely this is why no more was heard of it.

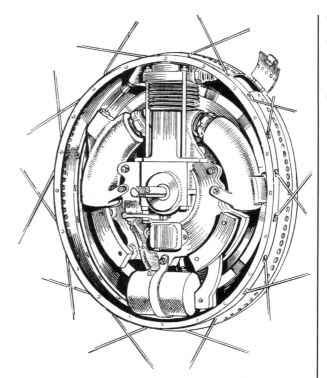

Above **The assembled Powerwheel with the cylinder balanced by the magneto armature. The door in the hub shell gave access to the sparking plug, although a special spanner was needed to extract it**

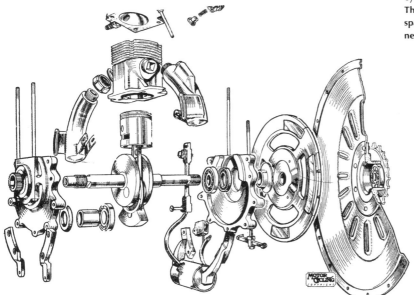

Progress

Pullin

This was the name of an imported German scooter that appeared in 1956, which was joined for 1957 by models with Villiers engines. There were three of these, all of which used the same chassis with fibreglass bodywork. This sat on a welded tubular frame with pivoted-fork front and rear suspension, while the wheels with 16 in. rims were larger than usual for a scooter.

For the Anglian model, the engine was the 147 cc 30C, while the Briton had the 197 cc 8E, both being fan-cooled. The Britannia also had a 197 cc engine, but this was a 9E with four speeds and electric start.

Sadly, the machines lacked the style and line of the Teutonic models, and by late 1958 had been discontinued. They were never seen again.

After the Powerwheel exercise (see page 148), Cyril Pullin turned his attentions to the scooter field, and in 1955 offered a design and prototype to any manufacturer willing to produce it. The machine was planned to need minimal and inexpensive tooling, while much that was under the skin came straight off the shelf.

The engine unit was a 197 cc Villiers with fan-cooling and Siba electric start, which went into a monocoque type of chassis. The rear body was formed from sheet alloy with cross-members and was bolted to the front section. Both wheels were suspended on pivoted arms with 8 in. rims and 6 in. brakes, the front one being enclosed by the combined apron, mudguard and headlamp housing.

The appearance was acceptable and the model was shown fitted out with windscreen, dualseat, spare wheel and rear carrier, so offered the right menu to the scooter rider. However, this failed to suit the taste of any manufacturer, so only the prototype was ever built.

This was a pity because it worked well and could have had possibilities.

Progress scooter at the 1956 Earls Court show with its larger-than-usual wheels

Radco

This make of machine was produced by the Birmingham firm of E. A. Radnall from just before World War I. Their range was on the market for most of the 1920s, but tailed off in the next decade, with production coming to a halt in 1933.

For the next 20 years, they stuck to making components for the industry, but in 1954 returned to the fray with a single model called the Ace. In truth, there was little enough to distinguish it from many other utility mounts, for its motive power came from a 99 cc 4F engine with two speeds.

This went into a simple rigid loop frame, but a novel note was struck by the front suspension. This was by short leading links with external spring units and was supplied by Metal Profiles. For the rest, the equipment included a saddle with a cylindrical toolbox beneath it, a centre stand and direct lighting.

As happened with others in the 1950s, there was an announcement, a prototype, maybe a buyer's guide listing, and then silence. No more was heard of the model, and the firm went back to making components. They did have one more go in 1966 with a basic mini-bike, but this, too, failed to catch on and met with the same fate.

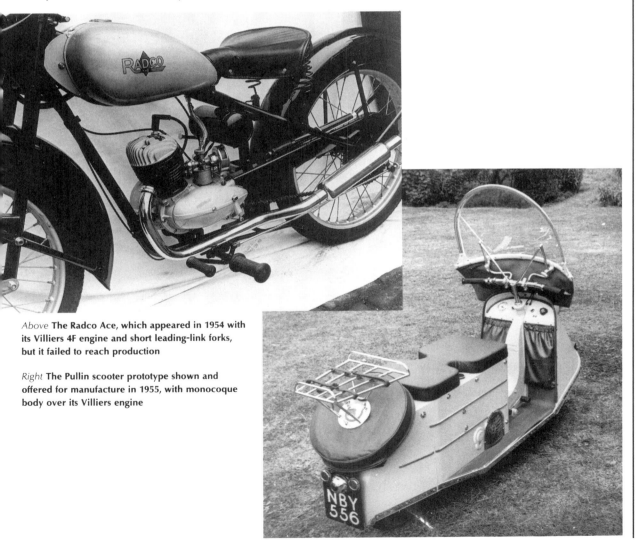

Above **The Radco Ace, which appeared in 1954 with its Villiers 4F engine and short leading-link forks, but it failed to reach production**

Right **The Pullin scooter prototype shown and offered for manufacture in 1955, with monocoque body over its Villiers engine**

Rainbow

Raleigh

This machine was built as a prototype in 1950 by a gentleman of the same name who wanted to create a link between cycle and motorcycle. In some respects, it was likened to an autocycle but, once an allowance was made for the restricted facilities of the builder, it could be seen more as a step-through.

This was reinforced by the design parameters Rainbow set himself; low centre of gravity, enclosed engine, easy mounting of the machine by the rider, and legshields, all of which can be found in current step-through models. For the 1950 designer, there was little option, other than to use a 99 cc Villiers 1F engine unit with its two speeds, but the rest of the machine was less usual.

The frame had twin tubes, which ran down from the headstock, under the engine and then up and back to the rear wheel. Vertical tubes supported the saddle and rear carrier, while the cylindrical fuel tank was mounted behind the headstock. There were legshields and, in addition, there was a cover that enclosed most of the engine unit. Part of the machine's neat appearance came from the use of a circular, drum silencer, which went on the left of the crankcase to match the flywheel magneto on the right.

Front suspension was by single tube girders with rubber-band suspension, and the forks carried a 26 in. wheel, much as a heavy bicycle or autocycle. This pattern was not repeated at the rear, where a 20 in. wheel was installed, its use allowing a low seat height. It would have been easy enough in production to have amended the front end to accommodate a smaller wheel, and this could have given the project a more balanced line.

Unfortunately, this was not to be and the Rainbow stayed as a prototype only, in recognition of the ingenuity of its designer. There was no production and, thus, no further mention of the machine.

Raleigh are best known for their bicycles, but have dabbled with power from Victorian times. This involved motorcycles, three-wheelers and the sale of engines and gearboxes to others in pre-war times, but from 1935 they concentrated on their first love – the bicycle.

In 1958 they returned to powered machines in a modest way and produced a moped late in the year, which was typed the RM1. It had a 49.5 cc Sturmey-Archer two-stroke engine with V-belt drive to a countershaft, and chain to the rear wheel. Inside the engine, there was an overhung crankshaft with a Lucas flywheel magneto on its end, outboard of the V-belt pulley.

The engine was made for Raleigh by BSA, but they kept the cycle parts to themselves and used

The Sturmey-Archer engine used by the Raleigh moped when launched in 1958 as the RM1

a woman's model as the basis for the frame, which lacked rear suspension and had rigid bicycle front forks. The wheels were of the normal 26 in. cycle size, but did have drum brakes in the hubs, while the rear wheel had a sprocket on each side.

The fuel tank went between the twin down-tubes, and there was a saddle, rear carrier and toolbag. The engine was clamped to the down-tubes, with the pedal shaft running though the countershaft, and there was a means by which the rider could simply pedal the device home if the engine failed or the fuel supply ran out. There were guards over the chains and belt drive, a centre stand, and a single twistgrip control, which operated both throttle and decompressor.

Accessories such as screen and legshields were offered, and during 1959 the original model was joined by the RM1C, which had a clutch. Both were replaced for 1960 by the RM2C, which had a larger fuel tank with a fairing over it, among other detail improvements.

At the end of 1960 this, too, was dropped, for Raleigh changed course to use imported engines and designs for the rest of that decade.

Raynal

This company led the way to the autocycle in pre-war days by building a production version of the Jones prototype in 1937. The Jones had been made in conjunction with Villiers, and the original engine had provision for the pedal shaft to run through the middle of the clutch shaft.

The arrangement was fine, until the machine toppled over, or was even parked, bicycle fashion, with one pedal on the kerb. Then, sooner or later, the shafts would bend and bind, giving trouble. For production, this was avoided by relocating the pedals to a normal bottom bracket and moving the engine forward a little.

The power unit became the Villiers Junior, and the machine the archetype of the autocycle. The frame was an open bicycle type with a simple sprung fork, while both wheels had drum brakes. In 1939 it was joined by a model with rigid forks.

Post-war, the JDL engine was used to produce the Popular, which was much as the pre-war model, but with girder forks. After a season, it was renamed the De Luxe for 1947, with no real change, and in this form ran on until late 1950.

A suffering Raynal autocycle struggling with too much of a load for its 98 cc JDL engine in 1948 – actually a 1938 machine

RCA

Greeves with 349 cc RCA twin engine on test in 1958

This was an engine, rather than a machine, which first appeared in 1957. The name came from R. Christoforides and Associates, but the design was that of Peter Hogan. He, and brother John, had been at the forefront of British 125 cc racing in the early 1950s with a pair of Bantams, John winning many events.

Peter's first twin was built by coupling two Bantam engines, and with the experience gained from this venture he laid out the 349 cc RCA twin. It was modern in concept, with a horizontally-split crankcase, full flywheels and twin Amal carburettors, following bench tests with a single Zenith. Electric starting was provided by a Siba unit, and the one unusual feature was the location of the exhaust ports. These were in each side of the iron block, alloy adaptors being bolted to this and then connected to the exhaust pipes. The cylinder heads were separate and in alloy, as the Hogans had made and sold these for Bantams at one time.

The engine drove an Albion gearbox, and an alloy chaincase, carrying the RCA badge, enclosed the drive. The complete assembly was first tried in a Greeves, which was altered to suit where necessary, and in this form was the subject of a road test. The report gave a top speed of 75 mph, which was about par for stock models that year, although sports machines, such as the Velocette Viper, were good for 90. The RCA did, however, pull well, which mattered when only four speeds were to be had.

The RCA engine was tried by Dot for two models in 1959, one for scrambles and the other a road machine. This exercise only lasted for two years, for the power curve was unsuited to the off-road task and engine supplies were limited anyway. There was a brief attempt at road racing, for which the engines had the exhaust adaptors reversed to point to the rear, where they were fitted with short open pipes.

These machines failed to provide any impact on the racing scene, although that same year a race-kitted Yamaha twin made an appearance on some British circuits. For one make it was to be oblivion, and for the other further development and years of success.

Reynolds

Royal Enfield

Reynolds Tubes were much involved with the motorcycle industry and, as well as producing the raw material, often helped with the development of frames, forks and complete machines for both road and competition use. From all this background activity, one exercise was shown at the 1955 London show and in the following year during TT week.

It was a prototype moped, built to show what could be done, but without any intention of Reynolds themselves becoming involved in selling a complete machine. The design followed European practice in most respects, and the engine unit was a two-speed German Victoria.

This went into a beam frame with pivoted-fork rear suspension, while at the front there were leading links for the show, but telescopics at the TT. For the rest, there was a tank, saddle and rear carrier, so the model conformed to the accepted standards of the day.

It was an interesting project, but no-one stepped forward to take it further, and Reynolds wisely stuck to their main business of making tubing, so nothing further was heard of it.

Royal Enfield were masters of the technique of using a small number of major assemblies in various ways to create a model range to cover most requirements. They did this before the war, and even during it to some extent, and were to use the trick throughout most of their post-war years.

This was not too apparent when their 1946 range was announced with just three models, although two, at least, had common cycle parts and nearly identical engines. These were the 346 cc ohv model G and 499 cc J, which were based largely on earlier Enfield practice.

The engines differed in bore only to obtain the two sizes, so the stroke was common and really only the head and barrel varied. Both of these were in iron, which was normal then, but much else of the design was less so, although common to the Redditch firm.

Thus, the connecting rod was forged in light alloy with a plain big-end bearing. The crankshaft was built up conventionally and ran in a crankcase that was split on the centre line, but which also had a compartment for the oil of the dry-sump lubrication system. The timing gear was by a train of gears, the mag-dyno being sited behind the cylinder, and the valve gear was fully enclosed. The timing cover shape was typical for the marque, for it also encompassed the twin oil pumps, their drive and an oil filter chamber.

The engine drove a four-speed Albion gearbox, which had an extra external pedal. This allowed the rider to select neutral from any gear, except first, and was to remain an Enfield feature for a long time. These two assemblies went into a rigid cradle frame, which had twin tubes that ran under the massive crankcase to protect it. At the front were telescopic forks, and both wheels had 19 in. rims and 6 in. brakes in offset hubs. There was a deeply valanced sprung mudguard at the front and a two-part guard at the rear. Most of this was easily removed, which made dealing with punctures a little less of a problem.

Both the G and J were fitted with the usual Amal carburettor, Lucas electrics, saddle, toolboxes, and speedometer, although the last was always listed as an extra, rather like purchase tax. Both were not always wanted, but were compulsory in Britain.

In addition to these two models, the firm carried out factory rebuilds of its wartime C and CO models. These were both of 346 cc, but with side or overhead valves respectively, and while the cycle parts were much as for the G and J, the wartime girder forks were retained. The CO used the same engine as the G, but the C had a side-valve head and barrel.

These models were reworked to meet the intense demand for transport in the immediate post-war years, at a time when there were great shortages. Most new machines went for export, and ex-army models filled the gap. Many were simply sold off by the services, but Enfield had this involvement for a couple of years.

The third 1946 model was in complete contrast and effectively new on its home market, although it had first been seen in 1939 and was quite familiar to many service users. It was the 125 cc two-

stroke model RE, which was known to the forces as the Flying Flea and based on the pre-war 98 cc DKW model RT.

This last had been handled in Holland by a Jewish-owned firm in the 1930s, but in 1938 the concession was abruptly removed. Undeterred, the firm looked to Britain and arranged for Enfield to build them a copy, right down to the finish, but with a 125 cc engine. It was to be called the Royal Baby, or RB, not too far from the German RT.

By April 1939 prototypes were in Holland, and a few machines were sold just before war broke out. While that closed one door firmly, it left Enfield with a fully-developed lightweight, ready tooled up, and the army was soon a customer. Around 55,000 were built, some being supplied in a parachute crate for airborne use. They proved invaluable in action and for general duties. After the war, Enfield simply changed to black paint in the spray shop, added a touch of chrome, and continued to build them.

The RE engine was built in unit with its three-

Royal Enfield 125 cc model RE based on the wartime Flying Flea, as it was in 1950 when it had gained telescopic forks prior to a redesign in the following year

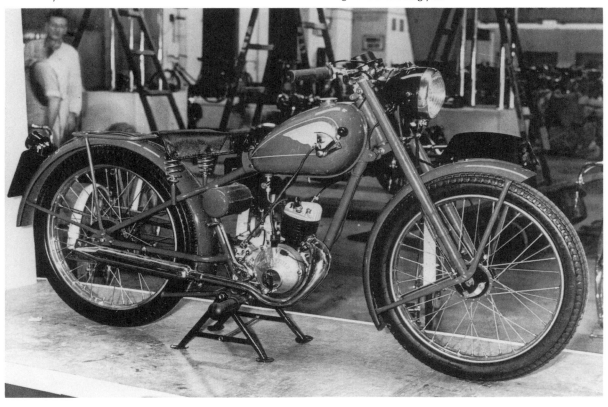

speed hand-change gearbox and had conventional construction. Inside, there was a flat-top piston and bobweight flywheels with a pressed-up crankshaft, while the head was in alloy and the barrel in iron. A Miller unit on the right looked after the lights and ignition, and a pressed-steel cover on the left enclosed the primary drive.

The engine unit went into a simple rigid frame, which picked up on lugs at each end. Front suspension was by girders with rubber bands as the medium, and the wheels had 19 in. rims and small drum brakes, 4 in. at the front and 5 in. rear. The fixtures and fittings were simple and included a saddle, cylindrical toolbox, centre stand and rear carrier.

With production so important, there were no real changes for two years, and for 1948 it was the RE that had a little amendment. This was to the exhaust pipe, which was given a distinct bulge as it curved down from the exhaust port, but other changes were minimal. This continued for 1949, when the 500 single became the J2 model, thanks to a change to a twin-port head and the addition of a second exhaust system for the left side of the machine.

The real Enfield news for 1949 was the introduction of two new models, one reviving a pre-war single name and the other a vertical twin. The single was the Bullet, the name of which went back to 1933 and which had always been associated with sporting models. During 1948 the post-war prototype had been seen in action in various trials and had already raised eyebrows by using rear suspension, then unheard of for such events.

The model was released in three forms for road, trials or scrambles use, but the essentials were the same for all. The engine followed many Enfield principles, but these were amended to suit, so the oil compartment was moved to the rear of the crankcase to move the engine's weight forward. The length was then held to a minimum by bolting the gearbox to the rear of the crankcase and driving it with a duplex chain. This was tensioned with a slipper and enclosed in a cast alloy case with single fixing for the outer, so the resulting assembly was much as unit construction.

The engine itself followed Enfield practice in most areas, but had the iron cylinder deeply spigoted into a much taller crankcase. On top went an alloy head with separate rocker housings, so this, too, differed from the touring engines. Internally, things were less altered in design or layout, but were improved in detail and materials.

The engine and gearbox assembly went into an open frame with pivoted-fork rear suspension and telescopics at the front. The wheel and brake sizes were as for the tourers, but blade mudguards were used, along with generally more modern features, except for the saddle. The result was a smart motorcycle that stood out during a drab period, its silver-grey finish being topped off by a chrome-plated tank with frosted silver panels.

For trials, the machine was fitted with a Lucas racing magneto, wide gear ratios, raised exhaust and more suitable wheels and tyres. Both lights and a mag-dyno were available, for it was an era when most competitors rode their machines to and from events, as well as in them. The scrambler received a similar treatment, but without the options, and had close gears and an open exhaust.

The second new model was the 500 Twin, which never had any other name, but annoyed Triumph by being listed as the 5T. It had a brand-new, 495 cc ohv vertical twin engine with separate heads and barrels in alloy and iron respectively. The crankshaft was a single alloy-iron casting with plain big-ends and ball and roller mains. There were two camshafts, which were driven by chain, with a further chain from the inlet camshaft to the dynamo. This ran at engine speed with a skew-gear-driven points housing and distributor for the coil ignition system built into it.

Lubrication was by the normal Enfield pumps, and the oil was kept in a crankcase sump, as on the Bullet. Like that model, the gearbox was bolted to the rear of the case, and from then on, the Twin followed the lines of the road Bullet, except for details, such as an ignition and lights switch, plus ammeter set in a box beneath the saddle. Only the sprung front mudguard spoilt the machine's fine lines.

Despite launching two new models, Enfield kept at it, and for 1950 the RE was fitted with telescopic front forks, which picked up on the girder mountings. There were other details, but it was only the cast alloy fork top cover for the Bullet and Twin which was notable.

The smallest model received a major redesign for 1951, when its engine unit became more streamlined and went into a new frame. Internally, the engine was much as before, but the works were housed in a new set of alloy castings of much neater style. Changes were to an external ignition coil, crankshaft-mounted clutch and foot-change for the gearbox.

Prosaic model J2 Royal Enfield from 1952 with its iron engine, separate gearbox and rigid frame

The new frame gave more support to the engine, as it had a full loop. It was still rigid, but the telescopics at the front were revised to normal yokes, the top one carrying the speedometer and handlebars. These had been cleaned up with welded-on pivot blocks, alloy levers and axial cables for throttle and decompressor. The front brake size was increased to 5 in. to match the rear, but the cycle parts remained much as before. Thus, the RE2, as it was called, stayed true to its roots as a light, handy machine.

The other models ran on with little change for 1951 and 1952, although for that year, the trials Bullet gained a sleeved alloy barrel, and the Twin had its switches moved around and was given the option of a dualseat. The G and J models continued as they were, with no real alteration. The former was dropped in 1954, and the latter a year later.

There were more additions for 1953, with new models at both ends of the range. Smallest newcomer was the Ensign, which had a 148 cc version of the RE2 engine. This was installed in a frame that appeared to have plunger rear suspension with exposed springs, although it was, in fact, a pivoted fork. The springs were simply held in the same manner as for a plunger frame and, thus, copied a pre-war European style. Otherwise, the Ensign was very much as the RE2, which continued unchanged to the end of the year and was then dropped.

The 346 cc Bullet had some internal changes and was joined by a 499 cc version. This duplicated the smaller model on most points, but it was fitted with a larger rear brake and sidecar lugs. In addition, the forks were available with extended wheel lugs to give sidecar trail. These, along with a steering damper, were also available for some other models.

The Twin had some new parts, but more important was the appearance of a larger version, the 693 cc Meteor. This was much as the smaller model, but it had dual 6 in. front brakes, the 7 in. rear brake and a larger fuel tank. Despite the fact that the machine was their new top model, a dualseat remained an option.

More new models and changes were introduced for 1954, the Bullets and both twins being fitted with a styling cowl at the top of the forks. This carried a small pilot lamp at each top corner, plus the headlamp, enclosed the top of the forks, and provided a mounting for the instruments and switches. Enfield called it a casquette, and it was to be a styling feature for many years.

The Bullet range was extended by introducing a road-racing version, but this looked far from competitive when compared to the well developed BSA Gold Star. The same options were also offered for the larger Bullet, but few took them up. For the Twin, there was a mag-dyno option, which was a curious move at a time when

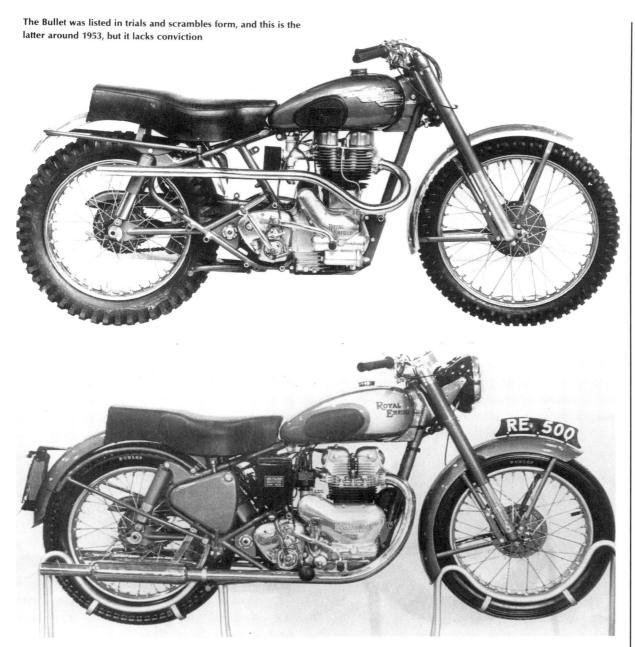

The Bullet was listed in trials and scrambles form, and this is the latter around 1953, but it lacks conviction

First of the Royal Enfield twins was the 495 cc model listed as the 500 Twin and shown here in 1953 form

the industry was turning to alternators. It involved alterations to the drive to achieve the correct magneto speed.

The final new models were for the 250 class, which the firm had ignored in post-war years. To deal with this, they built a 248 cc version of the model G engine and produced the model S by fitting this in an open-diamond, rigid frame with a light, four-speed Albion gearbox. At the front

were telescopic forks, and the cycle parts were as for the G model. Unlike the other models, it had coil ignition and a Miller alternator on the left-hand end of the crankshaft.

The model S was only built for the one year, but the Clipper, which was launched with it, ran on for a little longer. This used the same engine and gearbox in a pivoted-fork frame with tele-scopics, so was a cross between the Bullet and G models.

The Clipper was fitted with a casquette without pilot lights for 1955, while the road Bullets were given a dualseat and dual front brakes. These items appeared on the Twin, too, where the mag-dyno became standard. This also went on the Meteor. All the larger models had the gearbox amended so that the pedals were on concentric spindles, and the Ensign continued with covers to hide its rear springs.

The range of Bullets was modified for 1956, and the two road versions changed to an alternator for charging, although they kept the magneto for ignition. This led to an enlarged chaincase, while the models also had a new frame and many detail alterations. All the competition machines were dropped, to be replaced by a Moto-Cross Bullet in each size for that year only.

The utility 250 Clipper was joined by a similar 350 model, which retained the same separate engine and gearbox format. It kept to a saddle, so was cheaper than the Bullet, and appeared to follow the typical Enfield trick of clearing the stores of excess stocks by building a model to use them.

At the bottom of the scale, the two-stroke became the Ensign II with some detail changes and a dualseat, which gave it a much more solid look. For the twins, the smaller stayed as it was and the larger was renamed the Super Meteor. In

A 1956 Royal Enfield 693 cc Super Meteor on test, where its power and low-speed pulling came in for praise

this form, it produced more power and had an alternator for charging, while retaining the magneto. The engine unit went into a new frame, and the result was a fast, beefy motorcycle.

A new model was introduced for 1957 as the 248 cc Crusader, which was to lead to many versions and be a mainstay of the firm well into the next decade. It featured unit construction, but otherwise followed Enfield methods in most respects, if not all.

The engine had a short stroke and iron top half. Inside, there was a one-piece, cast-iron crankshaft with plain big-end and alloy rod. A single alloy cover enclosed the rockers, but the location of the camshaft on the left was not usual. It was driven by a chain outboard of the primary and, in turn, drove the oil pump, which had a cross-shaft to the points on the right. The alternator was also on the right, and the oil for the dry-sump system in a chamber in the crankcase, as usual.

The complete unit went into an open frame with telescopic front and pivoted-fork rear suspension. The wheels were 17 in. with full-width hubs and 6 in. brakes, while the rear was driven by a fully-enclosed chain. There was a dualseat and a centre section with a lid on each side to carry the electrics and tools.

Alongside the new Crusader, the two Clippers continued for 1957 only, as did the two road Bullets, Ensign II and both twins, although the smaller of these did gain an alternator and coil ignition. A Clipper II appeared for 1958 as a low-cost version of the Crusader, and an Ensign III ran alongside the II with a higher specification level. The two Bullets continued much as before and were joined by another 346 cc Clipper, which was based on the Bullet engine with iron top half, alternator electrics and Crusader-type cycle parts, but with 19 in. wheels.

The Crusader itself was little altered, but became available with a factory fairing during the year. Earlier, in 1956, the firm had co-operated with The Motor Cycle to build a full fairing for a Bullet, so had learnt much from this project, which was known as the Dreamliner. That had been a complete front and rear enclosure with dual headlights, but the 1958 design was simpler, being a basic dolphin type plus a deeply valanced front mudguard. It was called the Airflow, and within two years was offered for all the road models as a factory fitment.

Thus, it appeared for the 250 and 350 Clippers in 1958, as well as for the twins, which had other

Above **The Royal Enfield Dreamliner on the Isle of Man in 1957 where it drew the crowds as always, despite its basic Bullet engine**

additions and alterations. The Super Meteor alone had little change and did not get its Airflow until 1959, but the 500 Twin was replaced early in the year by a new model. In addition, the larger twin was joined by a high-performance version.

The new small twin was the Meteor Minor, which was listed in Standard and De Luxe forms. It followed the lines of the earlier machine, but had a short-stroke, 496 cc, ohv engine and a number of detail amendments. The cycle parts were much as for the Crusader and, thus, in a style which had become a standard for the firm. An Airflow version of both models was offered from the start.

The performance 700 was the Constellation, which had yet more power, a TT carburettor, magneto and siamezed exhaust system. The cycle side was much as for the Super Meteor, but more sporting with chrome-plated mudguards.

Even the Ensign III was given an Airflow for 1959, when it was joined by the Prince model, which used the same engine. It did, however, finally receive full-circle flywheels and went into a pivoted-fork frame with extensive chaincase and side covers, much as the larger models. An Airflow version was offered, as it was for the two road Bullets, which had other changes, including 17 in. wheels for the 346 cc model only.

The Crusader was given an alloy head and joined by a Sports version, while the two sizes of Clipper model continued, all with the Airflow option. All the twins ran on, with just a change

The later small twin was the Meteor Minor, shown here in 1958 standard guise with saddle rather than dualseat

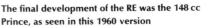

The final development of the RE was the 148 cc
Prince, as seen in this 1960 version

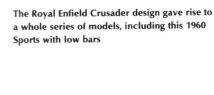

The Royal Enfield Crusader design gave rise to
a whole series of models, including this 1960
Sports with low bars

to siamezed pipes for the Super Meteor, but the
Standard Meteor Minor was dropped at the end
of the year.

The one new machine for 1959 was the 346 cc
Works Replica Trials model, which was the final
version of this long-running type. It had the all-
alloy engine with heavy flywheels and a well-
tucked-in exhaust system, but really came along
too late, for the two-stroke engine was taking
over in trials.

The range ran into 1960 and the new decade
with limited changes. The Ensign was dropped, to
leave the Prince, while the standard and Sports

Crusaders continued, as did the Bullets, the trials
model and the Clipper II. The larger Clipper was
revised with an alloy head and 17 in. wheels, so it
became a cheap version of the Bullet.

For the twins, there were changes for the Super
Meteor and twin carburettors for the Constellation. The Meteor Minor ran on as one model
only with a new silencer, but was joined by a
Meteor Minor Sports with increased power and
more sporting fittings.

It made a good range, typical of the marque,
for the future, and they carried it on for quite a
while.

Scott

The Scott is perhaps the strangest of production motorcycles, and it kept its unique layout from its earliest days. There may have been odder machines built as prototypes, or in short runs, but only the Scott could lay claim to a more or less constant build for some 60 years. Certainly, it was an acquired taste for any enthusiast and, while the company had its best days in the 1920s, they kept going through the bad times as well.

They returned to motorcycles in 1946 with a Flying Squirrel, little altered from that of the late pre-war days. There was the same 598 cc, twin-cylinder two-stroke engine with its water-cooling, single Amal and two-into-one exhaust pipe. The block was inclined, as it had always been, and the central primary chain drove a three-speed gearbox.

A duplex rigid frame carried the engine and gearbox, along with the traditional Scott radiator and fuel tank. At the front were Brampton or Webb girder forks, which carried the one new post-war feature, a dual front brake in a full-width hub. The rear hub was also full-width, and the

model was promised with a roll-on centre stand in place of the older rear one.

Few machines were built with girder forks before these were replaced by Dowty telescopics, using air as the suspension medium and oil for damping and lubrication. These were similar to those also used by Panther and Velocette; all depended totally on the air seals to keep the model on an even keel.

In this form, the Scott continued until 1949, when a change was made to coil ignition with a distributor on the right. This was driven by skew gears from the Pilgrim oil-pump drive, while a pancake dynamo went on the left. The changes and removal of the magneto drive chain allowed for a separate oil tank, which went on the right, below the saddle. The roll-on centre stand now made its appearance, and in this form the Flying Squirrel continued for 1950.

Unfortunately, the Scott had become a rather expensive anachronism, with a price tag well above most four-stroke twins and on a par with an Inter Norton. It also failed to offer a comparable performance, and the few sales to enthusiasts were not enough to prevent the firm going into voluntary liquidation.

The result of this was the sale of the old Saltaire works, while manufacture was transferred to the Aerco Jig and Tool Company in Birmingham, a firm owned by Matt Holder, who was a keen Scott enthusiast. They announced that the 1951 model would continue as before, but it was some time before new machines were made, and for a while only those which had been part of the purchase as stock were available.

The 1946 Scott Flying Squirrel with girder forks prior to the fitting of the Dowty telescopics

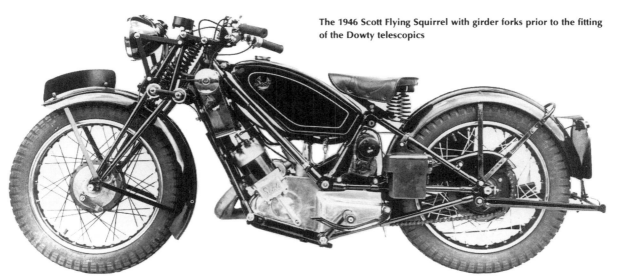

The Scott Swift of 1958 with the smaller 493 cc engine, but which failed to go into production

It was 1954 before there was any further news, and a further two years before machines were available again. The new model was much as the old one in the engine department, but was available in 497 and 598 cc sizes. Rigid and pivoted-fork frames were made available, both being new and of the duplex type. At the front were telescopic forks, and there was a Lycett dualseat for the rider. The fuel tank lost its traditional, sharp-edged style, which had always been so very distinctive, and the line seemed to suffer from this.

Thus, the Scott continued in small numbers, and for 1958 was fitted with an alternator in place of the dynamo. This called for a rectifier, rather than a regulator, and that year the speedometer was mounted in an extended headlamp shell.

During 1958 a new model, the Swift, was seen. This had a revised 493 cc engine with flat-top pistons. Six prototypes were built, but the model did not go into production. At the end of the year, the rigid models were dropped and the smaller-capacity model was to special order only.

In this way, the Scott ran to the end of the decade and on for another. For those who understood the machine, there was no other way, and for the rest – well, they did not know what they were missing.

Sun

As with so many others in the motorcycle industry, this firm had its roots in Birmingham and the cycle trade. In 1911 they built their first powered two-wheeler and continued with them, apart from a break during the war years, until 1933. They then dropped their line, but continued to make parts and machines for others until 1940, when they reappeared with an autocycle.

This machine was offered in three versions, and it was one of these that was their first post-war model in 1946. It used the 98 cc Junior de Luxe Villiers engine in a rigid frame with blade girder forks to provide the most basic motorized transport.

The Autocycle was listed with the JDL engine up to 1948, but for the next year was revised to use the 2F unit. At the same time, it was joined by the Motor Cycle, which had the two-speed 1F engine in a rigid frame, also with girder forks, and was equally basic. These two machines continued for 1950, at the end of which, the Autocycle was dropped and the Motor Cycle revised and joined by two more models.

Its main change was to tubular girders in place of the blades, while it retained its saddle and rear carrier, but gained a nice maroon finish. The other two models shared cycle parts and had a loop frame with plunger rear suspension and telescopics at the front. The specification was intended to be better than standard, hence the rear springing, and, thus, also included battery lighting and an electric horn.

The power units were the 122 cc 10D or 197 cc 6E Villiers engines with three-speed gearbox, and the models were called the 122 de luxe and the Challenger de luxe. Both had 19 in. wheels with 5 in. brakes, adjustable footrests, and a good saddle.

The three models continued for 1952 with detail improvements, and in March a 197 cc Competition machine was announced, although it did not reach the market until 1953. It was listed as the Competition Challenger and was first seen with a plunger frame. However, it became rigid for production, but was a full loop type with the saddle raised on its own little subframe. The telescopic forks carried a 21 in. front wheel, while the rear stayed at 19 in., and there were alloy

The 1953 Sun Challenger with 6E Villiers engine in rigid frame with telescopic forks

165

mudguards and wide-ratio gears with options of a tuned engine and close gears.

The road models also had changes for 1953, the smallest having the 4F engine unit, and the 122 cc version the 12D. The largest model became available in a rigid frame, while a dualseat was offered as an option.

For 1954 the 122 and 197 cc Challenger road models went into a new pivoted-fork frame and kept their battery lighting. Despite the frame change, a saddle was still the standard fit, although a dualseat was listed as an option. The engine of the larger machine became the 8E, which allowed the model to be offered in three- or four-speed forms.

The competition model stayed in its rigid frame, but was now offered in three forms, all powered by the 8E engine. The basic model was listed as the C1, but with a tuned engine, it became the C3, and with this engine plus a four-speed box, the C4.

The range was completed by the 99 cc model, which was unchanged, and extended by the addition of the Cyclone, which used the 224 cc Villiers 1H engine unit. This went into a new pivoted-fork frame with telescopic forks. The machine also had battery lighting and a dualseat.

The Cyclone continued with little alteration for 1955, as did the 99 cc model, which had a new tank and a new name – Hornet. The smaller Challenger had a change of engine to a 147 cc 30C unit, becoming the Mk 1A, while the larger became the Mk IV. On the competition side, just two models were listed, one of which, the Trials, was much as the C4, but the other, the Scrambler, was new. This last had a pivoted-fork frame and Earles leading-link forks with a standard or tuned engine and three or four speeds.

The road range of Hornet, Challenger 1A and Cyclone continued as they were for 1956, while the larger Challenger became the Mk V. It was joined by the Wasp, which used the 9E engine in a pivoted-fork frame with Armstrong leading-link forks and a degree of rear enclosure. The same engine and forks were also used for the Wasp Competition model, which replaced the Trials and Scrambles machines and had a raised saddle and alloy mudguards to suit its intended trials use.

There were more changes and additions for 1957, the Hornet becoming Saxe blue in colour and the smaller Challenger becoming the Mk IV with a 148 cc 31C engine unit. The 197 cc version stayed as it was with its 8E engine, as did the

Wasp with the 9E, but there was also a new machine of the same capacity. This was the Century, which used the 8E engine with three speeds in a pivoted-fork frame with telescopic front forks and a degree of rear enclosure. The Wasp Competition continued, as did the Cyclone, and a second new model was the Wasp Twin with the 249 cc 2T Villiers twin engine. The cycle parts were much as for the Wasp, so included the Armstrong leading-link forks, and the name was soon changed to the Overlander.

One further model was proposed for 1957, which was the Geni scooter with a 99 cc 4F engine unit. It differed from most scooters in having a distinct tunnel behind the apron, but this allowed the engine to sit well forward. In addition, it had 15 in. wire-spoked wheels, which added to the stability. The frame had pivoted-fork rear and leading-link front suspension, and the rear was enclosed by a body that extended up to the dualseat.

When the Geni reached production, it was fitted with the 6F engine with foot-change and incorporated other detail alterations. In this form, it went forward for 1958 as part of a much reduced range. At the start of the year, this totalled four machines, including the Geni, but the Hornet was soon dropped, as were both Challengers, the Century, the Cyclone and the Wasp Competition. Left were just the Wasp and Overlander, which continued with the same cycle parts.

In June 1958 the Geni became the Mk II, thanks to some improvements, and went forward with the Wasp and Overlander for 1959. The last two had their rear enclosure improved to give a smoother line, but both were dropped during the year. This left the Geni, but during 1959 it was joined by another scooter called the Sunwasp. This shared its bodywork with Dayton and Panther (see pages 77 and 140), while under the skin went a tubular frame and a 174 cc 2L fan-cooled Villiers engine with three-speed gearbox and Siba electric start. The suspension was by leading links at the front and pivoted fork at the rear, while the wheels were 10 in. pressed steel with 6 in. brakes.

The Geni and Sunwasp both continued for 1960, but there were no longer any Sun motor-cycles. The smaller model went at the end of that year, while the other continued, but only for one more year. The family that had run the concern from Victorian times retired and sold out to Raleigh, who soon removed the name from the cycle and scooter market.

The Wasp Twin, which soon had its name changed to the Overlander, but kept its Villiers 249 cc 2T engine and leading-link forks

The Sun Geni scooter, which was powered by a 99 cc 6F Villiers engine and had a style similar to that of the DMW Bambi

The larger Sunwasp scooter, which shared body panels with Dayton and Panther and was driven by a 174 cc 2L engine

Sunbeam

The Sunbeam originated in Wolverhampton, where John Marston, a Victorian in manner and outlook, demanded the highest standards of work from himself and his employees. Their cycles and motorcycles reflected this, and for many years the Little Oil Bath Chain Case and the phrase 'The gentleman's motorcycle' meant Sunbeam.

In 1928 they became part of ICI and soon felt the dull hand of accountancy upon them, as well as the chill wind of the depression. Neither suited a firm which specialized in quality work, so profits fell and the business passed to AMC in 1937, and then to BSA in 1943. There were to be no more Marston Sunbeams, but post-war the firm did produce one of the few really new British models, although the parent group failed to support it as well as they might have.

The new machine was first described in the press early in 1946 and offered a great deal that was new on the British market. Features of particular note were the in-line vertical twin engine, its overhead camshaft, unit construction, shaft drive, plunger rear suspension, fat 16 in. tyres and a variety of interesting details.

The short-stroke engine, another innovation for the time, had a capacity of 489 cc and was an all-alloy unit. The cylinders had sleeves with a lip at the top, and the block and crankcase were cast as one down to the alloy sump plate. Above went the alloy head, with a single camshaft, which had the distributor at its rear, and the valves in an angled row. The rockers were supported by pillars, and a cover enclosed the entire mechanism.

The camshaft was driven at the rear by a pair of timing gears and a short chain with a Weller tensioner. The gear also drove down to the single oil pump of the wet-sump system. The one-piece, cast-iron crankshaft carried a pancake dynamo on its nose. The connecting rods were forged alloy and had shell big-end bearings.

The whole engine made a very neat unit, for there were no external pipes. On the left went the two sparking plugs, and on the right a single Amal carburettor, flanked by the two exhaust pipes. These swept down into one and then on to the silencer.

The engine had the gearbox and clutch housing bolted directly to it, with the clutch on the back of the crankshaft. The gearbox had four speeds and was of the indirect type, which allowed the drive to step over for the final shaft. Despite the in-line nature of the layout, both gear and kickstart pedals were on the right and moved in the normally accepted planes. An open shaft took the drive to the rear wheel. It had a rubber-coupling universal joint at the front end and a Hardy-Spicer at the rear. The drive to the wheel was by an underslung worm, rather than the more usual bevels, and the rear brake was incorporated into the housing.

The engine unit was housed in a duplex frame with plunger rear suspension and telescopic front forks. The latter were a little unusual in that a single spring was housed between a bridge bolted to the sliders, with its upper end attached to the top crown. A small rebound spring was included, but there was no damping in the fork legs, only a little oil for lubrication.

The wheels were interchangeable and had 16 in. rims carrying special 4.75 in. section Dunlop tyres. The brakes were 8 in. offset drums, the cable and lever of the front one being hidden inside the backplate. Massive mudguards protected each wheel, while rider comfort was looked after by a pan saddle. This had rubber mountings and a long spring housed in the frame top tube and linked to provide support.

Beneath the saddle were two boxes that housed the battery, on the left, and the coil, regulator and cut-out on, the right. The latter box also carried the ammeter and lights, plus ignition switch, in its cover, while tools were stored in another box mounted low down on the left, beside the gearbox. A roll-on centre stand was provided with a ratchet to lock it, and the machine was topped off with a handsome fuel tank with twin taps and kneegrips.

That was 1946, and during the year there was also news of a sports model, which had a revised cylinder head. This gave a crossflow layout, so the carburettor moved over to the left. The extra power pushed the maximum speed up.

Unfortunately, all was not well, for the machine suffered from bad vibration, a peaky power

Above **The S7 Sunbeam twin with its fat tyres and in-line engine with shaft drive to the rear wheel**

Left **A sectioned Sunbeam twin engine on display**

output, torque reaction geared to throttle movement and rapid wear of the worm wheel. The solutions chosen were to restrict the engine speed and power, which removed the torque and wear troubles, although it did leave the model underpowered. In this form, a batch was made with improved forks, as there had been dangerous breakages, and sent to South Africa, only to be returned as unrideable.

The original designer, Erling Poppe, had by now left the company, so BSA personnel had to deal with the problems and endeavour to tame what was meant to be a group flagship. They decided the answer was to mount the engine on rubber, which was done with two mountings and two sets of snubbers. This entailed the addition of a flexible section of pipe between the exhaust and silencer, plus flexible petrol lines. As the engine no longer contributed to the frame's stiffness, a small cross-bar was added ahead of the engine. A 4.50 in. ribbed front tyre was also fitted.

Finally, in 1947, the model went into production as the S7 and, in the meantime, had acquired a cast alloy cover over the sparking plugs. There was also one for the carburettor, and the exhaust pipes had elbows between them and the head.

The performance was hardly vivacious, for the weight was over 400 lb, and the meagre power gave a top speed of only 72 or 75 mph in contemporary road tests. Even allowing for the pool petrol of the time, this was not the expected performance of a 500 cc twin, for the docile 3T Triumph was as fast. In addition, the ride induced by the combination of the fat tyres, long saddle spring and undamped suspension was lively and the machine snaked in fast bends. It was also an expensive machine to produce, for there was nothing about it in common with other BSA products to help keep the price down.

The result of these problems was a revision, plus a second model for 1949. The original became the S7 de luxe, and the new machine the S8 with narrower tyres and a lighter line. Both kept the same engine unit, rear drive and frame, but the forks became standard BSA for the S8 and stock legs in special yokes for the S7. The S8 also used a 7 in. BSA brake at the front, where a 19 in. rim with a 3.25 in. section tyre was fitted. At the rear, that model used a 4.00 × 18 in. tyre.

The S8 had a different cast alloy silencer and a conventional saddle. The mudguards were reduced in width to suit the tyres, and the handle-bars had stock controls, not the inverted ones with hidden cables used by the S7. A new air cleaner and cover appeared, as did a prop-stand, while the S8 took the black finish previously used by the S7, which now was painted mist green. There was also an option of silver grey for the S8.

From then on, the two models continued to be built in small numbers, the S8 being the more popular, but neither sold well, for the market demanded more for its money. There were detail improvements, but also problems that remained. One was the engine's habit of cutting out when the machine was braked a trifle hard for traffic lights. The cause was the float chamber being ahead of the mixing chamber, which could be starved of sufficient fuel to allow this.

As the 1950s rolled by, the two Sunbeams continued without change, year by year, but fewer and fewer buyers came forward. BSA made no real attempt to improve it, although a variant known as the S10 was built. This had the power-sapping worm replaced with bevels, while a crossflow head moved the performance up to a level comparable with its rivals. However, it was not proceeded with.

The models were announced for 1957, but production ceased before then, although new machines were stuck in showrooms for another year or two. It was not, however, the end of the name, because BSA found another use for it.

To the horror of Sunbeam enthusiasts, it appeared on a scooter. When the group finally did get round to this fast-selling type of transport, they chose to produce both BSA and Triumph

The lighter looking S8, as it was in 1951, with its cast alloy silencer

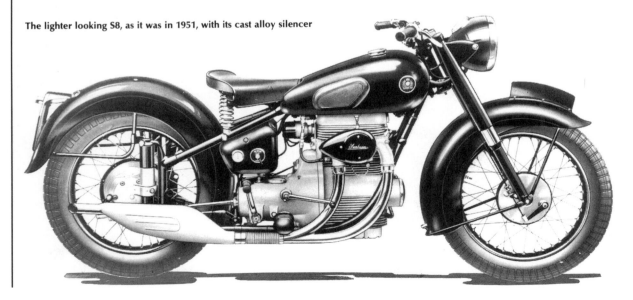

machines, by changes of colour and badges, and labelled the first a Sunbeam.

For both marques, there were two models, one with a 172 cc two-stroke engine and the other with a 249 cc ohv twin, offered with electric or kick starting. Both were launched in 1958 after a long development period, but it was 1959 before the twin reached the shops, and nearly 1960 before the single joined it.

The two engines differed totally, but otherwise the machines were nearly the same, with common transmission and chassis, except for minor details. The single was based on the D7 Bantam, although there were few common parts, as the barrel differed, the flywheels were smaller and the mainshafts longer. A flywheel magneto went on the right, with a fan to assist the cooling, and the clutch was on the left.

Right **An S7 serving with the police in Wellington, New Zealand, in 1952. It has a white finish and is fitted with radio**

Below **Sunbeam S7 pictured in 1973, but still much as it was when it left the factory**

The Sunbeam scooter built with single or twin engine and in these or Triumph colours, here with matching sidecar

The twin engine sat across the frame with a gear-driven camshaft to the rear. It was an all-alloy unit with one-piece forged crankshaft, generator on the right, points and oil-pump drive on opposite ends of the camshaft, and a Zenith carburettor to provide the mixture.

From then on, both twin and single drove back from the clutch by gears to a four-speed gearbox based on that used by the C15 and the Cub. The positive-stop change was retained, with control by a single rocking pedal, and final drive was by a duplex chain. This was enclosed in alloy castings, which also acted as the rear suspension pivoted arm to carry the 10 in. pressed-steel wheel and its 5 in. drum brake.

The chassis was in scooter style, but with duplex front tubes, to which the headstock tube was bolted. The front fork was telescopic, but with a single leg on the left, which had two tubes, one each for the spring and damper. The front wheel and brake were as for the rear. The bodywork was built up from pressings, but access to the mechanics was limited by the small panels provided. The dualseat was hinged to allow refuelling, and the one or two batteries were carried in boxes on the back of the apron.

All Sunbeam models were given a polychromatic green finish and listed as the B1, B2 and B2S to distinguish single, twin and electric-start versions. There was a long list of accessories in typical scooter style, which were essential for the dealer, who could do good business with them.

The machines continued with little change until the mid-1960s, but were never able to challenge the chic Italian models in the mass market, or the sophisticated German ones at the top end. As time moved on, the market shrank, so BSA went in other directions.

Sunbeam motorcycles were no more.

Swallow

This company was best known for its sidecars, but in the early post-war years it also built an elementary scooter which they called the Gadabout. Details were first released late in 1946, the model taking the form that the Italians were to make so popular a few years later.

The Gadabout lacked the performance produced by the foreign models, as it was heavier than them and its 122 cc Villiers 9D engine was a pre-war design. This unit, with its three-speed gearbox, was just ahead of the rear wheel in a rigid duplex frame with unsprung forks. Suspension was the province of the 4.00 × 8 in. tyres on their split rims, which were attached to hubs with 5 in. brakes.

The rider was given a slab seat, which was hinged for access to the engine, while the fuel tank went behind the seat, over the wheel. This was protected by a simple mudguard, which kept the worst of the dirt at bay and, in addition, there

The Swallow Gadabout with the box sidecar available for commercial use

was a complete rear body. Ahead of this was a flat floor, which rose to form an apron with a string holdall on its rear face.

The front section of the body was held by four quick-release Oddie fasteners, so it was very easy to remove. The remainder could also be detached quite easily. A rear stand and prop-stand were provided, and among the novel details was the use of the frame side tubes as silencers, so each had a tailpipe. Direct lighting and a bulb horn took care of those areas, and the controls were much as a motorcycle, but with a hand-change in the form of a long lever on the right of the body.

Thus, the Gadabout went its rather slow way in 1947, but was able to keep up with the traffic of those days. It was available with a box sidecar for commercial use, and for this had its gearing lowered, along with its performance.

For 1950 it became the Mk II with a 10D engine, fan cooling and foot-change, as well as a little more power. Rider comfort was improved by a change to leading-link forks with bonded rubber in torsion as the suspension medium, but the seat and tyres stayed as they were. The body was revised so that the rear section could be lifted up, and battery lighting was fitted.

The Gadabout continued in this style, but was now becoming upstaged by the Vespa and Lambretta, which had much sleeker lines. The days when anything with power and wheels would sell were sliding away, and buyers were starting to demand rather more than a crude scooter.

It continued for 1951, when it was joined by the Major model, which had a 197 cc 6E engine and was intended to go with the sidecar. There were a number of changes that appeared with this machine, while the smaller one ran on as it was, but at the end of the year, both were dropped. From then on, the firm concentrated on its sidecars.

Tailwind

Tandon

This was an enterprising clip-on design, which featured a disc valve and two speeds, that was seen in 1952 and built by a Mr Latta of Berkhamsted. The engine was a 49 cc two-stroke positioned above the front wheel, and the disc was driven by a peg on the overhung crankshaft.

At the other end of the shaft was a flywheel magneto, and between it and the crankcase a two-diameter roller. The entire assembly could be moved from side to side by a left-hand twistgrip, and the rollers were spring-loaded into contact with the tyre. A conical section between the two diameters ensured a smooth transition, and the whole unit functioned well.

As so many have found before and since, building one prototype may not be easy, but production is another and far more difficult matter altogether. In addition, the clip-on boom was close to becoming a moped boom, so no more was heard of this interesting device.

This firm was set up by Indian-born Devdutt Tandon to build cheap lightweights for both home and export markets, their first model appeared in 1948. Initially, it was known as the Special, but later as the Milemaster, and had a generally simple specification.

The power unit was a 122 cc Villiers twin-port 9D with three-speed, hand-change gearbox, which went into a duplex loop frame. There was no rear suspension, but at the front were telescopics with compression and rebound springs, plus a preload adjustment. The wheels had 19 in. rims and 4 in. brakes, while a pillar-mounted saddle and angular fuel tank did nothing to update the elderly lines of the engine. This had the usual twin pipes running down to a cylindrical silencer, from which one pipe ran up and back to the rear. There was a rear carrier, a prop-stand and direct lighting. The petrol tank was a little unusual in that it had a channel in its top surface for the

The two-speed Tailwind clip-on, which drove the bicycle front wheel with one of two roller diameters

frame's twin top tubes and was hung from them. In addition, the cavity was used as a toolbox with a chrome-plated lid secured by knurled nuts.

This simple model continued with few changes for some years and was joined for 1950 by another of the same capacity, but with a very different appearance. The new machine was called the Supaglide and powered by the 10D engine with its three-speed foot-change gearbox. This went into a new loop frame, which had pivoted-fork rear suspension controlled by a rubber cartridge mounted beneath the engine.

Telescopic forks were at the front, and the tank continued to have a recess in the top for the tools, but was of a much nicer shape with conventional rounded lines. The machine now had rectified lighting with the battery mounted beneath the saddle. There was a single exhaust pipe and silencer, a centre stand and a blue paint finish. The rear brake size was increased to 5 in.

For 1951 the two 122 cc models were joined by the Supaglide Supreme, which had a 197 cc 6E engine in place of the 10D, but was otherwise the same, except for a 5 in. front brake. During the year, a further 125 appeared as the competition Kangaroo, which differed from standard in gearing, a 21 in. front wheel, tyres, the 5 in. front brake and alloy mudguards. In addition, the saddle was raised and the headlight quickly detachable.

All four models continued for 1952, at the end of which the Milemaster was replaced by the Imp, which used the 10D engine in a rigid frame with telescopic forks and wheels with 5 in. brakes. The two Supaglide models continued, with just a change to the 5 in. front brake for the smaller one, but the Kangaroo had rather more alteration.

It went into a new frame, the rear fork being controlled by conventional spring units and the saddle replaced by a trials seat. In other respects, it was as before and was joined by the Kangaroo Supreme, which had the 6E engine. The same frame type was also used with road cycle parts to create the Imp Supreme.

This was one of only two models to continue for 1954, but with an engine change to an 8E. The other was the Imp, which had a similar alteration to a 12D. The Supaglide and Kangaroo models were dropped.

To make the range up, there were four other models, the Imp Supreme De Luxe being much as the basic model, but with four speeds, a dualseat and extra equipment. It kept to the 8E engine, which was also used for the Scrambler. This had Earles-type leading-link front suspension, an open exhaust, no lights and a racing seat.

The remaining models were larger in capacity and used the best of the Imp cycle parts with a choice of engines. For the Monarch, which was

The 1948 Tandon with its 9D engine and crude tank, built more for export than home use

Above **The competition Tandon Kangaroo with 10D engine and rubber-block rear suspension, as built for 1951–2**

Below **Tandon Imp introduced for 1953, still with the 10D engine, but in a rigid frame**

initially called the Sprite, it was the 224 cc Villiers 1H unit, but the Twin Supreme had the 242 cc British Anzani twin with its rotary inlet valve.

Both had the frame improved for 1955, when it was also used by a new model, listed as the Viscount and fitted with the 322 cc British Anzani twin engine. All three were given full-width hubs front and rear with much needed 6 in. brakes and short leading-link forks, which also went on the Imp Supreme De Luxe. The other Imps continued, but the smaller one had an engine change to the 147 cc 30C unit. They were joined by the Imp Supreme Special, which had the 8E engine, three speeds, short leading links, rear suspension and direct lighting to reduce costs. For competition, the Scrambler continued, but with a 7E engine, and was joined by a 250 Scrambler, which used the British Anzani twin unit fitted with stub pipes.

However, time and finance were running out for the Tandon, and late in 1955 there was an order to wind them up. They had always operated on a knife edge, so it did not take much to push them over. This was not the end of the name, however, for they were back by the middle of 1956 with a simple two-model range.

This comprised the Imp Supreme Special and the Monarch, the former being fitted with the 8E engine with three speeds. The pivoted-fork frame had the short leading-link forks, a dualseat, wheels with 5 in. brakes and direct lighting. Four speeds and battery lighting were options, but standard on the Monarch with its 1H engine. Otherwise, this was similar, except for the use of the full-width hubs with the 6 in. brakes.

These models remained in the lists until 1959, when production finally ceased for good.

Teagle

Triumph

This was a clip-on engine made in Cornwall and first seen late in 1952. It was derived from one designed for garden power tools, so it was light and simple, and the company saw the powered bicycle as a method of expanding their market.

The 50 cc two-stroke engine was largely a single alloy casting, which formed the cylinder and crankcase, with an iron liner and separate head. An overhung crankshaft with forged alloy rod were used, the one running on the other for the big-end. The crankcase was open on both sides, with a bearing housing on one side and a simple door on the other. A drive roller went on the mainshaft, as did the Wipac flywheel magneto, which incorporated cooling fans.

The engine sat over the rear wheel, the cylinder being laid back close to the horizontal, and had its fuel tank mounted above it. The whole unit was pivoted, so it could be lifted clear of the tyre, and was spring-loaded to it when in contact.

It was 1954 before there was any more news of the Teagle and it remained on the market for some two years before the moped overtook it and all its brothers.

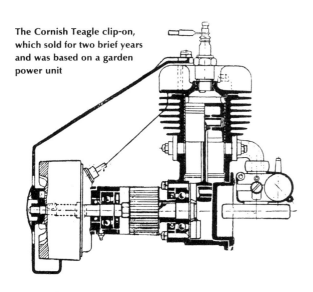

The Cornish Teagle clip-on, which sold for two brief years and was based on a garden power unit

Triumph were the first firm to announce their post-war range, and the news came in March 1945, well before the end of the war. Not only were they first off the mark but, unlike many others, their machines were not the wartime ones with a new civilian finish.

One reason for this was the vertical twin range, which they had introduced in the late 1930s and which set a style that the major firms were all to copy. However, Triumph had a ten-year start over the opposition, which they exploited to the full in their advertisements.

There were five models in the range, as announced, one single and four twins, the latter being sports and touring versions in two sizes, but only three models were to go into production. The single was one of the pair not destined to reach the public, although at first sight, it should have been the obvious choice, as it was the wartime model with a new paint finish.

As the army machine, it had been the 343 cc 3HW, based firmly on the pre-war 3H with ohv engine, four-speed gearbox, rigid frame and girder forks. In army service, it gained a one-piece head and rocker box cast in iron, and it was intended to keep this for the post-war model. After the announcement, it was realized that it made more sense for the firm to concentrate on the more profitable twins and leave 350 cc singles to other marques, so the 3H never reached production.

The two 499 cc twins were the Speed Twin and Tiger 100, and were much as they had been in 1939. There were changes, however, and the major one for the cycle parts was the adoption of telescopic front forks of a neat, slim style. These were based on a wartime design and had hydraulic damping, while the front wheel diameter was reduced to 19 in. to match the rear.

The engine was the trend-setting Edward Turner design, which had contrived to look like a twin-port single at its launch. It was compact, light and went well, so had few post-war changes. The design was based on a built-up crankshaft, the two shaft forgings being bolted to a central flywheel and the assembly supported by a ball race on each side.

The aluminium crankcase was split on the vertical centre line and carried the two camshafts high up, the exhaust being ahead of, and the inlet behind, the crankshaft line. They were gear driven via an intermediate gear, with a train in the timing chest on the right. This extended to the rear to drive the magneto. Unlike the pre-war design, which had a mag-dyno, the post-war version had a separate dynamo clamped to the front of the crankcase, where it was gear driven from the exhaust camshaft.

An iron block was bolted to the crankcase, with the two light-alloy pistons moving in unison in it, and to this was bolted the one-piece, iron cylinder head. The rocker box was in two parts, each an alloy casting, with access caps to the valve adjusters in the outer rocker ends. The pushrods ran up within tubes placed on the engine centre line and forward and aft of the block. Unlike the pre-war engine, the rockers were lubricated from the oil return line. This oil drained down through drillings and the pushrod tubes, which no longer had external drain pipes running to them.

The Tiger 100 engine had a higher compression ratio than the Speed Twin, and its internals were

polished, but otherwise the two were the same. On the outside, the sports model had a slightly larger carburettor, but its exhaust was no longer special, being the same set of parts as used by the tourer, including the tubular silencers.

Virtually all the transmission and cycle side were common to both models, only the finish and the petrol and oil tanks differing. The transmission was by the very typical Triumph four-speed gearbox with a foot-change that operated in the reverse manner to most others of that time. The multi-plate clutch continued to stick first thing in the morning and was housed, together with the primary drive, in a handsome alloy chaincase.

A rigid frame with telescopic front forks was used with wheels incorporating offset hubs and single-leading-shoe drum brakes. The oil tank went on the right, under the saddle, and the Tiger 100 had a wing-nut cap, as did some early post-war Speed Twins. The battery was on the left to match the tank, and the toolbox between the frame chainstays, on the right.

Although the speedometer was mounted on the top of the forks, the other instruments, plus the light switch, went into a tank-top panel, as in pre-war days. The tank itself was chrome plated with lined, painted panels. The machine's finish was the famous Amaranth red for the Speed Twin, and black with silver mudguards and tank panels for the Tiger 100.

These two models were to be matched by two smaller ones with 349 cc engines, to be known as the 3T and Tiger 85. On the face of it, they would

Nice 1947 Triumph Tiger 100 on test with sprung hub to enliven the ride

Smallest of the twins was the 3T, and this was the 1948 version

have been virtually the same models with revised engine dimensions but, in fact, the differences went much deeper.

The 349 cc engine used a wartime crankshaft design, in which the two halves were clamped into a central flywheel and, thanks to this, one-piece connecting rods could be used. They retained their plain big-ends, and the crank assembly still turned in a drive-side ball race, but there was a bush for the timing side.

Most of the rest of the lower half, and the valve gear, was as for the larger engine, but both head and block differed. Their fixing was by long through-studs with top bolts, which could be seen quite easily from either side of the engine. At the top, the head and rocker boxes were cast in one with alloy covers for each pair of valves and rocker adjusters. This also was easy enough to spot.

There were other differences, too, with a smaller carburettor and changes to both exhaust pipes and silencers. The gearbox remained the same, as did the forks and a number of the detail fitments, but the frame itself was smaller and lighter, which affected some of the parts that were bolted to it.

In the event, only the 3T went into production, having the same finish as the Speed Twin, but in black. The Tiger 85 would have mirrored the larger sports model in black and silver, but it made sense, at that time of acute shortages, for the firm to concentrate on the larger models.

With the Government screaming for production and exports, there were few changes over the next few years, but for 1947 there came the famous sprung hub. This was listed as an option, for it replaced the standard rear wheel and, at first sight, appeared to be a rather large, full-width hub.

This it was, but inside was a slider box, which allowed the wheel to move in a curve, centred on the gearbox sprocket, with a total of 2 in. of movement. Also within the hub were the compression and rebound springs, under considerable stress and preload, while to each side were caged ball races and their inner and outer cups. Due to the size of the hub, the rear brake was increased to an 8 in. drum, and it was necessary to take the speedometer drive from the gearbox instead of the rear wheel.

Otherwise, the range ran on with its three models, although during 1948 the 3T had the fixing of its head and block changed to that used by the larger engine. Rather more exciting for that year was the news that Triumph were to produce a real racing motorcycle in limited numbers. This was based on the machine used by Ernie Lyons to win the 1946 Manx Grand Prix and had a Tiger 100 engine with alloy head and block. It was called the Grand Prix.

The alloy top half came from a wartime generator unit and, due to this origin, was of a square format. This was to suit the enclosing cowl of the generator, and the castings retained the small bosses for its fixing screws. The layout also dic-

The Triumph Grand Prix, as introduced in 1948 with alloy top half and external oil filter in front of the gearbox

tated that both inlet and exhaust ports were parallel to each other, but despite this, twin Amal carburettors were crammed in and fed by a remotely-mounted float chamber.

Otherwise, the engine looked stock, but it had racing camshafts and magneto, a blanked off dynamo drive and a raised compression ratio. The standard gearbox was given close ratios and, in the style of the times, the primary drive was fully exposed, having a light top guard only. The cycle

parts were essentially standard and included the sprung hub, but the front brake size was increased to 8 in. There were alloy mudguards and wheel rims, a bigger oil tank and megaphone exhausts, but a saddle and rear pad remained.

On the circuits, the Grand Prix proved fast, but fragile, so it was competitive with the Manx Norton of the day while it kept going. The handling was not so good, the hub often being more of a hindrance than an asset, so as soon as the Norton

The sporting TR5 Triumph Trophy with the die-cast head and barrel used from 1951 in the short-wheelbase, rigid frame

Nice line of early 1950s Triumph twins

gained its Featherbed frame, there was no contest. In addition, engine technology moved on, pool petrol disappeared, and within two or three years, the GP was no longer able to stay with the front runners. By the end of 1950 production ceased and the firm concentrated on what it did best, building good road motorcycles.

Prior to that, it was 1949 before there was any real change to these, and then it was mainly cosmetic with the appearance of the famous nacelle for the front forks. This enclosed the upper part and extended forward to carry the headlight unit, while its upper surface accommodated the instruments and switches. This removed the need for the tank-top instrument panel, so its place was taken by an optional parcel grid.

That same year saw another model join the range as the TR5 Trophy, which was aimed at the sporting off-road and trials rider. The design was based on the machines used by the firm for the ISDT, hence the model name, but both engine and cycle parts were special to some degree.

The engine was mainly Speed Twin, but above the crankcase were the alloy head and block used by the Grand Prix, but with much lower-ratio pistons within. There were also softer cams, only a single carburettor and a lovely siamezed exhaust system, which curled round to a waist-level silencer on the left.

This unit went into a special frame with boxed-in front engine plates, and the wheelbase was reduced, so parts were a tight fit. The four-speed gearbox was used and the sprung hub was an option. The mudguards were short and sporting.

A 20 in. front wheel and 4 in. section rear tyre were fitted, along with quickly-detachable lights, so there was no nacelle. A saddle and pillion pad looked after the seating, and the finish was in chrome, silver and black to produce a very smart, dual-purpose machine.

The range had a revised gearbox for 1950, when the tank styling was altered to four horizontal bars, and an additional, larger model appeared as the 649 cc 6T Thunderbird. This took the Turner twin on to its next logical step, the increase in capacity coming mainly from a larger bore, although the stroke went up a little as well. The general details were as for the 5T, and both engines had the external oil drain pipes, as in pre-war days. For the rest, it was the same gearbox, frame, forks and cycle parts.

Changes for 1951 were limited to the sports models, as little altered on the three sizes of tourer. For the T100 and TR5, there was a new die-cast head and barrel in light alloy with close-pitched fins. The exhaust ports were splayed out, as they always had been for the T100, but this change meant a new exhaust pipe was needed for the TR5. The T100 also had a dualseat fitted as standard, it having been an option the year before, and all models had new filler caps and the parcel grid fitted as standard.

The Grand Prix was not continued for 1951, but in its place was an official racing kit for the T100. This included high-ratio pistons and better camshafts, along with twin carburettors, all the associ-

ated pipes and controls, megaphones and a big oil tank. It did the job well and allowed the firm to concentrate on production of their road models.

The 3T was quietly dropped at the end of the year, for it was never popular nor very profitable to the firm. The other four models and the race kit continued for 1952, with an SU carburettor for the 6T and little other alteration. It was much the same for the twins in 1953, although the 5T was fitted with an alternator and the race kit was replaced by a complete model in the form of the T100c. This was effectively the same thing, but was supplied with silencers and full electrics, as well as the tuned internals.

There was a second new model for 1953 and it was to lead to many versions, including a whole range for BSA. The newcomer was the 149 cc Terrier, which was aimed at the lightweight market, then the province of the Bantam, Enfield and a hoard of machines using the small Villiers engines.

The Terrier had an ohv unit-construction engine with four-speed gearbox. The iron cylinder was inclined forward and topped by an alloy head with integral rocker box, while the timing gear was of the simplest, with two gears, a camshaft, tappets and pushrods. The crankcase was a little unusual in that its vertical split line was on the left, so the pressed-up crankshaft went in from that side, while the drive main went into a casting

that acted as a door and the chaincase inner.

The crankcase also contained the gearbox, with a single cover on the right for both gears and timing side, plus an outer cover to conceal the gearchange mechanism. An alternator went on the left-hand end of the crankshaft in the primary chaincase, and the points for the coil ignition were in a housing behind the barrel. Their cam was skew-gear driven from the crankshaft, and the same shaft drove the twin-plunger pump for the dry-sump oil system. An Amal supplied the mixture, and the exhaust system ran low down on the right.

This engine unit went into a loop frame with plunger rear and telescopic front suspension, neither of which had any damping. Construction was simple, but the front end looks mirrored those of the twins with a nacelle. The wheels had offset hubs and 19 in. rims, while the rider had a saddle. The oil tank was beneath this, on the right in true British style, with the battery housing on the left to match it.

For 1954 the Terrier was joined by the larger 199 cc Cub, which had an upswept exhaust system as standard and a shell blue finish for the tank and mudguards in place of the overall Amaranth red of the Terrier. Both models were given a mechanical gear indicator and had common cycle parts, while the Cub had a dual-seat as standard.

Left **The Triumph Terrier single, at its launch at Earls Court late in 1952, with its typical marque line and plunger frame**

Right **Checking over a 1956 6T Thunderbird for fork and headrace wear. Front brake also needs attention with that cam-lever angle**

Other changes that year were to the 6T, which switched to alternator electrics, and to the T100. The latter was joined by a larger 649 cc version, listed as the Tiger 110, and both went into a pivoted-fork frame with dualseat and an 8 in. front brake to arrest progress. The other models stayed as they were, except for the T100c, which was dropped, but for 1955 all the twins went into the pivoted-fork frame and several had internal changes. For the singles, the Cub had the low-level exhaust system fitted as standard.

For 1956 the T110 was fitted with an alloy cylinder head and joined by the TR6, which used the same 649 cc engine in the TR5 cycle parts. Both now had higher-performance engines, so the old power style that suited the TR5 both on and off road so well had gone. The singles also had changes, the most noticeable being to the Cub, which went to 16 in. wheels.

The Cub continued alone for 1957, for the Terrier was dropped, but in a pivoted-fork frame with damped front forks. It was joined by the T20C competition model, which used the same frame, but had an upswept exhaust and came with trials tyres and a crankcase shield, although it retained the lights and headlamp nacelle.

There was also a new tank badge for the Cub models, and this was fitted on all the twins as well. In addition, the 5T, 6T and TR5 had a full-width front hub, and the TR6 an 8 in. front brake. They

were joined by one new model, which was the first of the unit-construction twins and listed as the model 21 or 3TA.

The new machine had a twin-cylinder, 349 cc engine, much as its predecessors, with a bolted-on flywheel, twin gear-driven camshafts, plain big-ends and separate rocker boxes. Ignition was by coil, with the points and distributor in a housing behind the iron block and driven by skew gears from the inlet camshaft, which also drove the oil pump.

The crankcase extended rearwards to carry the four-speed gearbox, while an Amal supplied the mixture and an alternator went on the left-hand end of the crankshaft. This drove the clutch with a duplex chain within a polished alloy case, and much of the transmission was stock conventional Triumph.

The engine unit went into a simple loop frame with pivoted-fork rear and telescopic front suspension. The fixtures and fittings followed Triumph practice in the main, with a nacelle for the headlamp and the new badge on the sides of the tank. The wheels had 17 in. rims and 7 in. brakes, the front one in a full-width hub, but the real feature of the model was its rear enclosure. This was extensive and, thanks to its shape, quickly became known as the 'bathtub', a name it was to keep through the years.

With this new model, the firm began to plan a

Triumph Tiger Cub in its 1958 form, before it was given a rear skirt

Below A 1959 Triumph Tigress TW2 scooter enjoying cobbles in the rain, but better than queueing for a bus

The two Cubs ran on with detail changes, which included a move to Zenith carburettors during the year.

At the end of 1958 the 5T and TR5 were dropped, the former being replaced by the 5TA. This was simply a bored-out version of the 3TA, finished in the traditional Amaranth red, and it kept the Speed Twin name. Of the older models, the T100, T110, 6T and TR6 ran on much as before, but were joined by one of the most exciting Triumphs of all time, the T120 Bonneville.

This was, in essence, a twin-carburettor T110 with the optional splayed-port head fitted as standard and was the final development of the original twin for Edward Turner. He maintained that 650 cc and 6500 rpm were as much as one could expect from the layout without excessive vibration problems. The Bonneville soon became a legend.

However, the Bonneville and the 5TA were not the only new models for 1959, as there were more, plus changes to the Cubs. Many of the latter were detail changes only, but for the road model, there was also some partial enclosure with rear skirts, which followed the lines of the unit twins, but not to the same extent. For the single, the rear wheel was left more exposed and there were cut-outs for the oil tank and toolbox.

The final new models were scooters and replicas of those in the Sunbeam range (see page 168),

new range, so there were few changes for the pre-unit models in 1958. All the twins were given the slickshift gearchange, where the clutch was withdrawn by the gear pedal movement, but this was never very popular with riders. The two Tiger models were given full-width front hubs for their 8 in. brakes, the same hub being fitted to the TR6.

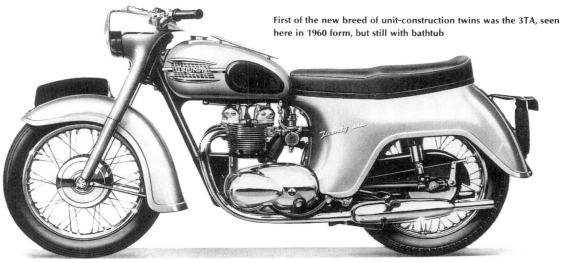

First of the new breed of unit-construction twins was the 3TA, seen here in 1960 form, but still with bathtub

Flagship of the Triumph line was the T120 Bonneville, which lost the nacelle for 1960 when it gained a new frame and an alternator

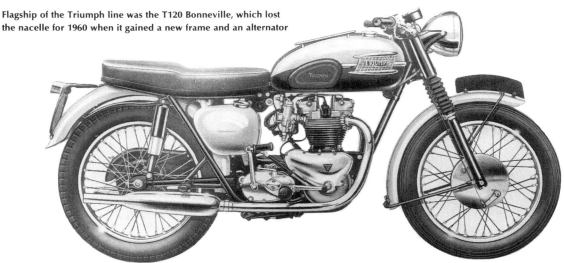

except for colour and badges. They were called Tigress with the Triumph badge, the single being listed as the TS1 and the twins as the TW2 and electric-start TW2S. All were in a shell blue colour. The single did not reach the lists until 1960.

For the new decade, Triumph kept nearly all their models from the previous year, but the T100 and T20C were both replaced. The first became the T100A and had a higher-powered version of the unit-construction engine with energy-transfer ignition. It used the same set of cycle parts, but in a black and ivory finish.

The T20S also had energy-transfer ignition, as well as direct lighting, no battery and a small, off-road-style headlamp. The front forks were heavy-duty and based on those of the 3TA with gaiters, while there were other detail improvements. The Cub changed to 17 in. wheels, and during the year, both models had a major engine change.

This concerned the crankcase split line, which moved to the cylinder centre-line, while the internals stayed as they were.

The scooters continued as they were, as did the 3TA and 5TA, while all the 649 cc models had a new duplex frame. The first version of this had problems, but these were soon overcome, and all four models also had revised forks. The 6T and T110 were both fitted with the 'bathtub' rear enclosure and its associated deep front mudguard, while the T120 lost its nacelle in favour of a separate headlamp shell. The T110, T120 and TR6 all retained their magnetos, but went over to an alternator to charge the battery.

Thus Triumph entered the new decade with a strong range, which became fully unit-construction in 1963. Later came the trauma of the Meriden sit-in, the co-operative and the difficult times of the 1980s.

Turner

This machine was one of the eccentricities of the motorcycle world and made its brief appearance in Brussels in April 1946. Its full name was the Turner Byvan, but there seems to be no record as to whether or not Turner was the builder, nor are there any details of his background.

The machine was an oddity because it had front-wheel-drive. The engine unit was a 125 cc Royal Enfield Flying Flea, but turned round so that the gearbox was at the front. The cylinder was special, having the carburettor on the right and the exhaust at the front, while the whole assembly ran in reverse to its normal direction.

This only called for the retiming of the Miller flywheel magneto. The gearbox sprocket drove the wheel by chain. A small petroil tank sat above the engine, which was started by a hand-operated recoil mechanism attached in place of the kick-start lever. The gear lever remained hand-operated in a gate and was positioned close to the twistgrip.

Special pressed-steel front forks carried the complete motor package, which had a small headlight in front of it. The whole of the remainder of the machine, from headstock to rear number plate, was fully enclosed to form a large parcel holder. There was a saddle on the top for the rider and a lid for access, but otherwise it simply acted as a carrier and held the rear wheel.

The machine had motorcycle-style spoked wheels, but with fairly fat tyres and was equipped with twin prop-stands. The finish was in bright red and the machine was run on the day it was shown, performing well enough on steepish Belgium slopes and cobbles.

It was far too radical, even for Europe, which was to have its share of show oddities over the years, so no more was heard of it.

The strange front-wheel-drive Turner Byvan, of 1946, being tried out in a Brussels street

Velocette

After the war, Velocette continued with their tradition of black and gold singles of high performance with ohv or ohc engines, and the range was little different from 1939. Missing were the KTS and, at first, the racing KTT, while the GTP only appeared briefly as an export batch of machines. Present and correct were the three sizes of M-range ohv models and the KSS.

The GTP had been in the range since 1930 and had a 249 cc two-stroke engine with throttle-controlled pump lubrication. The small post-war batch differed from its predecessors in having magneto ignition rather than coil, but the cycle side remained as it was, with a rigid frame and girder forks.

The ohv models were the 248 cc MOV, 349 cc MAC and 495 cc MSS. All had their roots in the 1930s, the first appearing in 1933 and the others following at the rate of one per year. All were similar in engine layout, with the camshaft set high up in the timing side, where it was driven by helical gears, which also drove the magneto.

The crankcase was typically Velocette, being narrow with the mains close in to the flywheels, and with the primary chain equally near the bearings. From this layout came the need for the gearbox sprocket to be outboard of the clutch, and for the clutch to have its own special design with a lift mechanism that few ever got to understand.

The very stiff crankcase carried an equally stiff crankshaft assembly within its walls, the cylinder and head being held to it by long bolts. The valve gear was fully enclosed, and engine lubrication was by dry sump, the gear oil pump being driven from the crankshaft. An Amal carburettor supplied the mixture, while a Miller dynamo was clamped to the front of the crankcase and was belt driven to provide the volts.

The four-speed gearbox had foot-change and a none-too-helpful kickstart ratio. The mechanics were housed in a cradle frame, which was improved from the pre-war one by the use of wartime developments for the army. The MSS had a heavier frame than the other two, and it also had a vertical seat tube, which made it easy to spot.

The frame was rigid, and at the front were Webb girder forks with friction shock absorbers and a steering damper. Both wheels had offset hubs and all used 19 in. rims. Tyre sizes were 3.25 in. front and rear for the MOV and MAC, but 3.50 front and 4.00 in. rear for the MSS. The brake sizes also differed, with 6 in. drums for the two smaller models and 7 in. versions for the largest.

The cycle parts were very much as British tradition required, with a saddle, oil tank beneath it on the right, and battery on the left to match it. The toolbox went above the right upper chainstay, and a pillion pad and footrests were included in the standard specification.

The KSS used the MSS cycle parts with its own 348 cc overhead-camshaft engine. This dated back to the 1920s, so by 1946 it was a very well developed assembly in a classic mould. Its design was based on the narrow crankcase common to the marque, and the iron barrel carried an alloy head with integral cambox. Thus, the camshaft rockers were fully enclosed, with access covers to the valves and their coil springs. The cam drive was by shaft and bevels, using a hunting tooth to spread the loads, and the right mainshaft also drove the oil pump and, via a chain, the rear-mounted magneto.

The engine was the major item to distinguish the KSS from its ohv brothers, but the wheels also differed, with 3.00 × 21 in. front and 3.25 × 20 in. rear tyres being used. The need for a high level of skill to set the engine up was reflected in the model's price, which was the highest of the road machines. It would only be exceeded by its racing cousin, the KTT, for 1947.

For that year, the other four models ran on, while the KTT reappeared, very much in its 1939 form, as the Mk VIII. Its overhead-camshaft engine had both head and barrel in alloy with massive finning. The valves were held shut by hairpin springs, but the head casting was extended to enclose them, while the rockers had return springs. They were mounted on eccentric pins for setting the gaps and were well lubricated.

The KTT bottom half was similar to the KSS and the others with a narrow crankcase, but with the parts designed for road racing. The four-speed gearbox had close ratios and some resemblance to the road units, but the frame was very different. It retained the cradle loop, but at the rear was pivoted-fork suspension controlled by oleo-pneumatic units. As in pre-war days, these used air for suspension and oil for damping, but were never easy to set correctly. At the front were Webb girders, and both wheels had high-tensile steel rims and conical alloy hubs with 7 in. brakes. There was a saddle and rear pad for the rider, a large oil tank and a rev-counter driven from the magneto sprocket.

There was no change to the range for 1948, but all the road models had to dispense with the girder forks, as they were no longer to be had from Webb. In their place, Velocette fitted Dowty Oleomatic telescopics, which used the same principles as the rear legs on the KTT. This model kept its girders, while the others had minor changes to suit the new forks. The two smaller M models also had their front brake size increased to 7 in.

At the end of the year, Velocette dropped the expensive KSS with its assembly problems, along with the MOV and MSS. The MAC continued as the most popular of the ohv singles, along with a limited number of KTT racers, but the sensation of the range for 1949 was the totally new LE.

This really broke with the firm's tradition, for it had a 149 cc, side-valve, horizontally-opposed, twin-cylinder engine with water cooling among its many radical features. It also had shaft drive, hand-lever starting, a monocoque frame and good weather protection. It was a very quiet-running machine.

The LE was aimed at the mass market and incorporated a host of ideas and ideals which, it was said, would ensure success in this fickle area of sales. Other firms had been along this path in the past and found that there were many obstacles. It was not until the scooter came along that there was much of a breakthrough, and it took the Honda Cub scooterette to reach a true world-wide market.

The Velocette came close, but was rather expensive, partly because the firm insisted on doing the job properly, as was their way. This led to looks without style, handling that the mass market would never appreciate, and too much of the mechanics on view. The social scene was no help either, for it was to be well into the 1950s before the scooter became accepted, and the LE was always too much of a motorcycle to fit the image.

The machine, one of the few really new post-war models to go into long-term production, had a side-valve engine to keep the width down, which seems odd in comparison with modern flat-twin BMW or Honda Gold Wing motors. However, in 1949 motorcycles were slim, so the LE had a small side-valve engine.

It was designed as one with the rest of the mechanics, so engine, gearbox, drive shaft and rear bevel box were effectively a unit, which was mounted to the frame. The engine had a built-up crankshaft, which went into the barrel crankcase from the front. There were iron barrels and alloy heads with tiny 10 mm sparking plugs, and the camshaft sat above the crankshaft with tappets to operate the valves.

A combined generator and ignition unit went on the front of the crankshaft, and just behind it a worm drove the pump of the wet-sump oil system. The camshaft was driven by gears at the rear of the crankcase, and there was no water pump, as the system relied on the thermo-syphon principle.

A special multi-jet Amal carburettor, with tiny jets, supplied the mixture to a long induction pipe, while the two exhaust pipes ran round to a common silencer box under the engine. It was very efficient, and the low noise level of the machine was one of its most outstanding features.

Unlike most flat-twins, the LE did not have its clutch hung on the back of the crankshaft, but drove this via helical reduction gears. These also moved the drive-line centre up and over, ready for the three-speed, all indirect gearbox. This was controlled by a hand lever working in a gate on the right, in car fashion, so neutral could be selected directly from top gear.

The hand-start lever lay below the gear lever and was connected to an internal quadrant via levers and shafts. The quadrant meshed with a gear in front of the clutch to give primary starting, and the lever was linked to the centre stand to retract this should the rider have left it down inadvertently. From the gearbox, the drive shaft ran down the left leg of the pivoted rear fork, having a universal joint at the front end. At the rear was a bevel box, to which the brake shoes were mounted.

The engine unit was hung from a frame made from sheet steel, the main part being a beam of inverted U-section, to which a massive rear mudguard was welded. At the front, the headstock was bolted in place, with the toolbox set just aft of it and welded into the top of the main pressing. Behind it, the petrol tank was bolted into place under the pressing and then came the battery chamber. This was open at the top, with the saddle above it and arranged to tip forward to give access.

The rear body had mountings for the suspension units, but in place of the usual bolt or stud, there was a slot on each side. This allowed the units to be laid down or made more upright to vary the stiffness of the suspension. The remainder of the frame comprised a tubular assembly at the front, which carried the radiator, two footboards that were bolted to it, and a steel pressing bolted to the back of the gearbox. This supported the rear ends of the footboards and provided the mounting for the rear fork pivot bearings.

The front suspension was provided by undamped telescopic forks, but these turned in taper-roller head races, a rare find in a small-capacity machine at that time. They carried a massive front mudguard, which partly enclosed them, and both wheels had 19 in. rims and offset hubs with 5 in. brakes.

This then was the revolutionary LE Velocette, which sold well, but not quite well enough to allow the firm to get the price down. They also had problems with it at the factory, for it needed a new production line and techniques far removed from those that had coped with the singles. It really was an extraordinary achievement by the

Goodman family, who always were Velocette, with their limited resources, and if they had had a BSA or Triumph purse they might have succeeded with it.

There were no changes for 1950, which was the last year for the KTT, and only the LE and MAC went forward for 1951. Both had changes, the first becoming the Mk II with its capacity raised to 192 cc, along with a good number of internal engine improvements. For the MAC, there was a change of front fork to a Velocette design using springs and damping oil in a conventional manner.

In June 1951 the MAC was further modified with a new alloy cylinder and head, and a cleaner timing cover. The new head included full valve-gear enclosure with a deep well in its top, into which the rocker assembly was bolted with a simple lid to complete the job. The barrel was of the Alfin type with the alloy fins cast on to the iron liner.

The two machines continued in this form for 1952, but for 1953 there was another MAC introduced with a sprung frame. This was similar to the rigid one, but with the chainstays formed as a loop to the rear. From each rose an ear made from pressings, and these were slotted for the attachment of the rear spring units. Thus, as on the LE, the suspension could be made hard or soft by altering the unit angle.

The rear fork was built up, each of the two legs being clamped to a spindle, which turned in bushes in a frame lug. Thus, the fork had to be aligned on assembly, but the arrangement worked

The Velocette MAC for 1951 when it gained marque forks and changed to an alloy top half

The MSS Velocette in 1954 with adjustable rear suspension and odd dualseat

well, as long as it was greased regularly. To go with the new frame, the gearbox had its end cover cleaned up and the change mechanism improved. The cycle parts were amended to suit the new frame and included a two-level dualseat. There was an alloy centre stand and a prop-stand, and both petrol and oil tanks were altered.

The rigid MAC and the LE continued, the former being unchanged and the second altered with an external oil filter. This was bolted to the right-hand cylinder head, while on the chassis side, the start

lever was no longer linked to the centre stand.

For 1954 the two MAC models and the LE ran on much as they were, but were joined by a new version of the old MSS model. The newcomer's appearance was much as that of the sprung MAC, for similar cycle parts were used and the engine was on the same lines. Unlike the old one, it had an equal bore and stroke, and alloy head and barrel, so was a much sharper performer than in the past. The top end differed from the MAC in that the valves were closed by hairpin springs and

the head was machined off just above their wells. The rocker box was separate, with the rockers held in split housings, but the valve lifter remained in the crankcase.

There was another 499 cc model for 1955 in the form of the Scrambler, which used a tuned MSS engine with a TT carburettor and open exhaust pipe. The frame and forks had minor changes to suit, plus alloy mudguards, an undershield, competition tyres and a smaller fuel tank. The other singles also had minor changes, while the LE gained an induction-pipe heater, using the cooling water, and an option of a two-level dualseat. During the year, the twin switched to a die-cast alloy rear fork, which replaced the original arrangement.

There were more new models for 1956, but the LE carried on as it was for most of the year before its wheels were changed to 18 in. rims and full-width hubs, while the carburettor became an Amal Monobloc. The rigid MAC was dropped, and the sprung one and the MSS ran on as they were, as did the Scrambler. An Endurance model appeared, which was based on the Scrambler, but was fitted with lights and was street legal. However, the best news for Velocette single enthusiasts was the appearance of the Viper and Venom models.

These were high-performance sports models with 349 or 499 cc engines, $7\frac{1}{2}$ in. front brakes, full-width hubs, and a deep headlamp shell that carried the instruments in its top surface. The Viper engine differed from the MAC in that it had a shorter stroke and copied the design of the MSS unit, on which the Venom was based. Both sports models used the normal pivoted-fork frame, forks and 7 in. rear brake.

All the singles changed to a Monobloc carburettor and single-level dualseat, while the dynamo was driven by a V-belt in place of the older flat one. Early in the year, a second Scrambler appeared with the Viper engine in the same cycle parts as the 500, and later in the year, the deep headlamp shell went on to the MAC and MSS.

The range continued as it was for 1957 and was joined by the 192 cc Valiant. This had an engine based on the LE, but with air-cooling, overhead valves and twin carburettors. It was coupled to a four-speed gearbox with foot-change, and the whole unit was mounted in a duplex tubular loop frame. The forks and wheels came from the LE, and the engine unit was enclosed by a bonnet, which left the top halves out in the breeze. There was a dualseat for the rider and a good range of fitments, but the machine came to the market at a high price for a 200 and without the performance of a 250. Many felt that a revamp of

Left **The 192 cc LE Velocette on test early in 1955 when its water cooling was hardly needed**

Right **Velocette Venom, as tested in 1958, although the number appears on another Venom test in 1956 – naughty**

the MOV would have been much better and more suited to the impending capacity restriction for learners.

The whole range continued much as it was for 1958, with one addition. This was a Mk III version of the LE, which had the four-speed gearbox from the Valiant with foot-change and kickstart. In addition, the speedometer, ammeter, and light switch were moved from the top of the legshield into a deeper headlamp shell, which was shrouded with a cowl to the forks. The Mk II continued in production for that year, but then was dropped.

For 1959 the Valiant was joined by the Veeline, which had a neat dolphin fairing with a good sized screen as standard. The LE continued in Mk III form only, and the four single-cylinder road models were fitted with an enclosure around their lower engine half and gearbox. This was made in fibreglass and cleaned up the lines of the machine, while allowing the firm to omit the polishing of timing and gearbox covers. The two scrambles models were given a revised frame, and there was a Willow green colour option for the road machines and two-tone for the Viper and Venom.

For the new decade, there were two more models, listed as the Viper and Venom Clubman. Both came without the lower enclosure, but with a selection of extras from the options list to suit the needs of the sporting rider. The rest of the range ran on as it was and would do so for another decade, with even more variations on both the flat-twin and sporting singles.

The nadir was shared by the Viceroy and Vogue, but the zenith was the fabulous Thruxton.

Sporting S501 Steib sidecar hitched to a 1958 Venom during a road test

The 1959 Velocette Valiant Veeline with air-cooled, flat-twin engine based on the LE unit

The MSS and other models gained extensive side covers for 1959, but kept their own line – again, a 1956 number on a later model

Rather hard work for a 1959 MAC coupled to a Surrey Rambler sidecar, but it managed

The 1960 Velocette scrambler model was offered in both engine sizes, this one being the larger

Velosolex

This was a French design of power-cycle, which sold in enormous numbers in its own country and, for a while, was built under licence in Britain. It always came as a complete machine, although the design was effectively a clip-on, which drove the front tyre by roller.

The engine was a 45 cc two-stroke with upright iron cylinder and alloy head incorporating a decompressor, and the unit straddled the front wheel. The crankshaft had an overhung big-end and carried the drive roller in the middle, and the flywheel magneto on its left-hand end. Both inlet and exhaust ports were at the rear of the cylinder, with the transfer at the front, and the exhaust was piped to a small drum silencer.

The petroil tank was also drum-shaped and went to the right of the crankcase to match the magneto. Both were used to carry the registration number. A membrane fuel pump was used to raise the fuel to the carburettor and was activated by the pressure pulses in the crankcase. The carburettor, mounted behind the cylinder, was unusual in not having a float chamber. Instead, there was, in effect, a weir return to the tank and a simple main jet feed for the engine.

The engine unit was carried in plates so that it could be spring-loaded to drive the tyre or held free from it. The rest of the machine was pure bicycle, but in a French style, for it had an open frame with a single curved tube that ran down from the headstock, curved round above the bottom bracket and rose to the saddle. Smaller tubes supported the bracket and formed the chainstays, while the fittings were pure cycle.

There was only one control, which was a trigger connected to the throttle with a link to the decompressor. To suit the nature of the model type and its home country, it was spring-loaded to fully open, as Gallic logic dictated that it would spend all of its time in that position. It made the machine extremely easy to ride. There was no fuel tap, only a choke for brief use when starting from cold.

The Velosolex appeared in France in 1946 and was an immediate success. Two years later, a few reached Britain, and gradually British components were phased in, production being carried out by Solex in North London. This was well underway by 1949, and there were detail changes in 1951 and 1956. Otherwise, the model continued to be offered until 1957, when British production ceased.

It never enjoyed the sheer volume of demand as in its home country, where it continued for many a year to carry people from all walks of life around the French countryside and towns.

The Velosolex, which was built in vast numbers in its French homeland and in reasonable quantities in Britain

Villiers

The Villiers engine had been part of the British motorcycle scene from before World War I and served many marques, both at home and abroad. The latter market began to decline after the 1940s, but at home a great number of firms continued to rely on the Wolverhampton units right through the post-war era.

Villiers produced an enormous range of engines, of which the motorcycle versions were just a part. Even these were highly diverse, and for years a great company strength was the ability of their basic designs to be varied to suit the customer. Thus, the same engine may crop up in these pages at many different points, but sometimes with three speeds and at others with four. It may have an electric starter and fan-cooling for a scooter in one version, or have a mildly-tuned cylinder for a competition model in another.

The engines ranged in size from a 50 cc moped unit to a 324 cc twin, and the gearboxes from single to four speeds. All, bar a pair of scrambles units, had a Villiers carburettor, and most relied on the Villiers flywheel magneto for ignition and lights.

Smallest of the range was the 50 cc 3K engine unit with its two-speed gearbox, which differed from most Villiers models in having true unit construction. Otherwise, it followed normal practice, with iron barrel, alloy head and bobweights, but the clutch was on the right-hand end of the crankshaft, while the flywheel magneto was on the left.

At what was normally viewed as the bottom of the range were the 100 cc engines, and post-war, up to 1948, there was just one unit listed as the Junior de Luxe or JDL. It was of 98 cc with a horizontal cylinder incorporating four transfer ports and twin exhausts, one on each side. Below it was a substantial cast alloy silencer box, which was connected to the ports by a cast elbow on each side. A further alloy casting carried the carburettor on the left. The cylinder head was in light alloy with an 18 mm sparking plug and a decompressor. The crankpin was overhung, with alternate steel and bronze rollers in the big-end, and turned in twin races in the crankcase. The main part of this extended back to house a chain-driven clutch, which drove the rear wheel.

For 1949 the JDL was replaced by two new engines, both of 99 cc, with their cylinders only

One of the few unit-construction Villiers engines was the 50 cc 3K used by this 1959 Norman Lido

Above **The two 99 cc F-series engines, with one or two speeds, used for light motorcycles and autocycles**

Below **The 1950 Villiers 10D of 122 cc, which was built along with the very similar 197 cc 6E; plug position indicates which is which**

inclined a little from the vertical. The construction of both was similar, the 2F having the single speed and countershaft clutch of the JDL. The 1F featured a two-speed gearbox with hand-lever selection and a clutch. The flywheel magneto was moved to the right for both engines, which had a full crankshaft in place of the overhung type. Both engines were designed to fit into a frame, rather than hang from it, as in the past.

The 2F remained in use without any real change until it was dropped in 1958, but the two-speed model was replaced by the 4F for 1953. This was a more modern design, with the flywheel magneto enclosed and the ignition points remote from it on the left-hand side. The result was a streamlined appearance, more in keeping with the times, but inside there were still only two speeds. In 1956 they were given foot-change to become the 6F, and this last version ran on into the 1960s, while the 4F was dropped in 1958.

The next Villiers capacity was of 122 cc, and the immediate post-war model was the 9D, which had a three-speed, hand-change gearbox. It followed pre-war lines, for it dated from 1937, but was of true unit construction with a vertical split line for the main castings. Within them went a built-up crankshaft with roller big-end, and

outside was the flywheel magneto on the right and the primary drive on the left.

The top half was distinctively pre-war, the iron barrel having an exhaust-port elbow, cast in alloy, bolted to each side. Both had a short pipe to lead to a cylindrical silencer, mounted ahead of the crankcase, and below the left one was bolted a curved, cast alloy, inlet pipe. The cylinder head was also in alloy with sparking plug and decompressor.

This simple engine was replaced by the 10D for 1949, and this design reverted to a separate gearbox, which was bolted to the rear of the crankcase. This was a step to give the firm the freedom to ring the changes, while another was to make both halves of the primary chaincase separate from the crankcase. The flywheel magneto continued on the right under a polished, spun-aluminium cover, and the crankshaft continued to be built up. The cylinder was vertical and more up to date, with single inlet and exhaust ports at the rear and front, while the head continued in light alloy, but without the decompressor.

From this simple beginning came a range of builds with options of electric starting, fan-cooling, a reverse gear, wide or close gear ratios and a competition specification. This last was listed as the 11D for 1954, while the basic model became the 12D for that year, both with the option of three or four speeds. For 1953 the 13D was built as a utility model, using the 12D crankcase and the 10D head and barrel. In all these cases, however, the differences were minimal, and the engine size was dropped during 1954.

It was replaced by the 147 cc 30C, which was a bored-out 12D, but also with new crankcase castings to allow this. With it came the competition 29C, and both engines were closely modelled on the 122 cc versions. The 29C ran to 1956 and the 30C to 1959, but they were effectively replaced for 1956 by the 31C. This had both bore and stroke revised to give it a 148 cc capacity and kept the older construction form, but was modified to give a streamlined appearance. Most of this came from enclosing the magneto and gearbox end with a single cover, and recessing the carburettor into the top of both crankcase and gearbox castings. The result was the appearance of unit construction, while retaining the flexibility of build that the firm found so useful.

The same layout, and many common parts, were used for the 174 cc 2L engine, introduced for 1957 and soon joined by the fan-cooled 3L for scooters. As with the 148 cc model, there were options of three or four speeds, and the two engines were interchangeable.

The Villiers 197 cc engine was possibly their most popular of the 1950s, and it served thousands of owners on their regular ride to work each

A 1957 DKR Dove with 147 cc Villiers 30C engine, which was based on the D-series

day. In the immediate post-war period, they did offer the 5E, which was as the smaller 9D with twin exhaust ports, although it did have foot-change for its three speeds. Ambassador seem to have been the sole British firm to have used this engine, as others of those times stuck with the 9D.

Like that model, the 5E was replaced for 1949 by a new design, the 6E, which was a larger version of the 10D and one destined to follow the same route. It repeated the separate gearbox arrangement and three speeds with larger crankcase castings and many common parts. It was replaced by the 8E for 1954, and this was joined by the competition 7E, both being offered with four speeds, as well as the three. The list of options was as for the 122 cc engine, but the 7E was dropped in 1956, while the 8E continued to 1958. However, this was only in three-speed form.

Both were joined by the 9E for 1955, and this repeated the streamlined design of the 31C, while retaining all the options available for the others. It was to continue as the firm's mainstay for the 200 cc class and was joined by two other versions.

The final development of the E-series was the 9E, used here by a 1956 Panther 10/4

One was the 10E, which had the cylinder mounted vertically instead of inclined forward a little, and the other was the 11E for scooters, with electric start and fan-cooling. Both the 9E and 10E were also listed in competition form, and the former for scooter use. All ran on into the 1960s.

The next capacity class Villiers used was an intermediate one of 224 cc for their 1H, which appeared for 1954. It was the first to have the streamlined construction, as befitted what was then the top of their motorcycle range, and this extended to enclosing the carburettor as well. It was only built with a four-speed gearbox.

The engine had full flywheels, but retained the separate gearbox, as with the smaller models. The major castings were formed to flow together to maintain the unit looks, which they did very well, and were assisted in this by the use of a smaller flywheel magneto. This fed an external coil, which was an improvement, and the points were under an access plate on the right-hand cover, which also carried an ignition switch. For the rest, the construction followed Villiers practice.

The 1H was joined by the 246 cc 2H in 1957, but this was little used, although it remained in the range until the end of the decade. For most firms, its place was taken by the 246 cc A-series

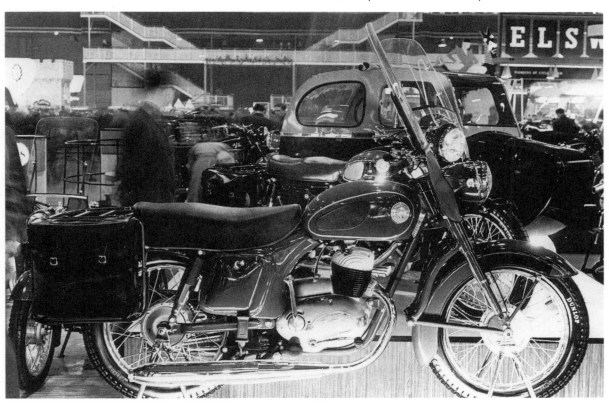

Another Panther, but with a 324 cc 3T Villiers twin engine, rather than the more usual 249 cc 2T

engines, which were built from 1958 on. In essence, they were the 9E, which had been bored out and fitted with a different rod to produce a whole range with many parts in common with the 197 cc units.

First to appear were the 31A and 33A, the former for road models and the latter for scrambles. All were to have four-speed gearboxes, but there was a great range of specification builds, some duplicated by the 9E and others special to the A-series. The 31A saw Villiers into the 1960s on the road, but for that year, the 33A was replaced by the 34A and joined by the 32A, which was built to trials specification. The two scrambles engines were among the few Villiers units to use an Amal carburettor.

The final Villiers engines were the twins, beginning with the 249 cc 2T of 1956. This followed the lines of the 1H and retained the separate four-speed gearbox, flywheel magneto on the right and ignition key in the cover. The twin-cylinder crankshaft was built up and had a centre web with bearing and oil seal so it could be bolted in between the two case halves. The alloy heads and iron barrels were separate, while a manifold was fed by a single carburettor. There were two sets of points under the access plate.

The 2T was joined by the 324 cc 3T, which became available for motorcycle use from 1958. Both twins could also be had with electric start, fan-cooling and reverse-running options in various packages to suit scooter and bubblecar use. The reverse was obtained by running the engine backwards, thanks to special wiring and controls, but its operation was tedious for a three-point turn.

Square barrel conversions should also be mentioned in connection with Villiers engines. The phrase refers to kits which came on the market in the late 1950s for both the E- and A-series engines. Their purpose was to improve the performance by changing both head and barrel, the latter invariably being cast in alloy with well-spaced, square-outline fins, hence the name. Marcelle and Parkinson were the best known, and some of these conversions enlarged the smaller engine to 246 cc. In the 1960s the kits progressed further to be used by a number of firms for their new models. They were also joined by an improved crankshaft and, later still, an entire bottom half.

Vincent-HRD

Monolever rear suspension, shaft drive, stub axle wheel mounting, hub centre steering, hydraulic clutch operation, enclosure and direct attachment of the suspension members to the engine and gearbox unit could all be features of a very modern motorcycle, but were all ideas propounded by Philip Vincent in 1943. His was a fertile mind, and while few of his ideas were to come to fruition in the hard practical daylight of the post-war years, they go a long way to show the man's advanced thinking.

The Vincent-HRD was a name to conjure with anyway, the pre-war 998 cc Rapide being a very different kettle of fish from the usual V-twins of the times with their side valves and sidecar calling. The Rapide was a grand tourer with plenty of power and high gearing for effortless riding at all speeds, which was how Vincent saw high-class motorcycling.

During the war years, he worked with his chief engineer, Phil Irving, to design a better and lighter Rapide, which would do the same job as the pre-war edition, but in an improved manner. The aim was to learn from the past and produce a very high-speed tourer with a host of rider features. They came pretty close to succeeding, too.

The pre-war model looked a mess, with pipes, plates, carbs, links and levers in a glorious disarray with no harmony at all. Post-war, all this was to change, with a shorter wheelbase, unit construction of engine and gearbox, the extensive use of light alloys, and a very clean appearance.

All this and a host of detail improvements were promised in a March 1945 announcement, for both Vincent and Irving had been hard at work on the new design, much of which was described by Irving in a talk given in June. This really whetted the appetite, but it was December before full details of the post-war Rapide were released.

The impact was tremendous, for the machine was as compact as a 500 single and incorporated many new features. The major part was the engine, which had the gearbox built in unit with it to provide a single, rigid structure. It was so rigid, in fact, that there was little frame at all, the rear fork being the major part, and even this was attached to the rear of the engine structure.

The rest of the frame comprised a beam over the engine, which had the headstock at its front end and also doubled as the oil tank. To its rear were fixed the rear spring and damper, which controlled the rear fork structure, while the tube itself was bolted to both cylinder heads. At the front were Brampton girders, as the two Phils considered telescopic forks to be inadequate for solo riding and totally unsuitable for sidecar work.

The engine was the heart of the machine and was a 50-degree V-twin with overhead valves and alloy heads and barrels. These were fitted to a massive crankcase casting, which was split vertically on the centre line between the two cylinders. These were offset to one another. Within the cases turned a large, built-up crankshaft, the mainshafts being pressed into the flywheels, which were drilled for balance.

The two big-ends each comprised three rows of uncaged rollers, running on a single crankpin, so the connecting rods sat side by side. Nuts pulled the pin into place, and the complete assembly was supported by two roller races on the timing side, and one roller and one ball race on the drive side.

The timing side on the right used a train of gears, with a large, central, intermediate gear meshing with each camshaft gear. The front one of these drove an idler, which meshed with the auto-advance magneto mounted ahead of the crankcase, under a protective alloy shield. Each camshaft looked after one cylinder, with cam followers and widely splayed pushrods running up to the unusual rockers and valve gear.

The pushrods, and the tubes in which they moved, had to be laid out to match the arrangement of the rockers, which lay across the engine, so the valve angle dictated the pushrod position. Each rocker was mounted in a pivot block, which was clamped into the head casting. Access to this, and the adjuster at the outer rocker end, was via a screwed cap carrying the firm's logo. There were further caps above the valves, which differed from normal practice in that the rockers engaged with them around the mid-point of their length, while the springs were above this.

The arrangement was as for the pre-war Rapide,

The Series B Rapide, as introduced in 1946, this one being photographed in Seattle, in the USA, in 1948

except that duplex coil springs were used in place of the earlier hairpins. This allowed the valve gear to be fully enclosed, while retaining the very short pushrod length and isolating the springs from engine heat. In some ways, it was a curious line to follow, for the engine was never meant to reach high speeds, hence the crowded roller big-end, and thus, had little need for ultra-light valve gear.

A single cover enclosed the timing side, an access plate being provided for the magneto gear. Under this was the oil pump, which was driven directly from the crankshaft. An oil filter went in a chamber in the lower front portion of the crankcases while the breather was driven by a timing gear.

Both cylinder heads had the exhaust port at the front, and the two pipes swept down to a single tubular silencer on the right. Thus, two Amal carburettors had to be used, each with its own float chamber, and these were fed by two petrol taps. The heads were cast with integral rocker chambers and fitted on long studs in the crankcase with mounting plates above them. These, in turn, were attached to the top frame beam-cum-oil tank, the details being designed to compensate for any differences in thermal expansion between the steel beam and alloy engine.

The primary transmission was by triplex chain within a large, polished alloy case, and this chain also drove the Miller dynamo, which sat above the gearbox section of the crankcase. The clutch was rather special to cope with the tremendous engine torque, which had proved too much for the Burman unit used pre-war. The new design was often thought to be operated by centrifugal force, but this was not the case all.

It was, in fact, two clutches in one, with most of the power being transmitted via a drum and shoes, not unlike a brake. This clutch was engaged by a simple plate type and, thanks to its servo action, it was able to transmit all the power, while remaining very light in action. So light were the original springs that excessive cable friction could prevent the clutch engaging fully, so they had to be strengthened.

The gearbox was of a very compact, four-speed, cross-over design, so the rear chain went on the right. The change mechanism was on the right of the engine case, under an outer cover, and was linked by shaft and bevel gears to the selector camplate, which was mounted above the two gear shafts. These were arranged with the main-shaft at the rear to place it as close to the rear fork pivot as possible. The kickstarter was on the right, along with the gear pedal, and had a long, curved lever, which ran under the footrest to give the rider the best chance of a long swinging kick when starting.

The complete engine and gearbox unit, with its minimal frame, rode on spoked wheels, each with two single-leading-shoe brakes. Twin drums for the wheels dated from the pre-war models, and the rear ones each carried a sprocket. Thanks to some good detail design, the wheel could be very quickly taken out and turned round to provide an easy change to sidecar gearing.

Sporting alloy mudguards were used and there was a dualseat, rather than a saddle and pillion pad. The seat was supported at the rear by struts from the rear fork structure, so it rose and fell a little as the suspension worked. The rear fork carried a rear stand, which was held up by a small T-bar screw, and at the front of the crankcase there was a prop-stand on each side. By means of a minor adjustment, these could be used as one to become a front stand.

The stands made it very easy to work on the machine, and it was a simple task to remove either the whole of the front end, plus the frame top beam, or the rear fork complete with wheel. In both cases, this left the engine unit ready and accessible for working on. This philosophy of making it easy for the owner to maintain the machine was continued throughout its design, while long-term appearance was enhanced by the use of stainless steel for many parts.

The result of all this work was a motorcycle with a shattering performance, despite the low-octane pool petrol the engine had to suffer in its early days. The weight came out at around 450 lb, and the 45 bhp produced by the relaxed and stress-free V-twin was sufficient to propel it quite fast enough for the road conditions of the times, when few were straight and most were excessively bumpy.

Inevitably, there were problems in getting the new design into production, and it was May 1946 before the very first machine was fired up and taken out on to the Great North Road by Phil Vincent, minus hat, gloves or goggles. Phil Irving was next and then Arthur Bourne of *The Motor Cycle*, with cap and goggles, followed by Graham Walker of *Motor Cycling*. The two editors were very impressed, while the factory personnel must have been thankful it had all worked out so well.

Thus was the post-war Vincent-HRD Rapide born, and it was soon, correctly, advertised as 'the world's fastest standard motorcycle – this is a fact, not a slogan'. It was September before the first production machine was built, and it went to Argentina. More followed, many for export, while

the firm struggled with the shortages of materials and parts then so common.

Because the pre-war twin had been the model A, the post-war version became the Series B. It proved to be a real grand tourer, with the maximum speed in top simply 'not obtained' during one 1947 road test. Another managed 112 mph, and this with a low compression ratio, pool petrol, a riding coat and an engine with a docile tick-over for town use.

Early in 1948 the Rapide was joined by a faster version! This was the Black Shadow, which had larger carburettors and a small rise in compression ratio to produce a top speed beyond the 120 mph mark with little loss of docility or easy town riding. To match the name, the engine was finished in black, and the result looked wonderful. In addition to the engine improvements, the brakes were given ribbed drums and, best of all, a large 5 in. speedometer, reading up to 150 mph, appeared and sat boldly at the top of the forks.

Never ones to rest on their laurels, the two Phils, Vincent and Irving, had more new offerings for 1949 to expand the range and provide even better motorcycles for the discerning rider. The two Series B models continued, but were joined by the Series C, which had totally new front forks, called Girdraulics, and a damper for the rear suspension. The series C Rapide and Black Shadow were listed in the same form as the Series B, except for the suspension, and were joined by two singles and a racing model called the Black Lightning.

The singles were the Series B Meteor and Series C Comet, which had the same suspension variation and a good deal in common with the V-twins. They reversed the events of pre-war days, when Phil Irving created the Rapide by mounting two single top halves on a common crankcase. For 1949 he simply replaced the rear cylinder with a cast alloy frame member and added some gearbox plates so that he could use a separate four-speed Burman gearbox. The crankcase was modified to suit the needs of the single and, thus, the front cylinder and general line remained, but the dynamo was driven from the timing gear train. On the cycle side, the singles followed the twins with minor alterations, so the two looked much the same, the Meteor differing from the others in having a saddle and no pillion rests.

The Black Lightning was built for road racing, so its engine was tuned with TT carburettors and straight-through exhaust pipes. It had a rev-counter, but no kickstart, lighting equipment or

The 1948 Vincent-HRD
Series B Black Shadow
with its big, upright
150 mph speedometer

The Vincent-HRD was also built as a
500 single, and this is a 1949 Series
C Comet with the Girdraulic forks

Series C Black Shadow with 120+ mph
potential on pool petrol

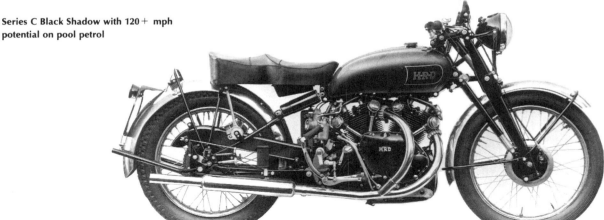

stands. Both wheels had alloy rims and alloy brake backplates, while the tyre sizes were 3.00 × 21 in. front and 3.50 × 20 in. rear. There were short alloy mudguards and a racing seat, which used the standard mountings.

The new forks used for the Series C models were still of the girder type, as the two Phils continued to consider telescopics poor for solos and useless when a sidecar was hitched to a machine. Their design was based on a pair of forged alloy blades linked to the headstock by forged links, the top one alloy and the lower one steel. As these were in one piece, they did not twist relative to one another, as separate links were prone to do, and the blades were further braced by a plate bolted to their front faces, just below the bottom link pivot.

This point had a further ingenious arrangement, for the link moved on an eccentric bush fixed to the spindle. As this bush was turned, it moved the pivot point and, thus, effectively altered the link position which, in turn, changed the trail. The dimensions were arranged so that the positions available gave solo or sidecar trail, and the change-over could be carried out in a few minutes.

Each eccentric bush also carried the top mounting for a long, slim spring unit, which ran down to the lower end of the fork blade. This allowed long, low-rated springs to be used to give a comfortable ride, while damping was dealt with by a separate hydraulic unit mounted between the fork links in the normal girder fork spring position. One final touch was to place the spring mountings on the eccentrics so that their loading was increased in the sidecar setting.

For 1950 the range continued with one more single in the form of the racing Grey Flash. This was a Comet built on the lines of the Lightning, with tuned engine, no road equipment and the racing fitments. It was listed in three forms, one of which was the basic road racer. Another was a road machine, effectively a Comet with a tuned engine, and the third was the same, but came with a kit of parts to convert it to the racer.

The Series B was dropped during 1950, so only the Series C continued for 1951, together with the three V-twins, the Comet and the three versions of the Grey Flash. The last was dropped for 1952, while the Lightning was built to special order only. However, the two road twins and single continued to offer the same high-speed touring as always.

It was the same for 1953, with minor improve-

ments, but during the year, the firm tried a totally different line with a clip-on engine unit. This was, in truth, developed and launched by the Miller company, who supplied Vincent with electrical parts, and was first seen early in 1952. The engine was designed to fit under a cycle's bottom bracket, to keep the weight low and to drive the rear tyre with its friction-roller.

The 48 cc, two-stroke engine had a horizontal cylinder and was made as narrow as possible to fit between the pedals, in the same manner as the German Lohmann. The engine was conventional, having an iron barrel, alloy head and pressed-up crankshaft with conical expanders for the crank-pin and roller big-end. A flywheel magneto was on the right with an external ignition coil, while a gear on the left drove a countershaft carrying a large-diameter roller. The engine was held so that it could drive or be free, and its mixture was supplied by a small Amal, while a silencer box went under the barrel. The petroil tank was mounted on the frame downtube, and the ignition coil housed in a recess in its base.

In the middle of 1953 it was announced that Vincent had taken over both production and sales of this unit, which became known as the Firefly. It was soon offered with a Sun bicycle that had been specially designed for it. This had a semi-open frame that was able to deal with the added weight, power and vibration. It had drum brakes front and rear, plus a widened bottom bracket to ensure that the cranks cleared the engine.

To the deep chagrin of members of the Vincent Owners' Club, the Firefly unit was listed alongside the three twins and the Comet for 1954. The Lightning was given caged roller big-ends, and there were a number of minor changes to the motorcycles, which otherwise ran on as before.

To augment their range, Vincent did a deal with the German NSU company, and for a year imported the Quickly moped, which pointed the way to the future and killed off the clip-on engines. In addition to the moped, there was a range of small motorcycles listed as NSU-Vincent. These had German engine units, frames and forks, but British wheels, tyres, tank, carburettor and other equipment. This arrangement side-stepped the tariff rules applicable at the time.

Four models were to be available. All had unit construction of the engine and four-speed gearbox, a spine frame, leading-link front forks and pivoted rear fork, which was controlled in much the same way as the big Vincents. The

A modified 1950 Black Shadow with many stainless-steel parts and other detail improvements

larger machines had hydraulic damping at both ends, but the smaller ones had to make do with friction units.

The smallest model was the 98 cc Fox, which had an ohv engine and was offered in standard or de luxe forms. The former had direct lighting and a saddle, while the latter was given a battery and dualseat, which was supported as on the Vincent, but with spring-loaded struts at the rear.

The Vincent Firefly taken over from Millers and never discussed by the Owners' Club

Next, came the 123 cc Fox, which had a two-stroke engine and similar specification, but neither Fox model was made in any numbers to speak of.

The larger models were the 199 cc Lux two-stroke and 247 cc Max, with overhead camshaft driven by eccentrics and connecting blades. This system worked well, and the German Max had a fine reputation, enhanced by the racing successes of the Rennmax model. For the venture with Vincent, both machines proved too expensive for the market, and neither went into production.

The exercise continued for 1955, but was then dropped, for Vincent had something far more

exciting to offer that year in the shape of the fully-enclosed Series D range. This was a remarkable development for the time and was to lead the firm into grave problems, but the object, as always, was to provide the discerning rider with a high-speed tourer; a two-wheeled Bentley, as Phil Vincent put it.

The enclosure began with a large and deeply valanced front mudguard, which ran outside the fork blades. Above it was a cowl, which carried the headlamp, extended outwards to protect the hands, and had a fascia for the instruments, and a windscreen to keep rain off the rider.

The rear of the machine was enclosed by a single moulding mounted on a subframe and carrying the seat. It enclosed the rear wheel to below the spindle and was hinged to give access to the rear end once two bolts had been slackened. A normal petrol tank was used, but below it was a panel on each side. These ran forward to form legshields, each topped by a forward-facing beak.

Under the mouldings went the familiar engine, frame and forks, but with a number of alterations. Both carburettors were on the right and became Monoblocs; ignition was by coil, with the points in the old magneto position; and the oil tank was fitted in the rear body, which simplified the frame's top beam. The rear suspension was controlled by a single Armstrong hydraulic spring unit, and the tyres were changed to 3.50 × 19 in. front and 4.00 × 18 in. rear. Only one brake was used in the rear wheel, although two remained at the front. The tommy bars on the spindles disappeared and the stands were revised. The prop-stands were no longer fitted and, in place of the rear stand, there

was a central stand operated by a long hand lever, much as on a pre-war Rudge.

With their new clothes, the models were given new names; the Rapide became the Black Knight, the Shadow the Black Prince, and the Comet the Victor, but only one of these was built. The models created a sensation at the show that year, but production problems arose with the mouldings, which Phil Vincent insisted should be to his usual high standards.

As a stop-gap, he decided to build Series D models without enclosure to Rapide and Black Shadow specifications. There was also one Comet, but this was later fitted with enclosure for a show. The open Series D V-twins had a tubular subframe to support the dualseat, but retained all the other new features. The mudguards reverted to the usual Series C type, and a toolbox appeared on the left of the subframe.

The machines kept the factory going, but the new seat and subframe lacked the lithe lines of the earlier models, and the company was, by now, once more in financial trouble. At the bottom end of the scale, the Firefly was offered as a complete machine, but in September 1955, at an Owners' Club dinner in Cambridge, Phil Vincent announced that the motorcycles would no longer be produced.

They had to build another hundred or so machines to fulfil outstanding orders, but in December the last official machine, a Black Prince, was completed. The Firefly continued for 1956 as a machine, and for two more years as a clip-on attachment, while the firm moved to other industrial uses for its engines.

Left **Open Series D Black Shadow built as a stop-gap with tubular subframe, but minus the lovely lines of the earlier models**

The Series D Vincent Black Prince with Shadow engine under the full enclosure

The Series D created a sensation at Earls Court, and there was a queue to sit on one for most of the show

The NSU–Vincent Max with 247 cc ohc engine seen at Earls Court, but never put into production

Wabo

This was a Dutch make of scooter, but one which used Villiers power for the models imported into Britain. These were two in number and, except for the engine units and forks, they were identical.

Engines were the 99 cc 4F, with two speeds, or the 147 cc 30C, with three, and both went into a rigid duplex frame with light or heavy telescopic front forks. The wheels had 16 in. rims and wire spokes, so were larger than usual for a scooter, and the bodywork was extensive. It followed normal scooter lines, but included a very deep tunnel, which ran from near the top of the leg-shields to the rear body and had footboards on each side.

The front mudguard turned with the wheel. The fuel tank was at the rear with an access panel for filling, while the rear body could be quickly released, thanks to car-bonnet-type fasteners. In continental style, it carried a saddle each for both rider and passenger.

The models were fully equipped and had a certain style, but the enterprise was short-lived, for the make both came and went in 1957, having but a brief life on the British scene.

The Dutch Wabo scooter with Villiers engine under the extensive bodywork, which came and went in 1957

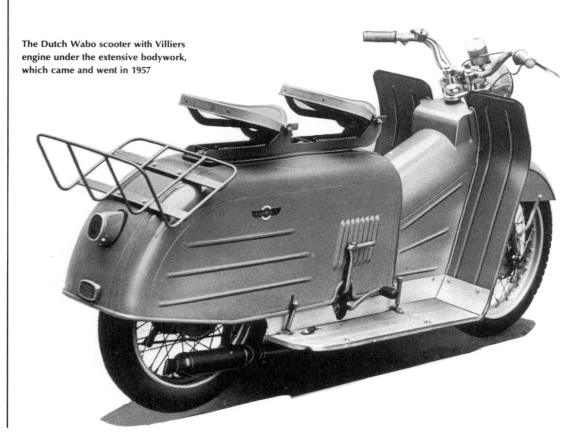

Watsonian

This sidecar firm built a prototype machine in 1950 to haul its products and, for a first attempt, it turned out rather well. For power, they chose a 996 cc V-twin JAP engine, which had side valves, but alloy heads and barrels, so was lighter than usual.

The engine was coupled to a four-speed Burman gearbox by a chain in an oil-bath case, and both went into a duplex loop frame. This had plunger suspension at the rear and Dunlop telescopic forks, which used rubber for the springs, at the front. Massive alloy hubs with 9 in. twin-leading-shoe brakes were used front and rear, so this was one outfit that defied convention and could stop quickly and easily.

The engine had coil ignition and an alternator housed in its timing cover, the distributor being fitted into the rear of this. A large battery went behind the rear cylinder and beneath the dualseat, and further back, between the right-hand chainstays, was the oil tank. This was made in alloy from a casting and sheet, its outer surface being ribbed. A large petrol tank of over five gallons capacity was fitted, and the whole machine was finished in pale green.

It made an excellent sidecar machine, but by 1950 the market for a rather thirsty V-twin of modest performance was vanishing. The low-down pull was tremendous and much appreciated when the going was bad, but in the showrooms the new 650 twins looked far more attractive. To settle the matter, JAP proved less than interested in supplying engines for a project with limited appeal, so the idea came to a halt. The machine itself existed at the time of writing and has modern lines, compared with pre-war haulers, so it was a good, but unsuccessful try.

Watsonian prototype, as built in 1950 and seen here some 35 years later, with its distinctive engine, oil tank and forks

Wooler

The Wooler was always one of the strange machines that make motorcycles so interesting. The industry is peppered with individuals who saw their way as being correct and often refused to deviate a fraction from their chosen path. They seldom built many machines, and those they did produce were frequently troublesome, but we all gained by the excitement they generated.

The Wooler was one such machine, and the first model, built in 1911, had a horizontal two-stroke engine with double-ended piston to avoid the need for crankcase compression. It also had plunger rear suspension and a similar arrangement on the front forks, while the fuel tank was extended round and in front of the headstock.

This tank style was to continue, and in the 1920s the firm built machines with flat-twin, four-stroke engines of rather more conventional form, although the plunger suspension for both wheels continued. They were entered for a couple of TT races, for which they retained the tank form, but were painted in a bright yellow, so were quickly named 'flying bananas'.

Other models were tried, the sole 1926 machine having a 500 cc ohc engine with the cams on the top end of the vertical shaft. Horizontal tappets and rockers took the movement to the valves, and the engine had twin exhaust ports. The machine had a more conventional rigid frame and girder forks, but even these had the Wooler touch. The frame differed from normal in having a series of flat plates to join the headstock to the duplex downtubes, while the fork springs, which were enclosed, were three in number and could be adjusted while riding.

It was back to the flat twin for 1927, but soon after that motorcycle production ceased, and all was quiet until 1945. When news of a new Wooler design and prototype came in May of that year, it was expected that the machine would be unusual. Press and public alike were not disappointed, for

it was unique in engine, frame, suspension and details.

The engine was the feature of greatest interest and was laid out as a transverse-four, the cylinders on each side being one above the other. This alone was far from normal, but really unique was the way in which they were connected to the crankshaft, for this was based on the beam engine. Capacity was 500 cc, and overhead valves were used.

The crankshaft ran along the machine, below all the cylinders, and was of a single-throw design. In fact, for the prototype, a modified assembly from a 150 cc New Imperial was used. Above the crankshaft was a T-shaped beam, which was pivoted at the junction of the leg and arms, this axis also lying along the machine. A master connecting rod joined the end of the T-leg to the crankshaft, so as this rotated, the beam oscillated. The arm of the T was set vertically, and each end was attached to two connecting rods, which pointed in opposite directions and ran out to the pistons. Thus, these moved in pairs, and the two pairs moved in opposition.

Engine construction was fairly simple, despite the complex linkage within, and a single alloy casting formed the block for all four cylinders, which had liners pressed in for the bores. It also included the section between the cylinders and extended down as the upper part of the crankcase. One alloy cylinder head went on each side and had vertical valves in a row. The rocker box was fixed to the head and had a lid held by three bolts.

Arrangement of pistons, rods, T-beam, master rod and crankshaft for the Wooler beam engine

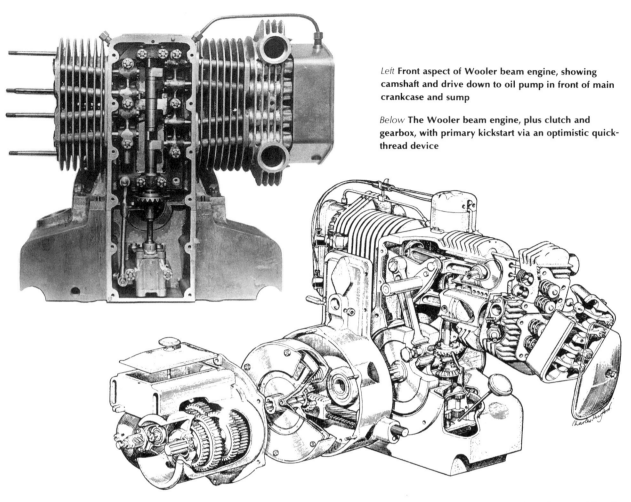

Left **Front aspect of Wooler beam engine, showing camshaft and drive down to oil pump in front of main crankcase and sump**

Below **The Wooler beam engine, plus clutch and gearbox, with primary kickstart via an optimistic quick-thread device**

A massive sump-cum-lower crankcase was bolted to the base of the block, with cover plates to front and rear. The plate at the front concealed the camshaft, which ran up the front of the engine and was driven by a bevel gear on the crankcase nose. Thus, it was able to operate the valves via pushrods and also drove the oil pump from its lower end and a distributor at the top. The front cover also provided a mounting for a pancake dynamo, which was driven by a further bevel gear from the camshaft gear.

It was suggested that a supercharger could be substituted for the dynamo, in which case, a single carburettor would feed it and long pipes would take the mixture to the inlet side. However, for normal use, twin carburettors, one on each side, were to be used. The exhaust pipes from each side swept down to join and then connect to the frame, which acted as the silencing system.

This extremely interesting engine was not the end of the matter, for bolted to its rear was to be either a four-speed gearbox or an infinitely-variable gear. This was to take the place of both clutch and gearbox, be purely mechanical in operation, and controlled by a twistgrip with a lock-up for the highest ratio. After all this, it was positively prosaic that the output should be stepped over by a pair of spur gears and then taken by shaft to the rear wheel. The shaft had a universal joint at the rear and a rubber coupling at the front, while spiral bevels were used to turn the drive.

The frame was constructed from tubes brazed into lugs that, in the main, were formed in welded steel, with a single top tube and widely splayed down tubes. These ran down to a large cross-tube, from which the bottom tubes led straight back to the rear plungers. Further tubes linked the tops of the plungers to the seat, with bracing tubes from there to the bottom tubes.

The front cross-tube had an aluminium manifold at each end, to which the exhaust pipes were connected, and the gases passed right along the bottom tubes to fishtail exhausts at the end. Quite what one did when the system eventually cor-

roded away was never discussed, and there was no mention of any provision against condensation.

Rear suspension was by twin plunger boxes on each side with the wheel spindle between them. Each box enclosed compression and rebound springs, but no damping, other than friction. At the front, the same arrangement was used at the bottom end of the forks, which gave them an odd appearance, but allowed the wheels to be interchangeable. The front fork had a massive lower crown only, with just a headrace adjustment and handlebar clamp above the headstock. The crown had a main tube running straight down to the rear plunger on each side, with a light one to the front. Again, there was no damping.

Both wheels had offset hubs with drum brakes, so they were very ordinary by Wooler standards, as were the mudguards that protected them. The saddle itself was normal, but not its springs, which were concealed in the two saddle tubes. The petrol tank followed the style of the past, stretching out ahead of the forks and bars, with the headlamp set in its nose. It certainly gave the machine an unusual line, but there were many other interesting details. The combined toolbox and air filter formed in the top of the gearbox was one, and the stand another, as it had two separate legs, the angle of which could be readily altered to create a prop-stand. Only three spanner sizes dealt with the entire machine, including the ignition, and there were no fixings with screwdriver slots. Access and servicing were all good

and easy, some operations requiring no tools at all since they could be done by hand alone.

The Wooler created great interest and gained much publicity, for it differed so much from the usual machines of the day. It also proved difficult to put into production, and it was late in 1946 before even a complete prototype was seen, although the engine had run some time earlier. Finally, in May 1947, this machine was shown to the trade, and an indication of the ease of servicing was provided by demonstration.

Once again, production was talked of as 'commencing next year', and it was much the same in 1948, although the firm did exhibit at the Earls Court show late in the year. Then, all went quiet, and it was late in 1952 before there was any further news of Wooler.

What was announced then was more new than old, for the engine had become a much more conventional 499 cc flat-four with air-cooling and overhead valves. The crankshaft ran along the frame and, for the best balance, the rods had normal and forked big-ends. They were forged in alloy with plain shells; the mains were also plain bearings.

The alloy cylinders were cast in blocks, as were the heads, which had separate rocker boxes. There were two camshafts, driven by one chain, and it was intended that one model would have alternator electrics, while a faster, sports machine would have a magneto. Wet-sump lubrication was specified, the oil pump being driven by the left-hand camshaft.

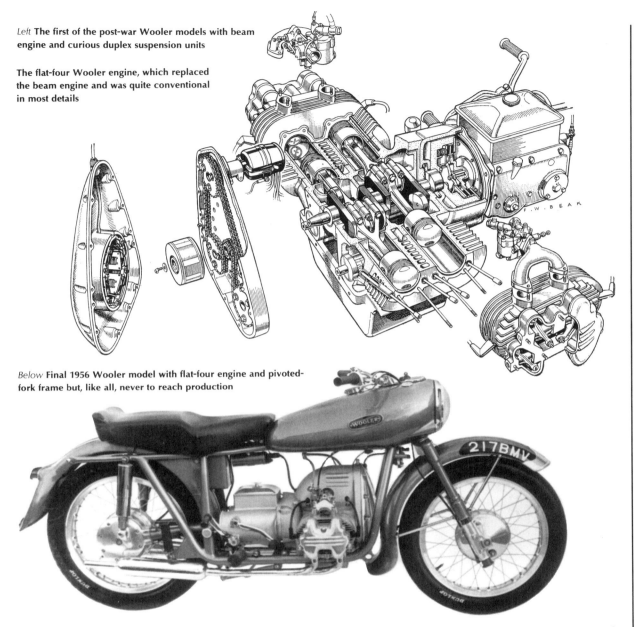

Left The first of the post-war Wooler models with beam engine and curious duplex suspension units

The flat-four Wooler engine, which replaced the beam engine and was quite conventional in most details

Below Final 1956 Wooler model with flat-four engine and pivoted-fork frame but, like all, never to reach production

One Amal supplied each pair of cylinders, and the exhaust pipes on each side joined and fed into a single silencer. The original four-speed gearbox was retained and bolted to the engine, while the shaft drive and rear bevel box also came from the 1945 model.

The frame was much as before, but the rear plungers only had one spring box on each side. At the front. the forks were similar, the plunger units being fitted at the ends of the fork tubes, which had the appearance of telescopics. The large lower crown still supported them, and the tank still extended forward to include the headlamp. Both wheels had full-width alloy hubs

with 7 in. brakes and could be interchanged, although the tyres were ribbed front and studded rear, so the practice was not recommended.

The next year, the Wooler was described, once more, as being close to production, and the press reported favourably on their rides of the prototype during development. It was the same thing late in 1954, when even extras were listed, in the form of a dualseat and crash bar, but for 1956 there was a revised frame. This had pivoted-fork rear suspension and a dualseat, but that was the end of the line for the Wooler, which never did make it into production, despite a decade of development.

Zenith

It is hard to believe that this firm ever returned to the market after the war. Their best days had been in the 1920s and prior to World War 1, but by the late 1930s, the range had dwindled to six models, all with JAP power.

After the war, only one appeared, and that was little altered from the 1939 version. It was the 750, powered by a 747 cc, side-valve JAP engine, which had its mag-dyno mounted on the side of the timing case, where it was bevel-gear driven. Total-loss lubrication was provided by a Pilgrim pump, and a single Amal carburettor was mounted between the cylinders.

Separate exhaust pipes ran back to twin silencers on the right, and the electric wiring from the engine was taken up under the tank via a vertical plated pipe. The engine drove a four-speed Burman gearbox, and both went into a duplex cradle frame, which was rigid at the rear and had Druid girder forks at the front. Later, these were changed for Dowty Oleomatics and, in either case, carried a 19 in. wheel, while at the rear the size was 18 in.

The appearance was, inevitably, pre-war, with a well valanced front mudguard, saddle, small oil tank and a three-gallon fuel tank. The last was finished in the traditional Zenith style of chrome and black with a red panel on each side.

The machine did not come on to the market until 1947, and production ended in 1950 after, it is said, some 250 examples had been built. Very few were ever seen, so most may have been exported, although one or two did survive at home.

The 1947 Zenith 750 with JAP side-valve engine in pre-war-style cycle parts and mainly for export

Model charts

These supplement the text to show how the model ranges varied through the years. Thus, each list gives the range for each year, and this includes models introduced during the year. Normally, the model year ran from October of the previous calender year, but in the 1960s this practice was to fall by the wayside.

The charts show the models and their capacity and engine type. The capacity is calculated from the bore and stroke, which is also given for many makes. Where a Villiers engine was used, its type number is given instead, and for some mopeds,

just the name of the engine manufacturer is shown. The model number, or name, is given under each year it was produced, with abbreviations where necessary. These are listed under each make.

The charts are arranged to run from the smallest to largest model by capacity groups; thus, sequences of a particular size of machine can be traced through the years. Singles are dealt with first, followed by twins, and then, in Ariel's case, the four. Reference to the main text should help clarify any doubtful points.

ABERDALE

	Engine	47	48	49
98 ts	JDL	Au	Au	Au

Au-Autocycle

ABJ

	Engine	49	50	51	52	53
49.9 ts	42 × 36				A M	A M
99 ts	2F	Au	Au	Au	Au	
99 ts	1F	M/C	M/C	M/C	M/C	

A M – Auto Minor   M/C – Motor Cycle
Au – Autocycle

AJW

	Engine	49	50	51	52	53	54	55	56	57
125 ts	JAP					FC				
494 sv tw	JAP	GF	GF							
498 ohv	JAP	SF	SF	SF	SF	SF	SF	SF	SF	SF
500 ohv	JAP					FF				

	Engine	58	59	60
48 ts	FBM	FC	FC	FC

FC – Fox Cub   GF – Grey Fox
FF – Flying Fox   SF – Speed Fox

AMBASSADOR

	Engine	47	48	49	50	51	52	53	54	55
197 ts	5E	I	II							
197 ts	6E			III	III	Cou				
197 ts	6E				Pop	Pop	Pop	Pop		
197 ts	6E				V	Emb	Emb	Emb		
197 ts	6E					Sup	Sup	Sup		
197 ts	6E							S/C		
197 ts	6E							SS		
197 ts	8E							Pop	Pop	Pop
197 ts	8E							Emb	Emb	Emb
197 ts	8E							Sup		
197 ts	8E							S/C	S/C	S/C
197 ts	8E							SS	SS	SS

	Engine	54	55	56	57	58	59	60
147 ts	30C			Pop				
148 ts	31C				Pop	Pop		
174 ts	2L				Stat			
174 ts	2L						Pop	Pop
197 ts	8E		En	En				
197 ts	9E			En	En	En	En	
197 ts	9E						Star	Star
224 ts	1H	Sup	Sup	Sup				
246 ts	2H				Sup	Sup		
249 ts tw	2T				Sup	Sup		
249 ts tw	2T						Super	Super

Cou – Courier   SS – self starter
Emb – Embassy   Star – 3 Star Special
En – Envoy   Stat – Statesman
Pop – Popular   Sup – Supreme
S/C – sidecar   Super – Super S

AMC – AJS

	b × s	45	46	47	48	49	50	51	52
348 ohv	69 × 93	16M	16M	16M	16M	16M	16M	16M	16M
348 ohv	69 × 93		16MC	16MC	16MC	16MC	16MC	16MC	16MC
348 ohv	69 × 93					16MS	16MS	16MS	16MS
348 ohv	69 × 93							16MCS	16MCS
348 ohc	74 × 81				7R	7R	7R	7R	7R
497 ohv	82.5 × 93	18	18	18	18	18	18	18	18
497 ohv	82.5 × 93		18C	18C	18C	18C	18C	18C	18C
497 ohv	82.5 × 93					18S	18S	18S	18S
497 ohv	82.5 × 93							18CS	18CS
498 ohv tw	66 × 72.8					20	20	20	20

	b × s	53	54	55	56	57	58	59	60
248 ohv	70 × 65						14	14	14
248 ohv	70 × 65							14CS	14CS
348 ohv	69 × 93	16M	16M	16M					
348 ohv	69 × 93	16MC	16MC	16MC	16MC	16MC	16MC	16C	16C
348 ohv	69 × 93	16MS	16MS	16MS	16MS	16MS	16MS	16	16
348 ohv	69 × 93	16MCS	16MCS	16MCS					
348 ohv	72 × 85.5				16MCS	16MCS	16MCS	16CS	
348 ohc	74 × 81	7R	7R	7R					
349 ohc	75.5 × 78				7R	7R	7R	7R	7R
497 ohv	82.5 × 93	18	18	18					
497 ohv	82.5 × 93	18C	18C	18C					
497 ohv	82.5 × 93	18S	18S	18S	18S	18S	18S	18	18
497 ohv	82.5 × 93	18CS	18CS	18CS					
497 ohv	86 × 85.5				18CS	18CS	18CS	18CS	18CS
498 ohv tw	66 × 72.8	20	20	20	20	20	20	20dl	
498 ohv tw	66 × 72.8							20std	20std
498 ohv tw	66 × 72.8							20CS	
498 ohv tw	66 × 72.8							20CSR	
593 ohv tw	72 × 72.8				30	30	30		
593 ohv tw	72 × 72.8						30CS		
593 ohv tw	72 × 72.8						30CSR		
646 ohv tw	72 × 79.3							31	31
646 ohv tw	72 × 79.3							31dl	31dl
646 ohv tw	72 × 79.3							31CS	31CS
646 ohv tw	72 × 79.3							31CSR	31CSR

The wartime Matchless G3L, on which the post-war range was based and which was sold off with many others to provide early post-war transport

AMC – Matchless

b × s		45	46	47	48	49	50	51	52
348 ohv	69 × 93	G3L	G3L	G3L	G3L	G3L	G3L	G3L	G3L
348 ohv	69 × 93		G3LC	G3LC	G3LC	G3LC	G3LC	G3LC	G3LC
348 ohv	69 × 93					G3LS	G3LS	G3LS	G3LS
348 ohv	69 × 93							G3LCS	G3LCS
497 ohv	82.5 × 93	G80	G80	G80	G80	G80	G80	G80	G80
497 ohv	82.5 × 93		G80C	G80C	G80C	G80C	G80C	G80C	G80C
497 ohv	82.5 × 93					G80S	G80S	G80S	G80S
497 ohv	82.5 × 93							G80CS	G80CS
498 ohv tw	66 × 72.8					G9	G9	G9	G9

b × s		53	54	55	56	57	58	59	60
248 ohv	70 × 65						G2	G2	G2
248 ohv	70 × 65						G2CS		G2CS
348 ohv	69 × 93	G3L	G3L	G3L					
348 ohv	69 × 93	G3LC	G3LC	G3LC	G3LC	G3LC	G3LC	G3C	G3C
348 ohv	69 × 93	G3LS	G3LS	G3LS	G3LS	G3LS	G3LS	G3	G3
348 ohv	69 × 93	G3LCS	G3LCS	G3LCS					
348 ohv	72 × 85.5				G3LCS	G3LCS	G3LCS	G3CS	
496 ohc	90 × 78						G50	G50	G50
497 ohv	82.5 × 93	G80	G80	G80					
497 ohv	82.5 × 93	G80C	G80C	G80C					
497 ohv	82.5 × 93	G80S	G80S	G80S	G80S	G80S	G80S	G80	G80
497 ohv	82.5 × 93	G80CS	G80CS	G80CS					
497 ohv	86 × 85.5				G80CS	G80CS	G80CS	G80CS	G80CS
498 ohv tw	66 × 72.8	G45	G45	G45	G45	G45			
498 ohv tw	66 × 72.8	G9	G9	G9	G9	G9	G9	G9dl	
498 ohv tw	66 × 72.8							G9std	G9std
498 ohv tw	66 × 72.8							G9CS	
498 ohv tw	66 × 72.8							G9CSR	
593 ohv tw	72 × 72.8				G11	G11	G11		
593 ohv tw	72 × 72.8						G11CS		
593 ohv tw	72 × 72.8						G11CSR		
646 ohv tw	72 × 79.3							G12	G12
646 ohv tw	72 × 79.3							G12dl	G12dl
646 ohv tw	72 × 79.3							G12CS	G12CS
646 ohv tw	72 × 79.3							G12CSR	G12CSR

ARIEL

	b × s	45	46	47	48	49	50	51	52
346 ohv	72 × 85	NG	NG	NG	NG	NG	NG		
346 ohv	72 × 85	NH	NH	NH	NH	NH	NH	NH	NH
499 ohv	81.8 × 95	VG	VG	VG	VG	VG	VG		
499 ohv	81.8 × 95	VH	VH	VH	VH	VH	VH	VH	VH
499 ohv	81.8 × 95								VHA
499 ohv	81.8 × 95						VCH	VCH	VCH
598 sv	86.4 × 102	VB	VB	VB	VB	VB	VB	VB	VB
499 ohv tw	63 × 80				KG	KG	KG	KG	
499 ohv tw	63 × 80				KH	KH	KH	KH	KH
995 ohv 4	65 × 75	4G	4G	4G	4G	4G	4G	4G	4G

	b × s	53	54	55	56	57	58	59	60
198 ohv	60 × 70		LH	LH	LH	LH	LH	LH	
346 ohv	72 × 85	NH	NH	NH	NH	NH	NH	NH	
346 ohv	72 × 85					HT3	HT3	HT3	
499 ohv	81.8 × 95	VH	VH	VH	VH	VH	VH	VH	
499 ohv	81.8 × 95	VHA							
499 ohv	81.8 × 95	VCH							
499 ohv	81.8 × 95		HT	HT	HT5	HT5	HT5	HT5	
499 ohv	81.8 × 95		HS	HS	HS	HS	HS	HS	
598 sv	86.4 × 102	VB	VB	VB	VB	VB	VB		
247 ts tw	54 × 54						Le	Le	Le
247 ts tw	54 × 54								Ar
499 ohv tw	63 × 80	KH	KH	KH	KH	KH			
499 ohv tw	63 × 80	KHA							
647 ohv tw	70 × 84		FH	FH	FH	FH	FH	FH	FH
995 ohv 4	65 × 75	4G							
995 ohv 4	65 × 75	4GII	4GII	4GII	4GII	4GII	4GII	4GII	

Ar – Arrow   Le – Leader

BAC

	Engine	51	52	53
99 ts	1F	Li	Li	
99 ts	1F			Ga
122 ts	10D		Ga	Ga
125 ts	JAP	Li		

Ga – Gazelle
Li – Lilliput

BANTAMOTO

	b × s	51	52
38.5 ts	38 × 34	Ba	Ba

BOND

	Engine	50	51	52	53
99 ts	1F	Mi	Mi	Mi	
125 ts	JAP		Mi	Mi	Mi

	Engine	58	59	60
148 ts	31C	P1	P1	P3
197 ts	9E	P2	P2	P4

Mi – Minibyke

BOWN

	Engine	50	51	52	53	54	55	56	57
47.6 ts	Sachs							50	50
99 ts	2F	AR	AR	AR	AR	AR			
99 ts	1F		MC	MC	MC	MC			
122 ts	10D			TT	TT	TT			

AR – Auto Roadster   TT – Tourist Trophy   MC – motor cycle   50 – Bown 50 moped

BRITAX

	b × s	49	50	51	52	53	54	55	56
48 ohv	39 × 40	En	En	En	En				
48 ohv	39 × 40					Br	Br	Br	
48 ohv	39 × 40							Sc	Sc
48 ohv	39 × 40							Hu	Hu

Br – Britax   Hu – Hurricane   En – engine unit   Sc – Scooterette

BSA

	b × s	45	46	47	48	49	50	51	52
123 ts	52 × 58				D1	D1	D1	D1	D1
123 ts	52 × 58						D1cp	D1cp	D1cp
249 sv	63 × 80	C10	C10	C10	C10	C10	C10	C10	C10
249 ohv	63 × 80	C11	C11	C11	C11	C11	C11	C11	C11
348 ohv	71 × 88	B31	B31	B31	B31	B31	B31	B31	B31
348 ohv	71 × 88		B32	B32	B32	B32	B32	B32	B32
348 ohv	71 × 88					B32GS	B32GS	B32GS	B32GS
496 sv	82 × 94	M20	M20	M20	M20	M20	M20	M20	M20
499 ohv	85 × 88			B33	B33	B33	B33	B33	B33
499 ohv	85 × 88			B34	B34	B34	B34	B34	B34
499 ohv	85 × 88					B34GS	B34GS	B34GS	B34GS
499 ohv	85 × 88				M33	M33	M33	M33	M33
591 sv	82 × 112		M21	M21	M21	M21	M21	M21	M21
495 ohv tw	62 × 82			A7	A7	A7	A7		
495 ohv tw	62 × 82					A7ST	A7ST		
497 ohv tw	66 × 72.6							A7	A7
497 ohv tw	66 × 72.6							A7ST	A7ST
646 ohv tw	70 × 84						A10	A10	A10

BSA

	b × s	53	54	55	56	57	58	59	60
34.6 ts	36 × 34	WW	WW	WW					
70 ts	45 × 44					Dandy	Dandy	Dandy	Dandy
123 ts	52 × 58	D1	D1	D1	D1	D1	D1	D1	D1
123 ts	52 × 58	D1cp	D1cp	D1cp					
148 ts	57 × 58		D3	D3	D3	D3			
172 ts	61.5 × 58						D5	D7	D7
249 sv	63 × 80	C10	C10L	C10L	C10L	C10L			
249 ohv	63 × 80	C11	C11G	C11G	C12	C12	C12		
247 ohv	67 × 70						C15	C15	C15
247 ohv	67 × 70							C15S	C15S
247 ohv	67 × 70							C15T	C15T
348 ohv	71 × 88	B31	B31	B31	B31	B31	B31	B31	
348 ohv	71 × 88	B32	B32	B32	B32	B32			
348 ohv	71 × 88	B32GS	B32GS	B32GS	B32GS	B32GS		B32GS	B32GS
496 sv	82 × 94	M20	M20	M20					
499 ohv	85 × 88	B33	B33	B33	B33	B33	B33	B33	B33
499 ohv	85 × 88	B34	B34	B34	B34	B34			
499 ohv	85 × 88	B34GS	B34GS	B34GS	B34GS	B34GS	B34GS	B34GS	B34GS
499 ohv	85 × 88	M33	M33	M33	M33	M33			
591 sv	82 × 112	M21	M21	M21	M21	M21	M21	M21	M21
497 ohv tw	66 × 72.6	A7	A7	A7	A7	A7	A7	A7	A7
497 ohv tw	66 × 72.6	A7ST	A7ST						
497 ohv tw	66 × 72.6		A7SS	A7SS	A7SS	A7SS	A7SS	A7SS	A7SS
646 ohv tw	70 × 84	A10	A10	A10	A10	A10	A10	A10	A10
646 ohv tw	70 × 84	A10SF	A10SF						
646 ohv tw	70 × 84		A10RR	A10RR	A10RR	A10RR	A10SR	A10SR	A10SR
646 ohv tw	70 × 84						A10Sp	A10Sp	A10Sp

D1cp – D1 competition
RR – Road Rocket
SF – Super Flash
Sp – Spitfire
SR – Super Rocket
SS – Shooting Star
St – Star Twin
WW – Winged Wheel

Another route was the scooterette, but the BSA Dandy was not to be the best example

COMMANDER

	Engine	53
99 ts	2F	I
99 ts	1F	II
122 ts	10D	III

CORGI

	b × s	48	49	50	51	52	53	54
98 ts	50 × 50	I						
98 ts	50 × 50	II	II	II	II	II		
98 ts	50 × 50					IV	IV	IV

COTTON

	Engine	54	55	56	57	58	59	60
197 ts	8E	Vu	Vu	Vu				
197 ts	9E		Vu	Vu	Vu	Vu	Vu	Vu
197 ts	9E			Tr	Tr	Tr	Tr	Tr
246 ts	33A							Sc
242 ts tw	Anz		Cot	Cot	Cot	Cot	Cot	
249 ts tw	2T				VT	VT	He	He
249 ts tw	2T							DG
322 ts tw	Anz			Cot	Cot	Cot	Cot	
324 ts tw	3T						Mes	Mes

Cot – Cotanza　　He – Herald　　Sc – Scrambler　　VT – Villiers Twin
DG – Double Gloucester　　Mes – Messenger　　Tr – Trials　　Vu – Vulcan

CYC-AUTO

	b × s	46	47	48	49	50	51	52
98 ts	50 × 50	Au	Au	Au	Au	Su	Su	Su
98 ts	50 × 50				Ca	Ca	Ca	Ca

	b × s	53	54	55	56	57	58
98 ts	50 × 50	Su	Su	Su	Su	Su	Su
98 ts	50 × 50	Ca	Ca	Ca	Ca	Ca	Ca

Au – Autocycle　　Su – Superior
Ca – Carrier

CYCLAID

	b × s	50	51	52	53	54	55
31 ts	35 × 32	Cy	Cy	Cy	Cy	Cy	Cy

CYCLEMASTER

	b × s	50	51	52	53	54	55
25.7 ts	32 × 32	Cy	Cy				
32.6 ts	36 × 32			Cy	Cy	Cy	Cy
32.6 ts	36 × 32			Me	Me	Me	Cym
32.6 ts	36 × 32				Pi	Pi	
32.6 ts	36 × 32				Ro	Ro	

	b × s	56	57	58	59	60
32.6 ts	36 × 32	Cy	Cy	Cy		
32.6 ts	36 × 32	Cym	Cym	Cym	Cym	Cym
124 ts	51 × 61	Pia	Pia	Pia		

Cy – Cyclemaster
Cym – Cyclemate
Pi – Pillion
Me – Mercury
Pia – Piatti
Ro – Roundsman

CYMOTA

	b × s	50	51
45 ts	38 × 40	Cy	Cy

Cy – Cymota

DAYTON

	Engine	55	56	57	58	59	60
174 ts	2L					AF	AF
224 ts	1H	Al	Al	Al	Al		
246 ts	2H				AS		
246 ts	2H				ACS	ACS	ACS
249 ts tw	2T			AT	AT		
249 ts tw	2T				AC	AC	AC
249 ts tw	2T				AE	AE	

AC – Albatross Continental
ACS – Albatross Continental Single
AE – Albatross Empire
AF – Albatross Flamenco
Al – Albatross
AS – Albatross Single
AT – Albatross Twin

DKR

	Engine	57	58	59	60
147 ts	30C	Dove	Dove	Dove	
148 ts	31C		Peg	Peg	Peg
148 ts	31C				Dove II
174 ts	2L				Peg II
197 ts	9E		Def	Def	Def
249 ts tw	2T			Manx	Manx

Def – Defiant
Peg – Pegasus

DMW

Engine	50	51	52	53	54	55	56	57
99 ts	1F	100	100						
99 ts	4F								Bambi
122 ts	10D	125	125	125	125				
125 ohv	AMC				125				
125 dohc	AMC					Hor	Hor		
147 ts	29C						Leda	Leda	
148 ts	31C								150P
170 ohv	AMC				175	175	175		
170 ohv	AMC					MX			
174 ts	2L								175P
197 ts	6E	200	200	200	200				
197 ts	6E			Comp	Comp				
197 ts	8E					200	200	200	200
197 ts	7E					Comp	Comp	Comp	
197 ts	9E							VI	VI
197 ts	7E							VII	VII
197 ts	8E								VIII
197 ts	9E							IX	IX
224 ts	1H					Cor	Cor	Cor	Cor
249 ohc	AMC					Dol	Dol		
249 ts tw	2T								Dol

Engine	57	58	59	60
99 ts	4F	Bambi	Bambi	Bambi	Bambi
197 ts	8E	VIII	VIII		
197 ts	9E	IX	IX	IX	IX
197 ts	9E				Mk 12
246 ts	32A			Mk 12	Mk 12
246 ts	33A			Mk 12	Mk 12
249 ts tw	2T	Dol	Dol	Dol	Dol
249 ts tw	2T		Mk X	Mk X	Mk X
324 ts tw	3T			Dol	Dol

Cor – Cortina   Hor – Hornet
Dol – Dolomite   MX – Moto Cross

DOT

Engine	49	50	51	52	53	54
197 ts	6E	200	DS	DST	DST	D	
197 ts	6E		RS	RST	RST	R	
197 ts	6E			S	S	S	
197 ts	6E				SC	SC	
197 ts	6E				SD	SD	
197 ts	6E				T	T	T
197 ts	6E				TD	TD	TD
197 ts	6E					DH	
197 ts	6E					RH	

DOT

	Engine	53	54	55	56	57	58	59	60
197 and 246 ts		SH	SH	SH	SH	SH	SH	SH	SH
197 and 246 ts		SCH	SCH	SCH	SCH	SCH	SCH	SCH	SCH
197 and 246 ts		SDH	SDH	SDH	SDH	SDH	SDH	SDH	SDH
197 and 246 ts		TH		TH					
197 and 246 ts		THX	THX	THX	THX	THX	THX	THX	THX
197 and 246 ts		TDH		TDH					
197 and 246 ts		TDHX	TDHX	TDHX	TDHX	TDHX	TDHX	TDHX	TDHX
197 and 246 ts						WR	WR	WR	WR

	Engine	51	52	53
248 sv	Bro	250	250	250

Note that the above models were all fitted with 6E engines up to 1953, with 8E for 1954–6 and 9E from 1957. From 1959 they were also available with 246 cc engines, the 31A being fitted for motocross, and the 32A for trials.

	Engine	56	57	58	59	60
48 ts	Vivi		Mo	Mo	Mo	Mo
48 ts	Vivi		Ra	Ra	Ra	Ra
48 ts	Vivi		Sc	Sc	Sc	Sc
48 ts	Vivi					Gu
197 ts	9E	Man	Man	Man		
249 ts tw	2T				SCH	
349 ts tw	RCA				SCH	SCH
349 ts tw	RCA				SR	SR

Bro – Brockhouse
Gu – Guazzoni
Ra – racer
Sc – scooterette
Man – Mancunian
Mo – moped
SR – Sportsmans Roadster

DOUGLAS

	b × s	47	48	49	50	51
348 ohv tw	60.8 × 60	T35	III	III		
348 ohv tw	60.8 × 60		Sp	Sp	Comp	Comp
348 ohv tw	60.8 × 60				IV	
348 ohv tw	60.8 × 60				IV Sp	

DOUGLAS

	b × s	50	51	52	53	54	55	56	57
125 ts	56.5 × 49			2L2	2L2	2L2	G		
124 ts	54 × 54						GL2		
124 ts	54 × 54						42L2	42L2	Std
124 ts	54 × 54								Magna
124 ts	54 × 54								Ultra
145 ts	57 × 57						GS	GS	GS
348 ohv tw	60.8 × 60	80	80	80	80				
348 ohv tw	60.8 × 60	90	90	90	90	90			
348 ohv tw	60.8 × 60		V	V	V	V	DF	DF	DF

Comp – Competition
DF – Dragonfly
Sp - Sports
Std – Standard

DUNKLEY

	b × s	57	58	59
49.6 ohv	39 × 41.5		Pop	Pop
61 ohv	44 × 40	Whi	Whi	Whi
64 ohv	44 × 42	SS	SS	
64 ohv	44 × 42		WS	WS
64 ohv	44 × 42		Sc	Sc
64 ohv	44 × 42			PM

PM – Popular Major scooter   Sc – S65 scooter   Whi – Whippet scooterette
Pop – Popular scooter   SS – Super Sports 65   WS – Whippet Sports

EMC

	Engine	47	48	49	50	51	52	53
125 ts	JAP						125	125
125 ts	Puch					racer	racer	racer
345 ts split single		350	350	350	350	350	350	350

EXCELSIOR

	Engine	46	47	48	49	50	51	52
98 ts	JDL	Au	V1	V1	V1			
98 ts	Goblin		G2	G2	G2	G2	G2	G2
98 ts	Spryt		S1	S1	S1	S1	S1	S1
98 ts	Goblin				M1			
122 ts	9D	0	0	0				
122 ts	10D				U1/U2	U1/U2	U1/U2	U1/U2
123 ts	Goblin				M2			
197 ts	6E				R1/R2	R1/R2	R1/R2	R1/R2
243 ts tw	Tal					TT1	TT1	TT1
243 ts tw	Tal							STT1

	Engine	53	54	55	56	57	58	59	60
98 ts	Goblin	G2	G2	G2	G2				
98 ts	Spryt	S1	S1	S1	S1				
99 ts	4F	F4	F4	F4	F4				
99 ts	4F			F4S	F4S				
99 ts	6F				F4	F4		F4F	F10
99 ts	6F				F4S	F6S	CA8	CA9	C10
99 ts	6F					SB1	SB1	SB1	
122 ts	13D		D12						
147 ts	Excel	C2	C1/C2	C3	C3/C4	C4			
147 ts	Excel							KS	MK1
147 ts	Excel							EL	ME1
147 ts	30C				C1		U8	U9	
148 ts	31C								U10
197 ts	6E	R1/R2							
197 ts	8E		R1/R2						
197 ts	8E		R3/R4	R4					
197 ts	8E			R5/R6	R6				

EXCELSIOR

	Engine	53	54	55	56	57	58	59	60
197 ts	9E				A9				R10
243 ts tw	Tal	TT1	TT1	TT3					
243 ts tw	Tal	STT1	STT1		SESTT2				
243 ts tw	Tal		TT2	TT2	TT3	TT3	TT4	TT4	TT6
243 ts tw	Tal		STT2	STT2	STT4	STT5	STT6		
328 ts tw	Tal						S8	S8	
328 ts tw	Tal							S9	S9

Au – Autobyk   Excel – Excelsior   Tal – Talisman

FLM

	Engine	51	52	53
125 ts	JAP	Gl	Gl	Gl

Gl – Glideride

FRANCIS-BARNETT

	Engine	46	47	48	49	50	51	52	53
98 ts	JDL	50	50	50	50				
99 ts	2F				56	56	56		
122 ts	9D	51	51	51					
122 ts	10D				52	52	52	52	52
122 ts	10D				53	53	53	53	53
122 ts	10D							57	57
122 ts	10D							59	61
122 ts	10D								63
197 ts	6E				54	54	54	54	
197 ts	8E								54
197 ts	6E				55	55	55	55	
197 ts	8E								55
197 ts	6E							58	
197 ts	6E							60	

	Engine	53	54	55	56	57	58	59	60
122 ts	13D		66						
147 ts	30C			69	73	78	78	78	
149 ts	AMC								86
171 ts	AMC						79	79	79
197 ts	8E	58	67	70	74	74			
197 ts	7E	62	62	62	76	76			
197 ts	7E	64	64	72	77	77			
197 ts	8E	65	65						
197 ts	10E						81	81	
199 ts	AMC								87
224 ts	1H		68	71	75	75			
249 ts	AMC					80	80	80	80
249 ts	AMC						82	82	82
249 ts	AMC							83	85
249 ts	AMC							84	84

GREEVES

	Engine	54	55	56	57	58	59	60
197 ts	8E	20R	20R	20R	20R			
197 ts	8E	20D	20D					
197 ts	8E	20S	20S					
197 ts	8E	20T	20T					
197 ts	7E				20R4			
197 ts	9E			20D	20D	20D		
197 ts	9E			20S	20S	20SA	20SAS	20SCS
197 ts	9E			20T	20T	20TA	20TA	20TC
197 ts	9E						20TAS	20TCS
246 ts	31A						24DB	
246 ts	32A							24DB
246 ts	31A						24TAS	
246 ts	31A						24SAS	
246 ts	32A							24TCS
246 ts	33A							24SAS
246 ts	33A							24SCS
242 ts tw	Anz	25D	25D					
242 ts tw	Anz		25R	25R	25R			
249 ts tw	2T				25D	25D	25DB	25DB
249 ts tw	2T					25TA		
249 ts tw	2T					25SA		
322 ts tw	Anz		32D	32D	32D			
324 ts tw	3T							32DB

GYS

	b × s	49	50	51	52	53	54	55	
									Mot – Motomite
50 ts	40 × 40	GYS	GYS	Mot	Moc	Moc	Moc	Moc	Moc – Mocyc

HERCULES

	Engine	56	57	58	59	60	
							Cor – Corvette
49 ts	JAP	HCM	HCM	HCM			HCM – Her-Cu-Motor
49 ts	Lav				Cor		Lav - Lavelette

HJH

	Engine	54	55	56	
147 ts	30C		Dn	Dn	D – Dragon
147 ts	30C			SpDn	DM – Dragon Major
197 ts	7E		Tr	Tr	Dn – Dragonette
197 ts	7E			Sc	Sc – Scrambler
197 ts	8E	D	D	D	SD Super Dragon
197 ts	8E		SD		SpD – Sports Dragon
197 ts	8E			SpD	SpDn – Sports Dragonette
197 ts	8E			SSD	SSD – Super Sports Dragon
224 ts	1H		DM	DM	Tr – Trials

INDIAN

	Engine	50	51	52	53	54	55
248 sv	Brock	R	R	R	R	R	R
248 sv	Brock					S	S

Brock – Brockhouse

JAMES

	Engine	46	47	48	49	50	51	52	53
98 ts	JDL	Su	Su	Su	Su				
99 ts	2F					Su	Su	Su	J1
99 ts	1F				Co	Co	Co	Co	J10
99 ts	1F						Com	Com	J4
122 ts	9D	ML	ML	ML					
122 ts	10D				Ca	Ca	Ca	Ca	J6
122 ts	10D				comp	comp	comp	comp	
197 ts	6E				Cap	J8	J8	J8	J8
197 ts	6E						J7	J7	J7
197 ts	6E							Col	
197 ts	6E				comp	comp	comp		

	Engine	53	54	55	56	57	58	59	60
99 ts	2F	J1	J1						
99 ts	4F	J3	J11	J11	L1	L1			
99 ts	6F					L1	L1	L1	L1
122 ts	13D	J5	J5						
147 ts	30C			J15	L15	L15	L15	L15	
149 ts	AMC							L15A	L15A
171 ts	AMC						L17	L17	
197 ts	7E	J9	J9	J9	K7T	K7T			
197 ts	10E						K7T		
197 ts	10E						K7	K7	
197 ts	8E		K7	K7	K7	K7			
197 ts	7E		K7C	K7C	K7C	K7C			
199 ts	AMC								L20
224 ts	1H		K12	K12	K12	K12			
249 ts	AMC					L25	L25	L25	L25
249 ts	AMC							L25T	L25T
249 ts	AMC							L25S	L25S

Ca – Cadet
Cap – Captain
Co – Comet
Col – Colonel

Com – Commodore
comp – competition
SU – Superlux

MERCURY

	Engine	56	57	58
48 ohv		Mer	Mer	Mer
49 ts	Ilo	Her	Her	
60 ohv			Wh	
99 ts	4F		Do	Pi
99 ts	6F		GS	GS

Do – Dolphin Mer – Mercette
GS – Grey Streak Pi – Pippin
Her – Hermes Wh – Whippet

MINI-MOTOR

	b × s	49	50	51	52	53	54	55
49.9 ts	38 × 44	unit	unit	unit	unit	unit	unit	unit

NEW HUDSON

	Engine	46	47	48	49	50	51	52
98 ts	JDL	Au	Au	Au				
99 ts	2F				Au	Au	Au	Au

	Engine	53	54	55	56	57	58
99 ts	2F	Au	Au	Au	Au	Au	Au

Au – Autocycle

NORMAN

	Engine	46	47	48	49	50	51	52	53
98 ts	JDL	Au	Au	Au					
99 ts	2F				C	C	C	C	C
99 ts	1F					D	D	D	D
122 ts	9D	MC	MC	MC					
122 ts	10D				B1	B1	B1	B1	E
122 ts	13D								B1S
197 ts	6E				B2	B2	B2	B2	B2
197 ts	6E								B2S
197 ts	6E								B2C

	Engine	53	54	55	56	57	58	59	60
47.6 ts	Sachs				Ni	Ni	Ni	Ni	SL
47.6 ts	Mi-Val								NiIII
49.9 ts	3K						NiII		
49.9 ts	3K							Lido	NiIV
99 ts	2F	C	C	C	C	C			
99 ts	4F		D	D					
122 ts	10D	E	E						
147 ts	30C			B1S	B1S	B1S	B1S	B1S	
148 ts	31C				B1S	B1S	B1S		
197 ts	8E		B2						
197 ts	8E		B2S	B2S	B2S	B2S	B2S		
197 ts	9E				B2S	B2S	B2S	B2S	B2S
197 ts	7E		B2C	B2C					

NORMAN

	Engine	53	54	55	56	57	58	59	60
197 ts	9E				B2C/S	B2C/S	B2C/S	B2C/S	B2C/S
197 ts	9E								B4C
246 ts	32A								B4C
242 ts tw	Anz			TS	TS	TS			
249 ts tw	2T						B3	B3	B3

Au – Autocycle   MC – Motorcycle   SL – Super Lido
Anz – Anzani   Ni – Nippy

NORTON

	b × s	45	46	47	48	49	50	51	52	53
348 ohv	71 × 88			Tr						
348 ohc	71 × 88			40	40	40	40	40	40	40
348 ohc	71 × 88			40M	40M	40M	40M	40M	40M	40M
490 sv	79 × 100	16H	16H	16H	16H	16H	16H	16H	16H	16H
490 ohv	79 × 100	18	18	18	18	18	18	18	18	18
490 ohv	79 × 100			Tr		500T	500T	500T	500T	500T
490 ohv	79 × 100			ES2	ES2	ES2	ES2	ES2	ES2	ES2
490 ohc	79 × 100			30	30	30	30	30	30	30
498 ohc	79.62 × 100			30M	30M	30M	30M	30M	30M	30M
634 sv	82 × 120			Big 4						
597 sv	82 × 113				Big 4	Big 4	Big 4	Big 4	Big 4	Big 4
497 ohv tw	66 × 72.6					7	7	7	7	7
497 ohv tw	66 × 72.6								88	88

	b × s	54	55	56	57	58	59	60
249 ohv tw	60 × 44						Jub	Jub
348 ohc	71 × 88	40	40	40	40	40		
348 ohv	71 × 88			50	50	50	50	50
349 dohc	76 × 76.85	40M	40M	40M	40M			
348 dohc	76 × 76.7					40M	40M	40M
490 sv	79 × 100	16H						
490 ohv	79 × 100	18						
490 ohv	79 × 100	500T						
490 ohv	79 × 100	ES2	ES2	ES2	ES2	ES2	ES2	ES2
490 ohc	79 × 100	30	30	30	30	30		
498 dohc	86 × 85.8	30M	30M	30M	30M			
497 dohc	86 × 85.62					30M	30M	30M
597 sv	82 × 113	Big 4						
597 ohv	82 × 113		19R					
597 ohv	82 × 113		19S	19S	19S	19S		
497 ohv tw	66 × 72.6	7	7					
497 ohv tw	66 × 72.6	88	88	88	88	88	88	88
497 ohv tw	66 × 72.6							88dl
497 ohv tw	66 × 72.6							Nom
596 ohv tw	68 × 82				77	77		
596 ohv tw	68 × 82			99	99	99	99	99
596 ohv tw	68 × 82							99dl
596 ohv tw	68 × 82					Nom	Nom	Nom

Jub – Jubilee   Nom – Nomad   Tr – Trials

OEC

	Engine	49	50	51	52	53	54
122 ts	10D	S1	S1	S1	S1	S1	
122 ts	10D		D1	D1	D1	D1	
122 ts	10D		C1	C1	C1		
122 ts	10D			SS1	SS1	SS1	
122 ts	10D			SD1	SD1	SD1	
122 ts	10D					D55	D55
122 ts	10D					D55RS	D55RS
197 ts	6E	S2	S2	S2	S2	S2	
197 ts	6E		D2	D2	D2	D2	
197 ts	6E		C2	C2	C2		
197 ts	6E			SS2	SS2	SS2	
197 ts	6E			SD2	SD2	SD2	
197 ts	6E					ST2	
197 ts	8E						ST2
197 ts	6E					ST3	
197 ts	7E						ST3
248 sv	Bro				Ap	Ap	Ap

Ap – Apollo   Bro – Brockhouse

PANTHER

	b × s	46	47	48	49	50	51	52	53
249 ohv	60 × 88	60	60	60	65	65	65	65	65
249 ohv	60 × 88				65St	65St	65St	65St	65St
348 ohv	71 × 88	70	70	70	75	75	75	75	75
348 ohv	71 × 88				75St	75St	75St	75St	75St
594 ohv	87 × 100	100	100	100	100	100	100	100	100

	b × s	53	54	55	56	57	58	59	60
249 ohv	60 × 88	65	65	65	65	65	65	65	65
249 ohv	60 × 88	65St							
348 ohv	71 × 88	75	75	75	75	75	75	75	75
348 ohv	71 × 88	75St							
594 ohv	87 × 100	100	100	100	100	100	100	100	100
645 ohv	88 × 106							120	120

	Engine	56	57	58	59	60
174 ts	2L					Pr
197 ts	8E	10/3	10/3	10/3	10/3	10/3
197 ts	9E		10/3A	10/3A	10/3A	10/3A
197 ts	9E	10/4	10/4	10/4	10/4	10/4
246 ts	2H		25			
249 ts tw	2T		35	35	35	35
324 ts tw	3T				45	45
324 ts tw	3T				50	50

Pr – Princess

St – Stroud

PHILLIPS

	Engine	54	55	56	57	58	59	60
49.2 ts		P36	P36	P36	P36			
49.2 ts	Rex						P40	P40
49.2 ts	Rex							P49
49.6 ts	Rex			P39	P39	P39	P39	
49.6 ts	Rex						P50	P50
49.9 ts	3K						P45	P45

PHOENIX

	Engine	56	57	58	59	60
147 ts	30C	pro	pro			
147 ts	30C			19S	19S	19S
147 ts	30C			19D		
147 ts	30C			150dl	150dl	
148 ts	31C			S150	S150	S150
148 ts	31C					150dl
174 ts	2L					S175
174 ts	2L					175std
197 ts	9E			S200	S200	S200
197 ts	9E					200 std
249 ts tw	2T			T250	T250	T250
324 ts tw	3T				T325	T325

pro – prototype

POWER PAK

	b × s	50	51	52	53	54	55	56
49 ts	39 × 41	unit	unit	unit	unit	unit	unit	unit

PROGRESS

	Engine	57	58
147 ts	30C	An	An
197 ts	8E	Br	Br
197 ts	9E	Bri	Bri

An – Anglian
Br – Briton
Bri – Britannia

RALEIGH

	Engine	58	59	60
49.9 ts	S/A	RM1	RM1	
49.9 ts	S/A		RM1C	RM2C

S/A – Sturmey-Archer

RAYNAL

	Engine	46	47	48	49	50
98 ts	JDL	Pop	DL	DL	DL	DL

DL – De Luxe
Pop – Popular

233

ROYAL ENFIELD

	b × s	46	47	48	49	50	51	52	53
126 ts	54 × 55	RE	RE	RE	RE	RE	RE2	RE2	RE2
148 ts	56 × 60								En
346 sv	70 × 90	C	C						
346 ohv	70 × 90	CO	CO						
346 ohv	70 × 90	G	G	G	G	G	G	G	G
346 ohv	70 × 90				G2	G2	G2	G2	G2
346 ohv	70 × 90				Tr	Tr	Tr	Tr	Tr
346 ohv	70 × 90				Sc	Sc	Sc	Sc	Sc
499 ohv	84 × 90	J	J	J	J2	J2	J2	J2	J2
499 ohv	84 × 90								JS
495 ohv tw	64 × 77				Tw	Tw	Tw	Tw	Tw
693 ohv tw	70 × 90								M

	b × s	53	54	55	56	57	58	59	60
126 ts	54 × 55	RE2							
148 ts	56 × 60	En	En	En	EnII	EnII	EnII	Pr	Pr
148 ts	56 × 60						EnIII	EnIII	
248 ohv	64 × 77		Cl	Cl	Cl	Cl			
248 ohv	64 × 77		S						
248 ohv	70 × 64.5					Cr	Cr	Cr	Cr
248 ohv	70 × 64.5						Cl II	Cl II	Cl II
248 ohv	70 × 64.5							CrS	CrS
346 ohv	70 × 90				Cl	Cl	Cl	Cl	Cl
346 ohv	70 × 90	G	G						
346 ohv	70 × 90	G2	G2	G2	G2	G2	G2	G2	G2
346 ohv	70 × 90	Tr	Tr	Tr				WRT	WRT
346 ohv	70 × 90	Sc	Sc	Sc	MX				
346 ohv	70 × 90		Ra	Ra					
499 ohv	84 × 90	J2	J2	J2					
499 ohv	84 × 90	JS	JS	JS	JS	JS	JS	JS	JS
499 ohv	84 × 90		Tr	Tr					
499 ohv	84 × 90		Sc	Sc	MX				
499 ohv	84 × 90		Ra	Ra					
495 ohv tw	64 × 77	Tw	Tw	Tw	Tw	Tw	Tw		
496 ohv tw	70 × 64.5						MM	MM	MM
496 ohv tw	70 × 64.5								MMS
693 ohv tw	70 × 90	M	M	M	SM	SM	SM	SM	SM
693 ohv tw	70 × 90						Con	Con	Con

Cl – Clipper   M – Meteor   Ra – Racer   Tw – Twin
Con – Constellation   MM – Meteor Minor   Sc – Scrambler
Cr – Crusader   MMS – Meteor Minor Sports   SM – Super Meteor
CrS – Crusader Sports   MX – Moto Cross   Tr – Trials
En – Ensign   Pr – Prince   WRT – Works Replica Trials

SCOTT

	b × s	46	47	48	49	50	51	52
598 ts tw	73 × 71.4	FS	FS	FS	FS	FS	FS	FS

	b × s	56	57	58	59	60
497 ts tw	66.6 × 71.4	FS	FS	FS	FS	FS
598 ts tw	73 × 71.4	FS	FS	FS	FS	FS

SUN

Engine		46	47	48	49	50	51	52	53
98 ts	JDL	Au	Au	Au					
99 ts	2F				Au	Au			
99 ts	1F				MC	MC	MC	MC	
122 ts	10D						DL	DL	
197 ts	6E						Ch	Ch	Ch

Engine		53	54	55	56	57	58	59	60
99 ts	4F	MC	MC	Hor	Hor	Hor			
99 ts	6F					Geni	Geni	Geni	Geni
122 ts	12D	DL	DL						
147 ts	30C			Ch	Ch				
148 ts	31C					Ch			
174 ts	2L							SW	SW
197 ts	8E		Ch	Ch	Ch	Ch			
197 ts	6E	Comp							
197 ts	8E		C1			Cen			
197 ts	8E		C3/C4	Tr					
197 ts	7E			Sc					
197 ts	9E				Wasp	Wasp	Wasp	Wasp	
197 ts	9E				WC	WC			
224 ts	1H		Cyc	Cyc	Cyc	Cyc			
249 ts tw	2T					Ov	Ov	Ov	

Au – Autocycle
Cen – Century
Ch – Challenger
Comp – Competition
Cyc – Cyclone

DL – De Luxe
Hor – Hornet
MC – Motor Cycle
Ov – Overlander

Sc – Scrambler
SW – Sunwasp
Tr – Trials
WC – Wasp comp

SUNBEAM

b × s		47	48	49	50	51	52	53	54
489 ohc tw	70 × 63.5	S7	S7	S7	S7	S7	S7	S7	S7
489 ohc tw	70 × 63.5			S8	S8	S8	S8	S8	S8

	b × s	55	56	57	58	59	60
172 ts	61.5 × 58						B1
249 ohv tw	56 × 50.6					B2	B2
249 ohv tw	56 × 50.6					B2S	B2S
489 ohc tw	70 × 63.5	S7	S7	S7	S7		
489 ohc tw	70 × 63.5	S8	S8	S8	S8		

SWALLOW

Engine		47	48	49	50	51
122 ts	9D	Gad	Gad	Gad		
122 ts	10D				Gad	Gad
197 ts	6E					Major

Gad – Gadabout

TANDON

	Engine	48	49	50	51	52	53	54	55
122 ts	9D	Mk1	Mk1	Mk1	Mk1	Mk1			
122 ts	10D			S	S	S	S		
122 ts	10D				K	K	K		
122 ts	10D						Imp		
122 ts	12D							Imp	
147 ts	30C								Imp
197 ts	6E				SS	SS	SS		
197 ts	6E						KS		
197 ts	6E						IS		
197 ts	8E							IS	IS
197 ts	8E							Sc	ISS
197 ts	7E								Sc
224 ts	1H							Mon	Mon
242 ts tw	Anz							TS	TS
242 ts tw	Anz								Sc
322 ts tw	Anz								Vis

	Engine	56	57	58	59
197 ts	8E	ISS	ISS	ISS	ISS
224 ts	1H	Mon	Mon	Mon	Mon

Anz – Anzani
K – Kangaroo
KS – Kangaroo Supreme
IS – Imp Supreme

ISS – Imp Supreme Special
Mon – Monarch
S – Supaglide
Sc – Scrambler

SS – Supaglide Supreme
TS – Twin Supreme
Vis – Viscount

TEAGLE

	b × s	54	55	56
50 ts		unit	unit	unit

TRIUMPH

	b × s	45	46	47	48	49	50	51	52	53
149 ohv	57 × 58.5									T15
349 ohv tw	55 × 73.4	3T	3T	3T	3T	3T	3T	3T		
499 ohv tw	63 × 80	5T	5T	5T	5T	5T	5T	5T	5T	5T
499 ohv tw	63 × 80	T100	T100	T100	T100	T100	T100	T100	T100	T100
499 ohv tw	63 × 80				GP	GP	GP			
499 ohv tw	63 × 80					TR5	TR5	TR5	TR5	TR5
649 ohv tw	71 × 82						6T	6T	6T	6T

TRIUMPH

	b × s	53	54	55	56	57	58	59	60
149 ohv	57 × 58.5		T15	T15	T15				
172 ts	61.5 × 58								TS1
199 ohv	63 × 64		T20	T20	T20	T20	T20	T20	T20
199 ohv	63 × 64					T20C	T20C	T20C	T20S
249 ohv tw	56 × 50.6							TW2	TW2
249 ohv tw	56 × 50.6							TW2S	TW2S
349 ohv tw	58.25 × 65.5					3TA	3TA	3TA	3TA
499 ohv tw	63 × 80		5T	5T	5T	5T	5T		
499 ohv tw	63 × 80		T100	T100	T100	T100	T100	T100	
499 ohv tw	63 × 80	T100c							
499 ohv tw	63 × 80		TR5	TR5	TR5	TR5	TR5		
490 ohv tw	69 × 65.5							5TA	5TA
490 ohv tw	69 × 65.5								T100A
649 ohv tw	71 × 82		6T	6T	6T	6T	6T	6T	6T
649 ohv tw	71 × 82		T110	T110	T110	T110	T110	T110	T110
649 ohv tw	71 × 82				TR6	TR6	TR6	TR6	TR6
649 ohv tw	71 × 82							T120	T120

TURNER

	Engine	46
126 ts	RE	Byvan

VELOCETTE

	b × s	46	47	48	49	50	51	52	53
149 sv tw	44 × 49				LE	LE			
192 sv tw	50 × 49						LE	LE	LE
248 ohv	68 × 68.25	MOV	MOV	MOV					
249 ts	63 × 80	GTP							
348 ohc	74 × 81	KSS	KSS	KSS					
348 ohc	74 × 81		KTT	KTT	KTT	KTT			
349 ohv	68 × 96	MAC	MAC	MAC	MAC	MAC	MAC	MAC	MAC
495 ohv	81 × 96	MSS	MSS	MSS					

	b × s	54	55	56	57	58	59	60
192 sv tw	50 × 49	LE	LE	LE	LE	LE		
192 sv tw	50 × 49					LE3	LE3	LE3
192 ohv tw	50 × 49				V200	V200	V200	V200
192 ohv tw	50 × 49						VL	VL
349 ohv	68 × 96	MAC	MAC	MAC	MAC	MAC	MAC	MAC
349 ohv	72 × 86		Vi	Vi	Vi	Vi	Vi	Vi
349 ohv	72 × 86			Sc	Sc	Sc	Sc	Sc
349 ohv	72 × 86							ViC
499 ohv	86 × 86	MSS	MSS	MSS	MSS	MSS	MSS	MSS
499 ohv	86 × 86		Sc	Sc	Sc	Sc	Sc	Sc
499 ohv	86 × 86			En	En	En	En	En
499 ohv	86 × 86			Ve	Ve	Ve	Ve	Ve
499 ohv	86 × 86							VeC

En – Endurance
Sc – Scrambler

Ve – Venom
VeC – Venom Clubman

Vi – Viper
ViC – Viper Clubman

VL – Veeline

VELOSOLEX

	b × s	48	49	50	51	52	53
45 ts	38 × 40	VS	VS	VS	VS	VS	VS

	b × s	54	55	56	57
45 ts	38 × 40	VS	VS	VS	VS

VILLIERS

	b × s	45	46	47	48	49	50	51	52	53
98	50 × 50	JDL	JDL	JDL	JDL					
99	47 × 57					2F	2F	2F	2F	2F
99	47 × 57					1F	1F	1F	1F	1F
122	50 × 62	9D	9D	9D	9D	10D	10D	10D	10D	10D
122	50 × 62									13D
197	59 × 72		5E	5E	5E	6E	6E	6E	6E	6E

	b × s	54	55	56	57	58	59	60
99	47 × 57	2F	2F	2F	2F	2F		
99	47 × 57	4F	4F	4F	4F	4F		
99	47 × 57			6F	6F	6F	6F	6F
122	50 × 62	12D						
122	50 × 62	11D						
147	55 × 62	30C	30C	30C	30C	30C	30C	
147	55 × 62	29C	29C	29C				
148	57 × 58		31C	31C	31C	31C	31C	
174	59 × 63.5				2L	2L	2L	2L
174	59 × 63.5				3L	3L	3L	3L
197	59 × 72	8E	8E	8E	8E	8E		
197	59 × 72	7E	7E	7E		10E	10E	
197	59 × 72		9E	9E	9E	9E	9E	9E
224	63 × 72	1H	1H	1H	1H			
246	66 × 72				2H	2H	2H	2H
246	66 × 72					31A	31A	31A
246	66 × 72					33A	33A	32A
246	66 × 72							34A
249 tw	50 × 63.5			2T	2T	2T	2T	2T
324 tw	57 × 63.5					3T	3T	3T

VINCENT–HRD

	b × s	47	48	49	50	51	52	53
499 ohv	84 × 90			BM	BM			
499 ohv	84 × 90			CC	CC	CC	CC	CC
499 ohv	84 × 90				CGF	CGF		
998 ohv tw	84 × 90	BR	BR	BR	BR			
998 ohv tw	84 × 90		BBS	BBS	BBS			
998 ohv tw	84 × 90			CR	CR	CR	CR	CR
998 ohv tw	84 × 90			CBS	CBS	CBS	CBS	CBS
998 ohv tw	84 × 90			CBL	CBL	CBL	CBL	CBL

VINCENT–HRD

	b × s	53	54	55	56	57	58
48 ts	38 × 42	F	F	F	F	F	F
98 ohv	NSU		Fox	Fox			
123 ts	NSU		Fox	Fox			
199 ts	NSU		Lux				
247 ohc	NSU		Max				
499 ohv	84 × 90			DV			
499 ohv	84 × 90	CC	CC	DC			
998 ohv tw	84 × 90	CR	CR	DR			
998 ohv tw	84 × 90	CBS	CBS	DBS			
998 ohv tw	84 × 90	CBL	CBL	CBL			
998 ohv tw	84 × 90			DBP			
998 ohv tw	84 × 90			DBK			

BBS – B Black Shadow
BM – B Meteor
BR – B Rapide
CBL – C Black Lightning
CBS – C Black Shadow

CC – C Comet
CGF – C Grey Flash
CR – C Rapide
DBK – D Black Knight
DBP – D Black Prince

DBS – D Black Shadow
DC – D Comet
DR – D Rapide
DV – D Victor
F – Firefly

WABO

	Engine	57
99 ts	4F	Scooter
147 ts	30C	Scooter

ZENITH

	Engine	47	48	49	50
747 sv tw	JAP	MC	MC	MC	MC

MC – motorcycle

Typical mount for the enthusiast of the 1950s was this 1956 Triumph Tiger 110, then one of the fastest available

Acknowledgements

This book completes the trio which covers British motorcycles from 1930 to 1970 and represents the period during which I did much of my riding and racing. Most of the machines discussed were outside the range of my pocket at the time, but many were sampled by one means or another, and all were seen or studied at Earls Court or close to hand at the local club.

Club riding was a disciplined pastime in the 1950s, well apart from the café racers, who could be seen grouped around the coffee stall outside the local railway station. Partly, this came from a strong road-racing section in the club, who actually went on to the circuits, so the café crowd were viewed as pseudo racers. Club members supported the racers at meetings and also ran local trials, the training scheme and rode discreetly in town, such social behaviour being encouraged to enhance the motorcyclist's image where possible.

The main help with this book concerned the pictures and, once more, I am indebted to the EMAP archives, which hold the old *Motor Cycle Weekly* files, and Malcolm Gough, of *Motor Cycle News*, from whence they came.

My thanks also go to old friend and fellow writer and racer Brian Woolley for kindly writing a foreword for this book.

A number of the pictures used would have carried the imprint of a professional and, normally, they would have been listed, as is the practice of both myself and the publishing house, but this is no longer possible due to the way in which the prints now reach us. However, our thanks, as always, go to those who drove their cameras in the past, when correct exposure owed more to the man behind the lens, than the electronics in front of it.

Finally, to both editors — Tony Thacker who commissioned this one, and Ian Penberthy who had to take it over in mid-sail — my thanks for support during its production. And, of course, to the staff at Osprey who, as always, did a great job, despite the change of editor and a move to a new office with all the trauma that brings.

Roy Bacon
Niton, Isle of Wight
December 1988